Blood Lines

Chicana Matters Series
Deena J. González and Antonia Castañeda, editors

Chicana Matters Series focuses on one of the largest population groups in the United States today, documenting the lives, values, philosophies, and artistry of contemporary Chicanas. Books in this series may be richly diverse, reflecting the experiences of Chicanas themselves, and incorporating a broad spectrum of topics and fields of inquiry. Cumulatively, the books represent the leading knowledge and scholarship in a significant and growing field of research and, along with the literary works, art, and activism of Chicanas, underscore their significance in the history and culture of the United States.

Blood Lines

Myth, Indigenism, and Chicana/o Literature

SHEILA MARIE CONTRERAS

University of Texas Press   *Austin*

Requests for permission to reproduce material from this work should be sent to:
Permissions
University of Texas Press
P.O. Box 7819
Austin, TX 78713-7819
www.utexas.edu/utpress/about/bpermission.html

∞ The paper used in this book meets the minimum requirements of
ANSI/NISO Z39.48-1992 (R1997) (Permanence of Paper).

Library of Congress Cataloging-in-Publication Data
Contreras, Sheila Marie.
Blood lines : myth, indigenism, and Chicana/o literature /
Sheila Marie Contreras. — 1st ed.
p. cm. — (Chicana matters series)
Includes bibliographical references and index.
ISBN 978-0-292-71796-1 (cloth : alk. paper)
ISBN 978-0-292-71797-8 (pbk. : alk. paper)
1. American literature—Mexican American authors—History and criticism.
2. Literature and myth. 3. Mexican Americans in literature. 4. Indigenous peoples
in literature. 5. Cervantes, Lorna Dee—Criticism and interpretation. 6. Anzaldúa,
Gloria—Criticism and interpretation. 7. Alurista—Criticism and interpretation.
8. Villanueva, Alma, 1944—Criticism and interpretation. 9. Identity (Psychology)
in literature. 10. Ethnology—Methodology. I. Title.
PS153.M4C67 2008
810.9'37—dc22
2007035061

In Memory of Guadalupe Flores and Feliciana Flores

Contents

Acknowledgments

It is generally true that writing can be lonely; another truth is that few books are written in total isolation. I have benefited from an enormous amount of support and companionship while writing this book, which began when I was a graduate student in Austin, Texas, developed during a year at Williams College in Williamstown, Massachusetts, and came to completion during my employment at Michigan State University.

For some time now, I have pined for Texas, its sun, its warmth, its *gente mexicana*. I also have often missed a community at The University of Texas, which, although now dispersed, had an undeniable impact upon me. We plotted, argued, and drank at the Hole in the Wall and then danced in small, book-lined living rooms until the early morning. As members of the (sub)TEX Collective, many of us contributed to the publication of that independent newspaper in 1994–1995. Communities shift and change, as ours did, but there are people whom I will forever associate with that time: Marco Iñiguez-Alba, Gordon Banner, Manolo Callahan, Nick Evans, Rebecca Gámez, Brendan Guilfoyle, Salah D. Hassan, Luís Marentes, Pancho McFarland, Leopoldo Rodríguez, Natasha Sinutko, and Sandy Soto.

Raúl Salinas and Resistencia Bookstore provided a crucial site for activism and literary culture in Austin. José E. Limón's encouragement was significant in the early development of my work in Chicano studies as a graduate student at The University of Texas at Austin. I also want to acknowledge the important contributions of Mia Carter, Ann Cvetkovich, Martha Menchaca, and Charles Rossman.

Although I still long for Texas, I have come to understand something quite profound. *El movimiento* is alive and well . . . and it's in Michigan. The political intelligence and sophistication of MSU MEXA-sponsored actions energizes me. The work of *veteranas* such as Diana Rivera and Theresa Meléndez is instructive and propelling. Diana Rivera has tirelessly built one of the best collections—if not the best—of Chicana/o Studies materials in the Midwest in the César Chávez Collection at The Michigan State University Libraries. As director of Chicano/Latino Studies at Michigan State, Theresa Meléndez's intellectual confidence and activist- and student-centered model of administrating reminds me that it is necessary to nurture relationships between Chicana/o Studies programs and off-campus communities.

At MSU, I have also enjoyed significant support from Doug Noverr, the chair of my department, and from a number of other colleagues, but especially my dear friend, Maria Bruno. I also was fortunate to receive from Michigan State University an Intramural Research Grant, which provided me with a semester's release from teaching.

I am grateful to Rachana Kamtekar, Doreen Piano, Antonia Castañeda, and Louis Mendoza who provided insightful and indispensable comments on the manuscript as it developed. Many thanks to Theresa May, editor-in-chief, University of Texas Press, for all her assistance, and to Sally Furgeson, who helped me immensely in preparing the manuscript for publication.

At a more personal level, I want to acknowledge people in my extended family: my *tías,* Adelita Summerlin and Dolores (Lola) Gigee, *mi tío,* Reynaldo Flores, my cousin, Michelle Goss Poole, and my brothers, Mario Ricardo and Jason Eric. To my father, Richard Joseph Contreras, I owe my perseverance as it was he who raised me to *know* that I would be educated. My mother, Eloisa Flores, continues to pass to me lessons that deepen and complicate my understanding of the larger historical context that is *Tejas.*

I have developed family ties to others in Michigan. I have been inspired by the Deardorff-Greens, Charlotte Deardorff and Don Green, and Ben, Tara, and Tenzin Green, whose garden and home in Lansing provide me and my family with a sanctuary. Mary Ann Martin of La Leche League of Lansing has seen me through my daughters' infancies and toddlerhoods, all occurring during the writing of this book.

Salah D. Hassan has rallied his intellectual resources, his generosity, honesty, and rigor—even when depleted by the demands of his own professional obligations and our shared family responsibilities—to be my most motivating critic, my staunchest advocate, my loyal and trusted friend, my partner in life.

Finally, I honor my daughters, Noor Feliciana and Paz Alejandra Hassan-Contreras, who have brought light and peace to my life in ways that I could not ever have imagined.

Blood Lines

Prelude

C hicanas and Chicanos are indigenous to the Americas. But in the United States, Indigenous relationships to land and Indigenous identity are determined by a system of categorization that privileges tribal affiliation and blood quantum. Even if Indigenous descent is recognized, the concepts of tribal identity and genealogy may appear unrelated to Chicana/o culture and history. This disassociation is rendered logical by the facts of Spanish fluency and Spanish surnames among contemporary U.S. Mexicans. We now well know, however, that the realities of cultural and racial *mestizaje* are not as simple as "Indian and Spaniard."[1]

On the other hand, the evidence of a Spanish cultural patrimony has not granted Mexicans much respect, even if it does mean that many speak *two* European languages. Chicana/o status in the racial hierarchy of the United States is determined, rather, by the historical connection to Native people. Yet physical manifestations of Mexican descent from Indigenous peoples racialize Mexicans in ways that confound the conventional Black/White dichotomy of U.S. popular discourse. And although Mexicans have been *accused* of being Indian (see the discussion of the "Edward Duran Ayres Report" in Chapter 2), they have ironically never been considered anything but foreign in the United States.

For many people socialized in the United States, including Chicanas/os, American Indian histories, cultures, and contemporary realities are primarily conceived in the terms laid out by the "vanished race" myth, the classic film genre of the Western, and the 1970s Keep America Beautiful campaign.[2] Within families, however, narratives circulate that tell the tales of Chicana/o indigeneity. Stories that speak of *abuelas indígenas* with pride exist simultaneously with fierce denials of Indianness that elevate European ancestral ties. This ambivalence about Indigenous descent has deep and historic roots. Seventeenth-century Indigenous chronicler, don Domingo Francisco de San Antón Muñón Chimalpahin Quauhtlehuanitzin, now known simply as Chimalpahin, documented the beginnings of a particular form of Mexican racism:

> Those who are worthy men, be they mestizos, or mestizas, recognize that they come from us [the Indians]. But others without reflecting, mestizos and mestizas, do not want to recognize that they have some of our blood, some of our color. Only vainly do they attempt to pass for Spaniards, they look down on us, they mock us.
> (Quoted in León-Portilla, *Endangered Cultures* 110)[3]

Chicanas/os bear the weight of this history of social relations of power as they attempt to conceptualize relationships both to Mexico and to the United States. Davíd Carrasco writes of the "intense pride" and "cutting shame at my Mexican ancestry" he felt at age fifteen during what he terms his first "Aztec moment." This moment was brought on by a visit to the National Museum of Natural History on Moneda Street in Mexico City, which was his initial encounter with pre-Columbian artifacts, including the statue of Coatlicue.[4] Borrowing the term from a Chicana medical technician with whom he and two other Mexican-Americans dine after a Latino medical conference in Mexico City, Carrasco defines "Aztec moments" as a space in which

> Chicanos are able to *re-member* their roots, to expand their sense of identity beyond either Anglo definitions or the black-white dichotomy that animates so much of race discourse in the United States. And we felt pride in this remembering and were coming to realize that our *mestizaje* was both a complex social location and also a symbolic meaning *from which* we viewed the world with complex eyes. (175)

The alteration of the word "remember," changing it from its conventional meaning of "recalling" into "reassembling," very much evokes Gloria Anzaldúa's treatment of the snake and the goddess Coatlicue in *Borderlands/La Frontera: The New Mestiza,* which I will discuss in Chapter 3. Carrasco's usage, like Anzaldúa's, suggests a conscious, intentional activity that at once represents intellectual development and cultural revitalization. In these moments, the link between contemporary mestiza/o identity and pre-Conquest Mesoamerica, specifically the Aztecs, is both forged and strengthened.[5] The conceptual space of the Aztec moment, according to Carrasco, enables Chicanas/os to recognize that the history of cultural and racial *mestizaje* results in multiple, complicated, contradictory, and even fleeting sociocultural positionings (Spanish, Indian, Mexican, Mexican-American, Chicana, Chicano, American, immigrant, etc.), and also that this history functions as both a metaphor and a medium that structures Chicana/o worldviews, what Carrasco calls "cosmovisions." His exposure to the Salón de Monolitos, which housed the Stone of the Sun as well as the Coatlicue statue, opened an aperture through which Carrasco saw that, in his experience to that point, "Mexico was a country valued only for its defeats, jokes, and folklore but not for its civilization" (176). He arrives at a place of appreciation, admiration, and respect for the ingenuity, creativity, and sophistication of the Aztecs, realizing that "the depth of Mexican culture was profound and fascinating" (176).

Carrasco's recorded visit to the Museum must have occurred before the monuments were moved to their current location in Chapultepec Park in 1964, although historical collections were moved in 1940 to Chapultepec Castle (Bernal 322). The Museum was previously located on Moneda Street, its creation part of the implementation of a national museum system after independence was achieved in 1821. The Moneda Street building underwent major remodeling in preparation for the centennial of Mexican independence, with an emphasis on the "reconstruction of a national history" (Florescano, "Creation" 94). In this reconstruction, Mexico's museum system drew from its rich reservoir of pre-Columbian cultural artifacts. Both the Moneda Street and Chapultepec incarnations share an overt and orchestrated centering of Aztec artifacts, which leads visitors to a specific understanding of the evolution of the Mexican nation. Writing of Moneda Street, Enrique Florescano argues that "through this great museum plan the ancient monuments came to function as the symbols of Mexican identity. They became the proud testimony of the creativity and cultural development of the Mexican people throughout their history" ("Creation" 94).[6] Carrasco's brief autobiographical sketch is evidence of the Museum's success.

The current Museum also continues this work of building national pride. After it opened in 1966, Ignacio Bernal, then director, published an article in *Current Anthropology* on the Museum's history, its holdings, its organization, its social function, and its unique and privileged place among world museums. In describing the layout of the then-new Museum, he writes that "[t]here comes a series of halls along the north side of the building which follow the cultural stages of the central valleys . . . since the Preclassic Horizon, to end in an immense central hall dedicated to the Aztec world" (323). Commenting on this feature of the Museum, Florescano tells us that "the atavism of the Aztec monuments in the Hall of Monoliths during the Porfirian period [during which the Museo enjoyed significant government patronage] now emerged with greater force in the new museum where the Mexica hall was the central focus of the building and a type of sacred cathedral of the exalted Aztec culture" ("Creation" 100). The floor plan of the Museum, according to Shelly Errington, was designed to guide visitors through this archaeological version of progress, toward the final, illustrious example of pre-Conquest technological and cultural sophistication, the Aztec Empire, symbolized by the Aztec calendar stone at the center of the room ("Progressivist" 234).

Octavio Paz has famously criticized the National Museum of Anthropology, writing that it is "an architecture built of the solemn matter of myth" ("Critique" 108). In "Critique of the Pyramid," written after the massacre of student demonstrators at Tlatelolco in 1968, Paz condemns the Mexican state as a continuation of "the Aztec model of domination in our contemporary history," censuring the Museum for its adulation of Aztec rule (111). The display of pre-Columbian Mexico, he argues, distorts history and diminishes horrific violence. Recognizing that the glorification of the Aztecs is the state's attempt to exalt itself, Paz calls for the dissolution of idols and the confrontation of realities both historical and immediate (112).

Nevertheless, Mexican state reclamation of an Aztec patrimony has a legitimacy that Chicana/o indigenism is unable to achieve, at least in a Mexican context. Later in his essay, Carrasco details another Aztec moment involving Mexican archaeologist Eduardo Matos Moctezuma. Following the excavation of the Aztec Templo Mayor, Matos is puzzled by the calls he receives from Chicanos in the United States "who claim they feel some deep connection to the Templo Mayor." Matos tells Carrasco that in Mexico "we know Aztlan was much closer to Tenochtitlan" and that "most Mexicans who migrate to the United States do not come from the territory of the Aztec empire" (Carrasco 177). He asks Carrasco for help in understanding this phenomenon of Chicano fascination with the Aztec ceremonial site and the Aztec homeland, Aztlán. Carrasco devotes the rest of the essay to reinvigorating the myth and the symbol of Aztlán, calling attention to sources in the colonial record, specifically Diego Durán's *History of the Indies of New Spain,* and interpreting contemporary Chicana/o art. He situates Diego Durán's account in an immediate post-Conquest period, during which conquered Indigenous people attempted to formulate a logic and recast mythic systems to make sense of what had happened to them and provide "hope for a return to paradise" (188). Aztlán, according to Carrasco, has *always* been a regenerative, recuperative, and transitional symbol. Yet, Carrasco never really addresses Matos' question of Chicano appropriation of the Aztecs. Why the Aztecs, when most Chicanas/os, according to Matos and with implicit confirmation by Carrasco, can assert no ancestral link to the Indigenous peoples of the Valley of Mexico?

My own answer to this question would redirect our attention to Mexico and to the nationalist project made apparent in the organization of the Museum of Anthropology. We could as easily ask, in that context, why the Aztecs, given the cultural diversity that existed among Indigenous peoples at the time of the conquest and that continues today? Errington speculates as to the reasons for this curious exaltation of the Central Valley of Mexico over all other regions of Indigenous Mexico. She argues that the Aztecs are the most prominent Indigenous group to have been conquered by the Spanish. Certainly there were others, but it was the Aztecs who saw their capital replaced, *literally,* by the Spanish capital when the Spaniards built their cathedral directly on top of the sacred space, Templo Mayor. In 1821, the capital of post-colonial Mexico remained in the Valley: "Events that count, events that matter, take place at the same site and are continuous with what went before" ("Progressivist" 239). The persistence of Mexico City as center makes it "the most visible site of the creation of the mestizo" (240). According to Errington, there is historical precedence for concentrating the ancient history of Mexico in the Valley as it is the site of most of the historical "action": migration, conquest, colonial rule, independence, the emergence of a nationalist identity. Although it is true that other Indigenous groups suffered at the hands of the Spaniards, even those that allied with them to defeat the Aztecs, it is the Aztec downfall that has perhaps captured most forcefully the imagination of chroniclers, historians, and explorers. The conquest of the Aztecs stands in as the conquest of Mexico in its entirety, and so the archaeological exhibition at the Museum, says Errington, is able to "assert that . . . the Mexica have as descendants all Mexicans, who are their heirs" (238). Thus, Errington continues, contemporary Mexicans are "present-day Aztecs."

It really is no wonder that Carrasco, and other Chicanas/os, have Aztec moments. Or that Carrasco would answer Matos with an extended meditative appropriation of Aztec mythology and cosmogony. What the Mexican case makes clear is that the glorification of the Aztecs is less about establishing a direct line of descent than it is about carefully crafting a national telos that moves from Teotihuacan to Tenochtitlan to present-day Mexico City. Thus, Mexican nationals like Matos may question Chicano affiliation with and emotional attachment to Tenochtitlan, and yet at the same time promote the Aztecs as the most glorified of cultural patrimonies the Mexican state has at its disposal.

Matos' reaction, of course, also reveals the cultural distance between Mexicans and Chicanas/os. Even as many Chicanas/os might look to Mexico as a homeland of sorts, Mexico does not necessarily return the affection. Chicanas/os remain "ex-Mexicans" or even "gringas/os," foreign to Mexico, but also to the United States. Chicana/o indigenist attempts to assert a pre-Conquest origin in the Americas should be understood in relation to this dual displacement and the need to create a narrative of belonging. Mexican state indigenism preceded Chicana/o cultural revitalization efforts and therefore helped put into play a conceptual system easily transported into U.S. Mexican America. More curious, however, than the apparent non sequitur of Chicana/o recuperation of Aztec gods and goddesses is the history of European appropriation of these same artistic forms and mythic pantheons.

This is not to say that Chicana/o indigenism, Mexican state indigenism, and European modernist primitivism operate in the same manner. Obviously, the contexts from which they emerge are highly specific. The motivations and goals of each are radically different as are, one could argue, their effects. The idea that Mexican state indigenism and European and Euro-American primitivism rely upon an anthropological and archaeological archive probably does not surprise anyone. *Blood Lines* undertakes an exploration of Chicana/o indigenism and its usage of this same archive, calling attention to a system of textual referencing that is both similar to and draws from preceding traditions of Mexican indigenism and European primitivism. What follows is not offered as a negative critique of the use of archaeological research and mythic reconstruction, but, rather, as a highlighting of it in order to complicate received ideas about Chicana/o indigeneity.

That Chicanas/os have looked to the writings of European and Euro-American archaeologists, anthropologists, and art historians in order to assert, theorize, and dramatize Chicanas'/os' relation to a pre-Conquest past is not in itself a problem. Victor Zamudio-Taylor has argued for placing Chicana/o art within the tradition of modernist art, and that doing so "creates a place and genealogy for it in qualitatively different terms, opening the way for the fashioning of new art histories" (344). Similarly, discussing, rather than diminishing, the significance of the archaeological and primitivist archive to Chicana/o indigenism mobilizes new understandings of Chicana/o cultural production and its relation to European and Euro-American traditions. Even as we recognize that Chicana/o indigenism occupies familiar terrain, we remain able to chart its reorganization of that terrain. Ultimately, this awareness should only strengthen the force of Chicana/o literary and other acts of appropriation, intervention, and resistance.

Myths, Indigenisms, and Conquests

C hicana/o indigenism draws from a wealth of source material, directly and indirectly, acknowledged and unacknowledged, creating cultural narratives that rely prominently on mythic accounts drawn from anthropology and archaeology. This study is about the complications and paradoxes of Chicana/o literary indigenism, most especially this reliance on the mythic. Focusing on Chicana/o critical discourse as it is articulated in the academy, fiction, poetry, and essay, *Blood Lines* examines a uniquely Chicana/o practice of valorizing the Indian. At the same time that I set out the distinct character of Chicana/o literary indigenism, I also place these writings within the context of dominant narratives of the Indian in the Americas, including Anglo-American and European modernist primitivism and the *indigenismo* of the post-revolutionary Mexican state. Made possible by the "techniques of knowledge" and "strategies of power" (Spivak, "Subaltern" 274) that previously assured subaltern silence, Chicana/o indigenism must be understood as yet another stage in the history of the representation of Indians.

Even as Chicana/o indigenist discourse puts forth its critiques of racial domination, colonial violence, and land removal, it remains embedded within the very "circuits" of knowledge and power that have advanced imperialist agendas. Gayatri Spivak calls it the "imbrication of techniques of knowledge with strategies of power" ("Marginality" 59), suggesting that modes of learning and claims of knowledge are informed by discourses of control and domination. Stuart Hall provides additional useful instruction on this topic as he addresses the question of cultural identity and representation. Challenging the simple binary of the *Présence Africaine* and the *Présence Européenne* in the Afro-Caribbean, he argues that the two are never exclusive, instead existing as mutually informing and transforming.

He contends, however, that it is the European presence that has fixed the Black subject "within its dominant regimes of representation: the colonial discourse, the literatures of adventure and exploration, the romance of the exotic, the ethnographic and traveling eye, the tropical languages of tourism, travel brochure and Hollywood . . ." ("Cultural" 233).

Hall's list ranges from the documents of colonial administrators and religious authority figures to accounts penned by explorers and travelers in colonial outposts and settler sites. Consider another context, for example, the documentation of the conquest of the Americas. Here, we find the recordings of Nahua myth, the translations and transcriptions of Aztec codices, the accounts of pre-Conquest civilization extracted from Native informants, and the first-person accounts of military and religious campaigns. These texts over time entered public discourse and attained, in many cases, the status of scientific observation. "The ethnographic and traveling eye" gained legitimacy as its narrative production was institutionalized in the fields of anthropology and archaeology. All of these narrative forms, from the documents of colonial administration to the unsanctioned accounts of those operating outside the institutions of state and religious power, have left their traces in the "tropical languages" popularized by contemporary touristic and media discourses.

Such texts perpetuate the colonial discourses that defined colonized subjects, established and legitimated the institutional power exerted upon them, and, often, unwittingly, eternalized the presence of those subjects.[1] But we must not lose sight of Hall's major point above, and that is that European representations of Black subjects have become "a constitutive element" of Black self-representation. In other words, such administrative and travel narratives not only instantiated the image of the colonized periphery in the minds of those in the colonial center, but also worked to produce identity for the very Indigenous subjects objectified in these accounts.

The Significance of Myth

Chicana/o indigenism is deeply influenced by these European and Anglo-American "regimes of representation," which structure Chicana/o indigeneity to an extent. It is impossible to consider pre-Columbian religion and history outside the context of their presentation. The artifacts that often engender indigenist response are accessed visually through museum exhibits, as well as through photographic and other forms of reproduction found in art books, anthropological texts, and explorer narratives. Thus, indigenism interlocks with the circuits of knowledge and power that I refer to above and that are evident in the distribution of pre-Columbian myth. The sustained and explicit use of myth in Chicana/o indigenist texts connects indigenist thematics to one of those circuits, specifically, anthropological discourse. Myth has been a primary realm of anthropological research and representation, from the translations of cave paintings and codices to attempts to collect the stories of a "vanishing race" in the western plains of the United States. In the case of the region known today as the state of Mexico, Western fascination with myth and its subsequent role in the circulation of information about Indigenous cultures and histories is evident in the numerous texts about the country, including the amateur anthropological travel accounts, which have taken the mythological as organizing theme.

Books like Neil Baldwin's 1998 *Legends of the Plumed Serpent: Biography of a Mexican God,* a tour through the "remote ruins" of Mexico, point to mythology as the defining feature of Mexico's pre-Conquest past, with almost complete disregard for Indigenous populations of the present. In recalling his decision to write the book, arrived at while lazing on the Isla Mujeres in some form of margarita-induced reverie, Baldwin recounts his dissatisfaction with the quality and quantity of materials designed to introduce the tourist to Mexico's past. Speaking about the site of Uxmal, he writes:

> There was no mythic background for the place, no sense conveyed of the intrinsic, underlying meaning, which predates the usual descriptions of what invading Spaniards saw and did when they arrived in the sixteenth century. (3)

Baldwin intends to address his concern by charting the trail of Quetzalcoatl in the archaeological ruins of Mexico. His remedy for the dearth of information is precisely this focus on the mythic, an apparent antidote to the "usual descriptions" of European invaders. It is myth, Baldwin suggests, rather than history, that reveals the essence of the country; it "predates" European accounts of the history of the Conquest and conveys "intrinsic, underlying meaning." It is through myth that we attain our deepest understanding of Indigenous Mexico, as we abandon the false constructs of European historical narratives and arrive at the essential. What Baldwin does not account for is that the fundamental meanings he purports to offer the reader are for the most part merely the explanations of non-Indigenous social scientists.

Indigenous mythologies have also received a fair amount of critical attention in the Western academy. The prominence of anthropologists such as Claude Lévi-Strauss in the theorization of myth makes evident the anthropological concern with the mythic. One could say that mythology is the province of anthropologists, who have expended a great deal of effort collecting and assembling myth and folklore as a way to explain primitive cultures. From the expansive four-volume *Mythologiques* to the condensed series of radio talks found in *Myth and Meaning,* however, Lévi-Strauss also advocated for an understanding of the role of myth in contemporary Western society. He rejected the idea that myth is simply the product of "primitive" thinking unable to move beyond the utilitarian aspects of existence, the search for survival, the struggle for the "next whole meal," and, in this proposition, he departed greatly from the theories of another prominent anthropologist, Bronislav Malinowski.[2] Lévi-Strauss understood myth as language and also as something different, a form of speech more complex than other linguistic forms or expressions. Using the Saussurean terms "langue" and "parole," he describes the first as the "structural side of language . . . belonging to a reversible time" and the second as "the statistical side of language . . . being non-reversible" (*Structural Anthropology* 209). Myth, he explains, is a combination of the two and bringing together these "time referents" creates a "third referent": "the specific pattern described is timeless; it explains the present and the past as well as the future" (209). Myth, therefore, both acknowledges and dismisses history; it is at once "historical and ahistorical" (210).

Lévi-Strauss' attempt to import linguistic methods into the study of myth has been roundly critiqued, as has his idea that myth depends upon a structural rigor and mobilizes systems of signification of which its tellers are unaware.[3] Although Jonathan Culler is convinced by Lévi-Strauss' structural approach when used to read groupings of myth that share a similar meaning, he remains decidedly unconvinced of the broader application of Lévi-Strauss' method. Most significantly, argues Culler, the anthropologist fails to provide evidence about meaning, ignoring the vital role that linguistic competence plays in the theorization of linguistics. "More than anything else," Culler writes, "it is the lack of data about meaning that vitiates the analogy with linguistics, for in the study of language the structural and the semiological cannot be dissociated: the relevant structures are those which enable sequences to function as signs" (49). Lévi-Strauss' method may bring together myths from vastly unrelated cultural contexts to reveal meaning, but it offers nothing to explain what the differences between those myths actually mean. In Culler's estimation, Lévi-Strauss invents meaning as he makes his argument for the structure of myth; however, the viability of that structure relies upon community understanding of its conventions. The fact that "[w]e know little about how to read myths" (Culler 51), that readers have no competency in Lévi-Strauss' system because meaning is contrived only by/in the quest to determine structure, means that myth, finally, is left unexplained. What Culler does grant Lévi-Strauss is ample credit for approaching "mythology as an institution" (50), and attempting to understand myth beyond the level of the local and the individual. Andrew Von Hendy similarly notes the contribution Lévi-Strauss makes by "establishing 'myth' as an object of study in its own right" (250), only the first of a series of accomplishments that Von Hendy ascribes to Lévi-Strauss.

What interests me most about Lévi-Strauss' approach is what the anthropologist had to say about the relationship between myth and history, which explains my choice of quotations in representing his work. Similarly compelling as we consider the interaction of myth with history is literary critic Roland Barthes' analysis, in which he defines myth as a "third level" of language. He elaborates this idea as a "second-order semiological system," one that takes the sign of the first-order semiological system of language as its signifier:

> [M]eaning loses its value, but keeps its life, from which the form of the myth will draw its nourishment. The meaning will be for the form like an instantaneous reserve of history, a tamed richness, which it is possible to call and dismiss in a sort of rapid alternation: the form must constantly be able to be rooted again in the meaning and to get there what nature it needs for its nutriment; above all, it must be able to hide there. It is this constant game of hide-and-seek between the meaning and the form which defines myth. (*Mythologies* 118)

Thus, according to Barthes, myth again is form, rather than content, a speech type, rather than the concept or idea itself. The tenacity of mythic speech is derived from its ability to deploy or reflect at will a meaning held in perpetual reserve. Myth is parasitic, drawing its life force from vapid "meanings" that persist despite their apparent worthlessness. And although any and all myths surely have historical origins, those origins are forgotten or discarded in the dissemination of myth. Yet, myth hides nothing; it is not sneaky or intentionally deceptive; it is, in fact, quite plain and straightforward. Its primary purpose is to naturalize its intentions, not to hide them as it "transforms history into nature" (128). Even more than Louis Althusser, who never actually defined his use of the term "myth," Barthes renders myth virtually synonymous with "ideology . . . by talking as if 'ideology' were something subsisting in practice entirely in its myriad networks of cultural 'mythologies'" (Von Hendy 290). More-over, what distinguishes Barthes' structuralist analysis of myth is its basis in a popular sense of myth as "widely propagated lie," a theoretical mo-bilization of the term inaugurated by Althusser (Von Hendy 290). From Barthes' perspective, the confusions and untruths enacted by myth are the workings of bourgeois ideology, which must be permanently and vigi-lantly critiqued.[4]

These contested propositions—that myth is a form of speech, that it reactivates the sign as form to initiate a further system of signification, that it depends upon history even as it erases it, and that it renders its motivations as part of a natural order—nevertheless can help us to discern the complexities of Chicana/o indigenist use of myth. Chicana/o indigen-ism relies upon an already established signifying order, one launched by the narratives of travel and exploration and later professionalized in the consolidation of anthropology as an academic discipline. Chicana/o ex-pressions of literary indigenism mobilize cultural conventions, investing them with new meaning. The Coatlicue statue that Anzaldúa presents, or the Aztec and Maya cosmogony that the poet Alberto Urista, more commonly known as Alurista, calls upon, bring with them not the unique historical fullness of the civilizations that created them but rather accepted notions about the pre-technological, the pre-modern, the pre-Christian, and the primitive. That all these ideas express something about people and societies that existed in the Americas before the arrival of the En-glish, the French, and the Spanish is unquestioned and critical for the purposes of Chicana/o indigenism. As the sign is redeployed as a signi-fier in this second-order system of myth, the new meaning attached to it says something now about Chicanas/os specifically, about their ancestral knowledge, about cultural genealogy, but most importantly about their historical primacy.

A recent example proves illustrative. In her address to the 2003 Mod-ern Language Association convention in San Diego, MLA president Mary Louise Pratt invoked Coatlicue in an attempt to recognize, or per-haps honor, the oppositional geographic entity of Aztlán, homeland of Chicanas/os:

> We're in the heart of Greater Aztlán, and in that spirit I'd like to call
> tonight on the company of one of its most gorgeous and powerful
> deities, Coatlicue, goddess of life and death, mother of the meditative

plumed serpent Quetzalcoatl, of the war-like Huitzilopochtli, and of his sister and archrival Coyolxauhqui. Coatlicue is recognized by her skirt of serpents and her necklace of skulls and hands. In this beautiful carving, recovered in 1790 when the main plaza of Mexico City was being paved, she has been decapitated, and a two-headed serpent has appeared where her head was. I'd like to imagine her tonight as a work of border art, standing on *la linea,* looking both ways. (417)

She identifies Coatlicue as a goddess of Aztlán, a discursive move made possible by Gloria Anzaldúa's *Borderlands/La Frontera: The New Mestiza,* published in 1987. Pratt introduces Coatlicue as a goddess of duality, presiding over life and death, giving birth both to the god of peace, Quetzalcoatl, and the god of war, Huitzilopochtli. Coatlicue also functions as a bridge across the U.S.-Mexico border, so very present yet also remarkably absent in the border city of San Diego, especially in its downtown convention district. Farther south, however, the militarization of *la frontera* and the toll it takes in human lives is evident in the barbed wire fences and guard towers of the port of entry, as well as in the traffic signs designed to warn motorists of women and children who might appear in the middle of the freeway in flight from *la migra.* Pratt's political reference to San Diego as "the heart of Aztlán" counterbalances her reference to Coatlicue's emergence in the form of a statue recovered from underneath the Zócalo in Mexico City. Pratt thus introduces a transnational Coatlicue, who originated in the ancient Aztec capital of Tenochtitlan and has become a goddess of Aztlán, the mythic mother of Chicanas/os. Such a rhetorical maneuver would have made little sense and, in fact, may have not been possible without the precedent set by Anzaldúa, who claimed and refigured Coatlicue in a form designed to empower Chicanas. Yet, Pratt's mobilization of the symbol of Coatlicue neglects to acknowledge Anzaldúa's initial intervention into pre-Columbian myth and its post-Columbian reception and, in this omission, says much about how effectively myth works and how quickly even its most recent transformations evaporate from memory.

Literary Primitivism and Mexico

The mythic in Chicana/o literary indigenism is entwined with literary primitivism, which finds its own sources in the narratives of anthropology and archaeology. Primitivism has been considered, to a large degree, as an art-historical term, which William Rubin, co-organizer of the 1984 Museum of Modern Art (MOMA) exhibit, "Primitivism" in 20th Century Art, defines as the "interest of modern artists in tribal art and culture, as revealed in their thought and work" (1).[5] In his deft critique of Rubin and co-curator, Kirk Varnedoe, Hal Foster challenges the "tribal-modern affinity" that is the organizing theme of the show. Despite the acknowledgment of modern interest in "tribal art and culture," according to Foster, the curators' more central goal is to position tribal and modern art alongside each other and to diminish the sphere of influence from tribal to modern. As an example, Foster cites MOMA's use of Picasso's *Les Demoiselles d'Avignon* as set piece for the show displayed in tandem with African masks, which have frequently been identified as source material for the painting. The argument for affinity, however, "runs that Picasso could not have seen these masks, that the painting manifests an intuitive primitivity or 'savage mind'" (46).[6] Furthermore, and perhaps most damning, is that the show suppressed the history of colonialism and the bribery, trickery, and theft that made primitive art available to Europe.[7]

Rubin's use of the term differs from cultural and/or chronological primitivism, in which practitioners celebrate instinct, simplicity, and an unmediated relationship with "nature" over "civilization," which is equated with the advent of capitalism, industrialism, and technology. Such beliefs may or may not be coupled with a glorification of a "golden age" of history, or "pre-history." They may find expression in the adoption of artistic forms and styles of so-called primitive peoples. Across these definitions, however, it seems that Maximillian Novak's assessment of primitivism in the eighteenth century continues to hold true in that it is "the idealization of a way of life that differs from our own in being less complicated, less polished, and less self-aware" (456).

Perhaps the most radical forms of cultural and chronological primitivism combined can be found in the deep ecology and some anarchist movements, which reject civilization and its oppressive mechanisms of capitalism and patriarchy. Fundamentally influenced by the writings of John Zerzan, these movements are called variously anarcho-primitivism, the anti-civilization movement, radical primitivism, or anti-authoritarian primitivism (See John Moore). Such iterations of primitivism demand the rejection of technology to reverse and overcome the damaging effects of a regimented and repressive division of labor designed in accordance with class and gender hierarchies. Deep ecologist and anarchist philosophies seek to combat the alienation of the worker that results from the segmentation and specialization of labor, which these philosophies identify as the foundation of modern civilization.

Apart from deep ecology and anarchist thinking, most versions of Western primitivist philosophy do not promote an actual "return" to modes of living that preceded civilization. Instead, as in the context of modern art, primitivism more likely attempts to incorporate, emulate, reproduce, or, by some accounts, appropriate the artistic forms of the "non-Western," or "tribal," peoples to which Rubin refers. In other cases, the emphasis is more explicitly on the idea of the primitive given human form: the tribal person, the African chieftain, the Caribbean "voodoo doctor," the Indian warrior and medicine wo/man, the Native woman, the Noble Savage. All versions of primitivism, however, rest to some degree upon this sort of imagining. They might idealize the pre-historical human who existed and thrived outside of the repressive confines of modern civilization or the anonymous Native artist/craftsman whose work expresses the sensibilities not of the individual but of the community to which that person belongs. We find primitivist projects that idealize an excavated ancestor whose visage, corporeal existence, and belief systems are accessible only through the documentations of his/her dispossessor. These documentations include images of goddesses and gods deemed worthy of preservation and legitimated in the present through the academic disciplines of archaeology and art history.

Foster provides a concise review of the primitive in Western culture as historically "articulated . . . in deprivative or supplemental terms" (58). Thus, the primitive is either abject barbarian or spiritual guide, pre-literate, pre-historical, culturally simplistic, or "a site of originary unity, symbolic plentitude, natural vitality" (58). Primitives are most often viewed as a source of regenerative energy, Sally Price points out, because they are "imagined to express their feelings free from the intrusive overlay of learned behavior and conscious constraints that mold the work of the Civilized Artist" (32). In the first extensive study of primitivism and art, Robert Goldwater also suggested the guiding logic behind the modernist desire to dig deeper into the collective psyche:

> It is the assumption that any reaching under the surface, if only it is carried far enough and proceeds according to the proper method, will reveal something "simple" and basic which, because of its very fundamentality and simplicity, will be more emotionally compelling than the superficial variations of the surface; and finally that the qualities of sim-

plicity and basicness are things to be valued in and for themselves: In other words, it is the assumption that the further one goes back—historically, psychologically, or aesthetically—the simpler things become; and that because they are simpler they are more profound, more important, and more valuable. (251)

This idea of profound simplicity stands in direct challenge to the meaningless complexities and ruptures of modern civilization and so the primitive has served many purposes since its emergence in the Enlightenment period. Indeed, from Montaigne to Rousseau to D. H. Lawrence to Georges Bataille, versions of primitivism have long been used to challenge accepted versions of the civilized. The primitive is structured as opposition; through its image, "Western" culture is revealed as spiritually lacking, morally corrupt, misdirected, and self-destructive. In its earliest formulations, primitivism—the transvalorization of the "non-civilized"— questioned the politics and policies of dominant cultures. Writers and artists continue to appropriate the idea of "the savage," of which the Indian is a version, as a vehicle for social critique, using it to express dismay over progress and modernization and to advance arguments for simpler, less complicated modes of living premised on a "return" to more "natural" philosophies of existence. Communitarian social structures and relaxed social mores, especially as related to sexual practices (although primitivist discourse has been decidedly heterosexist and patriarchal), are features of so-called primitive society glorified by writers past and present.

The primitive exists, in part, as a means through which and against which non-primitives define themselves and their own cultural contexts. This discourse that defines and appropriates Native cultures functions, ironically, to maintain the place of "the West" in the evolutionary order. Even if Western society is found to be corrupt and empty of "real" meaning, it continues to retain its place as civilized in relation to primitive societies and, in fact, is made the more enlightened precisely because of this recognition of the value of the "uncivilized." In their attempts to celebrate Indigenous cultures, primitivists identify features or practices that might be collected and imported into a Western context to make civilized life richer. In few cases do primitivists actually want to adopt fully a primitive lifestyle. The primitive, rather, is an exotic symbol that can be used to represent "man" in a condition of nature, as in the writings of Montaigne, or unconscious drives, as in the work of D. H. Lawrence. Academics, philosophers, and other writers have imposed an arduous task, that of charting a path of redemption for Europeans and European-Americans.

Mexico and Primitivism

In studies of modernist primitivism, little attention has been given to the place of Mexico as a site for European spiritual and cultural redemption, perhaps, in part, because European and Euro-American representations of Mexican culture emphasize a fascination with death that is traced back to pre-Conquest religious practices of human sacrifice. Goldwater, who was the first director of the Museum of Primitive Art in New York, an early historian of modern art, and considered one of the first experts in the study of African art, writes in *Primitivism in Modern Art* that because the Aztec and Inca civilizations had "long been destroyed and their lands occupied," they did not offer living examples of primitive simplicity (266). These societies did not conform to modernist ideas of the static nature of primitive societies or answer the need for contemporary examples of the perceived "immemorial" character of the primitive. Benjamin Keen, following Goldwater's lead, also contends that because of the "relatively high degree of formal complexity" of ancient Mesoamerican societies, discernable particularly in Aztec artifacts, Mexico had less influence than Africa and Oceania on modern primitivism (510).

Rubin, former director of Painting and Sculpture at the Museum of Modern Art, writes in the introduction to the catalog for the 1984 MOMA exhibit, "Primitivism" in 20th Century Art, that he considers Aztec art to be more "archaic" than "primitive" and more logically grouped with Egyptian art. Rubin bases this assessment on the apparent strict levels of hierarchy and specialization in Aztec social structure. It is, rather, the arts of "tribal" Africa and Oceania that are more properly classified as "primitive," whereas Aztec, Maya, and Toltec art, according to Rubin, issues from "court" cultures (74–75 n.14). These particular Mesoamerican civilizations, he writes, were exceptions in the context of pre-Columbian cultural forms, which, for the most part, have much more in common with what is more properly deemed "primitive" in the art world. Although he does acknowledge the interest in pre-Columbian art among modern artists, he argues that the influence emanated from the "Archaic sculpture of the Aztec, Maya, Toltec and Olmec cultures" (74–75 n.14).[8] Barbara Braun concurs with the previous assessments to a degree when she argues that although they had been circulating in Europe as curiosities and exotica since the sixteenth century, "Pre-Columbian artifacts were never central to the 'primitivist revolution'; unlike African objects, they played no important role in Picasso's generation of Cubism" (38).[9] Rubin includes a rather lengthy footnote documenting Picasso's ambivalent responses to "what he called 'l'art aztèque,' by which he meant the whole of Columbian art as he knew it" (333 n.5). In one case, in a conversation with Rubin, he calls pre-Columbian art "boring, inflexible, too big . . . figures without invention" (75 n.15). Yet Rubin quotes from a collection of interviews and conversations in which the Hungarian-born French photographer Brassaï documents Picasso's reaction to a photograph of pre-Columbian art: the "'Aztec head' makes Picasso pause abruptly, and then he cries: 'That is as rich as the façade of a cathedral'" (75 n.15).[10]

Braun also notes, however, that in the late nineteenth century, pre-Columbian artifacts began to "[inspire] Western designers, artists, and craftspersons to incorporate and imitate them in their own work" (21). She credits Paul Gauguin's interest in decorative arts to the inspiration he received from exhibitions at the Paris Expositions of 1878 and 1889 (38). The display of pseudo-ancient Mexican material culture was especially notable in 1889, where the ambitious, if anthropologically, architecturally, and historically confused Aztec Palace was constructed at the foot of the Eiffel Tower.[11] Vincent Van Gogh early expressed an interest in primitivism, most immediately recognizable in his praise of ancient Egyptian art, but also documented in his curiosity about "the tropics."[12] Although he did not see the History of Habitation display at the 1889 Exposition, he did see an image of a simulated ancient Mexican structure designed not by Mexicans, but by a French architect.[13] Van Gogh wrote to Emile Bernard that "I saw in one of the illustrated papers a sketch of ancient Mexican dwellings; they too seem to be primitive and very beautiful" (Read 48).[14] It was Gauguin's and Van Gogh's announcements of their own fascinations with the primitive that launched an interest in Aztec art in the 1930s, according to Rubin.

Ethnographic and archaeological information about pre-Columbian Mesoamerica, however, had been circulating in Europe for some time. Braun brings together a wide-ranging list of travelers, explorers, tycoons, and amateur archaeologists who began producing textual material in the early nineteenth century. Among these was the explorer Alexander von Humboldt, who traveled to Mexico in 1803, where he convinced authorities to disinter the statue of Coatlicue, which had been reburied shortly after it was excavated in 1790. Braun credits his work, *Vues des Cordilleres, et Monuments des Peuples Indigenes de l'Amérique,* part of a thirty-volume series on America, with "reshap[ing] the European vision of ancient Mexico and stimulat[ing] further explorations" (26). The photographic and other reproductions of Désiré Chanay, who in 1857–58 visited several Mayan archaeological sites in Mexico, were also significant in the dissemination of visual images and narrative descriptions of ancient Meso-america. Unlike France, Britain did not attract public support for the study of pre-Columbian artifacts, but in 1822, William Bullock, "collector of natural and ethnographic curiosities and a showman" (Braun 30) organized a show of antiquities that he had brought back from Mexico. This show, staged in London's Piccadilly Circus, peaked the interest of Lord Edward Kingsborough in pre-Columbian manuscripts and was influential in the production of his encyclopedic *Antiquities of Mexico*, which later served as a source for Diego Rivera (Braun 31, Brown 139). The most impressive British collections were amassed by Henry Christy and Alfred P. Maudslay. Christy's collection provided the basis for the British Museum's pre-Columbian permanent collection when it received a bequest in 1865. In the 1860s and 1870s, Braun writes, the first ethnographic galleries including pre-Columbian artifacts emerged in Paris and London, and in 1850, the Louvre opened its first Americanist exhibition containing approximately nine hundred objects. The Louvre collection, however, was eventually dismantled (31).

The first significant explorer from the United States was John L. Stephens, who traveled with Frederick Catherwood in the Yucatán and Central America during the period 1839–42. Stephens produced two volumes from these forays, *Incidents of Travel in Central America, Chiapas, and Yucatan* and *Incidents of Travel in Yucatan,* and both enjoyed immense popularity among the U.S. reading public. Catherwood's illustrations, engravings, and daguerreotypes remain the "most famous depictions" of the Mayan ruins partially because, Braun notes, William Prescott championed them in *The History of the Conquest of Mexico* (32).[15] The expeditions of Stephens and Catherwood were especially relevant in a time when the United States was struggling to establish its unique presence in relation to Europe. Thus, the artifacts of pre-Columbian civilizations, like the Indian mounds located within U.S. borders, provided material with which the country could assert an ancient patrimony to rival anything Europe had to offer. This type of collecting, in Braun's formulation, "became symbolic capital for both cosmopolitan status and confirmation of a national culture tied to the land" (32).[16]

Prior to the emergence of universities as the primary repositories of archaeological knowledge, it was, as Braun's overview summarized above makes clear, the museum that housed these knowledges. Museums were, according to Elizabeth Hill Boone, "the homeland of anthropology and archaeology" (329). In France, the Trocadero has been a place of signal importance for the modern public's access to ancient Mesoamerica. Harvard's Peabody Museum, endowed in 1860, became the "premier center of Pre-Columbian studies" (Braun 33) in the nineteenth century, and other important institutions included the emerging Smithsonian and the American Museum of Natural History. In the case of Britain, the British Museum was and continues to be a preeminent site of access for specialist and non-specialist alike.

The sculptor Henry Moore provides confirmation not only of Western artistic fascination with pre-Conquest Mexico, but also of the degree to which museums, and the British Museum in particular, function to instantiate versions of the primitive in the minds of their viewing audiences. Furthermore, articles in scholarly and popular journals, as well as book-length works provided details of archaeological expeditions, theories about life in pre-Conquest Mesoamerica, and, most importantly for Moore, reproductions that he modeled throughout his life.[17] Texts drawn from this archive proved invaluable to Moore, who consulted them as "sculptural pattern books, providing him with a repertory of images during the formative decade of his art" (Braun 98). Braun draws from Donald Hall's profile of the artist in a 1965 *New Yorker* series, noting that Moore was "something of a scholar of ancient Mexican sculpture" (97, n.17, 131). Rejecting Mayan sculpture as too similar to the Western tradition (Braun 107), Moore focused almost exclusively on Aztec sculpture, producing numerous works that not only evoke, but also clearly imitate particular Aztec artifacts. These works include masks; a series of sculptures entitled *Mother and Child,* the first carved in 1922; *Snake* (1924), a virtual replica of an Aztec coiled serpent; and the *Reclining Figure* series, famously modeled after the Chacmool, which appears throughout pre-Conquest Mesoamerica.[18] In keeping with conventional primitivist values, Moore intended for the "primordial vitality" of Aztec art to "miraculously infuse new life into modern art" (Braun 111).

In a 1941 essay, "Primitive Art," Moore offers his definition of the term he takes as his title, elaborating on it by narrating a "memory-journey" through selected galleries of the British Museum as he laments its closing (presumably during World War II). The sculptor attributes his knowledge of pre-Columbian art to his wanderings in the halls of the Museum, writing that "[e]xcepting some collections of primitive art in France, Italy and Spain, my own knowledge of it [primitive art] has come entirely from continual visits to the British Museum during the past twenty years" (269). On Mesoamerica in particular, he says that "Mexican sculpture, as soon as I found it, seemed to me true and right. . . . Its 'stoniness,' by which I mean its truth to material, its tremendous power without loss of sensitiveness, its astonishing variety and fertility of form-invention and its approach to a full three-dimensional conception of form, make it un-surpassed in my opinion by any other period of stone sculpture" (270). In his own reproductions of the Chacmool figure, Moore always feminizes his reclining figures, and in doing so, resituates his work in the realm of Western artistic conventions. His recumbent females are passive fig-ures that always look past the viewer. Their bodies are openly displayed, breasts prominent and pubic areas exposed, as if offered for consumption. "It is the old idealization of the female as a passive object of desire," Braun writes, "available to the determining male gaze as a symbolic release for lust, anxiety, and terror" (119). This represents, in Braun's final analysis, a "domestication of the primitive to Western culture by fusing its raw vitality, gravity, and mystery with familiar, acceptable content, such as the female figure, and conventional (sexist) attitudes towards it" (119).

This rehearsal of the relationship between the work of one of the most highly acclaimed modernist artists and the Aztec artifacts he sought out documents the impact of pre-Columbian culture in the post-Columbian art world, to draw upon the title to Braun's book. In Moore, we see the example of an artist searching for and then replicating what he believed to be truer forms of expression. Interestingly, in Braun's critique of Moore, we find a curious acceptance of the terms that primitivist thinking sets for itself, the vitality, the "spiritual fullness" that Foster earlier noted, the "mystery" of the unknown. But, more importantly, in the works of Braun, Foster, Rubin, and other art historians and critics, we have also been alerted to responses to pre-Columbian art—from Van Gogh, Picasso, and Moore—that suggest a rich variance of opinion among some of the most celebrated artists of the European modern period, even if none of them were motivated to claim Mexico as Gauguin did Tahiti.

Considering Indigenism

The term "indigenism" would seem to oppose primitivism as the former issues from a place of racial identification with, rather than strategic dis-tancing from, the "other." In Chicana/o writing, the term indigenism has been used to refer to texts that privilege and valorize Indigenous ancestry and culture.[19] Indigenism, however, has a complex history of negative criticism in Latin America. In the philosophy and practices of the post-Revolutionary Mexican state, "*indigenismo*" often refers to public policy initiatives spearheaded by mestizo intellectuals, such as anthropologist

Manuel Gamio, that pursued the explicit objective of "social realignment between the races" ("New Conquest" 143). Critical understandings of indigenista policies reveal the strategies of inclusion to be aimed at deracinating Indians, rather than redefining social legitimacy to include Indigenous communities and rectify the deep inequities in Mexican society. When outlining a "working policy for our study," in the May 1, 1924, issue of *The Survey Graphic,* Gamio writes that as the director of the anthropological branch of the Department of Agriculture, he is organizing "systematic efforts towards racial understanding, towards a fusion of the different cultures, towards linguistic unification and economic equilibrium. . . . We are convinced that it is only in this way that we may hope to achieve a coherent national consciousness, a true patria" (144). Couched in terms of hygiene, literacy, and economic readjustment, the project with which he has been charged and given the name "The New Conquest" is designed in such a way as to find little of value in the "backward civilization" (194) of the Indigenous communities of Mexico. Another Mexican anthropologist, Guillermo Bonfil-Batalla, well-known for his challenging of Mexican state indigenism, writes that "*[i]ndigenismo* did not contradict in any way the national plan that the triumphant Revolution had been crystallizing: to incorporate the Indian, that is, de-Indianize him, to make him lose his cultural and historical uniqueness" (116).

"Indigenism" also describes the stylistic appropriations of Indigenous cultural forms and traditions by non-Indigenous artists and intellectuals. It differs from primitivism in that the practitioners of indigenism have ancestral and cultural ties—however weakened by the passage of time—to Indigenous people. The origins of mestiza/o indigenism, according to Enrique Florescano, lie in a seventeenth-century "growing creole compulsion to identify themselves with the soil on which they lived and with the remote past of its original inhabitants" ("Creation" 82). In the late sixteenth century, the Spanish Crown blocked the collection and study of codices that could have preserved many more pre-Conquest histories. From the time of the Conquest, the collection of pictographic documents had been undertaken by missionaries, such as Juan de Tovar, Toribio Motolinía, and Bernardino de Sahagún, and the prevention of this practice had disastrous consequences for the Indigenous historical record in Mesoamerica. Some manuscripts escaped the Spanish authorities, Florescano writes, and these were "jealously kept by the descendants of the ancient native nobility and used as testimonies authenticating their lineage and patrimonial rights" ("Creation" 82).[20] But by 1780, Spanish authorities were beginning to support Creole examination and interpretation of pre-Conquest culture and history, which included excavations at Palenque

(Florescano, "Creation" 84). Unearthed monuments, such as the mono-liths excavated from the Templo Mayor in the Zócalo of Mexico City, were preserved, even if that meant reburying them, which was the case with the statue of the goddess Coatlicue. The statue was reinterred be-cause of Native responses to its presence, which included pilgrimages and displays of devotion that jarred religious and other authorities. Flores-cano points out that the functionaries in charge of the excavation and presentation of the artifacts to the public tried to transform a "living part of the beliefs and religious practices of the Indigenous population into an archaeological document" ("Creation" 86), ignoring the cultural practices and community beliefs of living Indigenous subjects. At the same time, these Creole elites appropriated an Indian past in order to construct a na-tional identity and provide a logic for Creole occupation of Native land. The reception of the Coatlicue statue at the time of its excavation is an important marker in historicizing the contradiction that remains at the center of Mexican state indigenism.

Although Mexican *indigenismo* preceded the Revolution, as an artistic trend it reached a zenith during Mexico's immediate post-Revolutionary period. Diego Rivera offers perhaps the most prominent example of a Mexican indigenist sensibility in his public murals commissioned by the Mexican state to adorn, for example, the halls of the National Palace and the Secretary of Public Education Building. Rivera brought images of the Indigenous into his panoramic visual narratives of Mexico and offered to the public astounding depictions of the agricultural, social, and techno-logical sophistication of a once-dominant civilization. Both in artistic ex-pression and public policy, *indigenista* activity by prominent artists, poli-ticians, and writers was considered to elevate Indians, to be executed on behalf of or in defense of them. For someone like Gamio, whose *Forjando Patria* (1916) is a founding text of state indigenism, incorporating the Indian both strengthened Mexican national culture and provided Indige-nous subjects access to the benefits offered by a modernized, homogenized nation-state, enabling them to move beyond their "backward" existence. Public policies designed to acculturate Indians—most especially through the institutions of schooling, anthropological projects, such as Gamio's world-renowned stratospheric excavations at Teotihuacan, and artistic projects, like those in which Rivera and other muralists participated—contrived to make past greatness visible and cement public acceptance of the desirable characteristics of Indigenous cultures. These approaches, however, belie the basic premise of Mexican state indigenism: the only good Indian is the mythic Indian.

Some, such as Bonfil-Batalla, have identified the problems with indigenism in the identities of its practitioners. It was non-Indians who devised *indigenismo* and decided "[t]he definition of what is 'good' and 'bad' in Indian cultures, what is useful and what should be discarded[. This] was not, of course, a matter in which the opinion of the Indians themselves counted. It was a matter, like all *indigenista* policy, in which only the non-Indians, the 'nationals,' those who exercised cultural control in the country and hoped to extend it further, had a voice" (Bonfil-Batalla 117). Historian Alan Knight echoes to some degree this perspective when he writes that "[p]ostrevolutionary *indigenismo* thus represented yet another non-Indian formulation of the 'Indian problem'; it was another white/mestizo construct . . . part of a long tradition stretching back to the Conquest" (77). Indigenism functions, according to the readings of Bonfil-Batalla and Knight, as an exercise in subjugation through which the dominant white/mestizo population was able to solidify and extend its control over Indigenous communities. Writing of indigenist literature, the Peruvian critic José Mariategui claimed that "it is still a mestizo literature and as such is called indigenist rather than indigenous. If an indigenous literature finally appears, it will be when the Indians themselves are able to produce it" (274). Bonfil-Batalla seems to hold out for a similar possibility, as his quotation above suggests that an indigenist policy directed by Indigenous people, one that takes into account their opinions and interests, would be viable, but he would call this philosophy and social practice "Indianismo/Indianism."

In the context of the United States, Ward Churchill offers a decidedly unconventional approach to the idea of indigenism. In his essay, "I Am Indigenist: Notes on the Ideology of the Fourth World," he advocates for an indigenist framework organized around action, rather than identity: "I have identified myself as being 'indigenist' in outlook. By this, I mean that I am one who not only takes the rights of indigenous peoples as the highest priority of my political life, but who draws upon the traditions—the bodies of knowledge and corresponding codes of values—evolved over many thousands of years by native peoples the world over" (*Struggle* 403). Churchill's anti-colonial indigenism depends upon a prioritized political commitment to Native rights as well as access to a cultural ethos handed down not only through filial ties, but also as part of a global reservoir of traditional knowledges held by Indigenous peoples. Churchill continues: "[T]he beginning point for any indigenist endeavor in the United States centers, logically enough, in efforts to restore direct Indian control over the huge portion of the continental U.S. which was never ceded by native nations" (415). What we find in this form of indigenism is again the emphasis on a traditional past that is able to inform a present course of action.

Churchill, however, weds this aspect of his indigenism to the Native land rights struggle, claiming that the initiation of any truly indigenist project must begin in the effort to restore Native control over Native land. The place of "tradition" in this iteration of indigenism is left unexplored as Churchill places most emphasis upon activism and land reclamation. Yet, his use of the term "indigenism" suggests that he is unaware both of its complex history and of its interpretation by anthropologists and historians. Citing Bonfil-Batalla as a "proponent," Churchill redefines indigenism, transforming it into a leftist mode of action. This transformation, however, is based upon a misreading of Bonfil-Batalla, a misrecognition of the context and the purpose of the anthropologist's work.

Churchill cites Bonfil-Batalla's *Utopía y Revolución: El pensamiento político contemporáneo de los indios en América Latina,* which he accesses through Roxanne Dunbar-Ortiz's *Indians of the Americas.* Bonfil-Batalla published the Indigenous political writings in *Utopía y Revolución* to demonstrate the concept of *panindianismo,* a term he uses to describe the autonomous political organizing of Indigenous peoples, distinguishing it against the indigenism of the non-Indigenous.[21] The political philosophy that Churchill outlines in "I Am Indigenist" would be called "Indianism" by Bonfil-Batalla. But the mestizo context of Bonfil-Batalla's work, in which many average non-Indigenous citizens "look Indian" and most people are biologically descended from Indigenous people, markedly differs from Churchill's Anglo North American frame of reference. Bonfil-Batalla is invested deeply in the argument that Mexico is essentially Indian, even though that Indianness is denied by many mestizo Mexicans, who, according to Bonfil-Batalla, associate being Indian with a negative primitive state of being "lazy . . . ignorant, perhaps picturesque, but always the dead weight that keeps us from being the country we could have been" (19). The anthropologist wants to emphasize the historical processes of de-Indianization that have produced cultural mestizos, people who are somatically and biologically, in terms of racial mixture and physical appearance, not really so different from the Native people who are segregated into separate social realms. As Bonfil-Batalla forces mestizo recognition of the persistence of the Indigenous in Mexican society, he also attempts to urge modern Mexico to reclaim indigeneity. This means, therefore, that all mestizos are potential Indians.

The distinctions become even more muddied and complicated when one considers closely the role of a mestizo academic such as Bonfil-Batalla in taking charge of defining who is or can be Indian and conceptualizing Indigenous political movements. Having taken his translated citations from Dunbar-Ortiz, Churchill nevertheless overlooks the critical formulation Dunbar-Ortiz advances as she presents Bonfil-Batalla in her own text. Focusing on the platform of the Indigenous Regional Council of the Cauca (CRIC/Columbia), Dunbar-Ortiz points to the organization's elucidation of "deviations" in Indigenous movements. The CRIC document reads as follows:

> La primera desviación, conocida por algunos como "racista" o "indigenista," consiste en darle absoluta primacía a los aspectos específicamente indígenas de la lucha, sin cuestionar en general el sistema clasista de dominación ni la situación de dependencia del imperialismo.
> [The first deviation, known to some as "racist" or "indigenist," consists in giving absolute primacy to specifically indigenous aspects of the struggle, without generally questioning the classist system of domination or the imperialist system of dependence.]

> Se forman organizaciones muchas veces con una ideología mística, que orientan las luchas contra el "blanco" en general y hacen alianzas más fácilmente con las clases dominantes y sus instituciones que con los demás explotados. El imperialismo mismo impulsa frecuentemente estas organizaciones que contribuyen evidentemente a desviar las luchas indígenas y a dividir las fuerzas populares.
> [Many times organizations are formed with a mystical ideology that orients the struggles against "whites" in general and makes easy alliances with the dominant classes and their institutions that also exploit the indigenous. Imperialism itself frequently drives these organizations that clearly contribute to the derailment of indigenous struggles and the division of the power of the people.]

> La segunda desviación es contraria a la anterior y se presenta cuando organizaciones políticas o gremiales pretenden imponerle al indígena sus programas y esquemas organizativos sin tener para nada en cuenta su realidad propia.
> [The second deviation is contrary to the first and is present when political or union organizations try to impose upon the indigenous their own programs and organizational plans without considering indigenous reality.] (302)

CRIC views indigenism as a myopic approach to the complex challenges that Indigenous communities face. In their broad sketch of deviations of indigenism, they identify the failure to address class oppression because of a sole emphasis on race, a reduction of the multiple layers of oppression experienced by Indigenous people. Furthermore, the cultural arrogance of non-Indians who presume to know what is best for Indians is exposed by CRIC as a form of the very imperialism that reduced the status of Natives in the first place. Finally, CRIC points to opportunistic appropriations of Indigenous causes used to advance non-Indigenous agendas.

It is not entirely evident that CRIC would implicate Bonfil-Batalla in this critique, but Dunbar-Ortiz obviously does: "It is not clear why Bonfil chose not to deal with CRIC's explicit critique of the ideology reflected in his essay, which CRIC describes as one of the two 'deviations' in the indigenous movement" (86). She does not elaborate her claim, although she later acknowledges Bonfil-Batalla's "solidarity and unqualified support" that, unfortunately, "has not translated itself into theory or strategy" (90). This solidarity can be seen in Bonfil-Batalla's role in organizing the Barbados Symposium in 1971 and his signing of the Declaration that emerged from those meetings.[22] The Symposium was held under the combined sponsorship of the World Council of Churches and the Ethnology Department at the University of Berne, Switzerland. The document it produced, called the Barbados Declaration, was endorsed by the World Council of Churches and signed by eleven anthropologists. It both formally exposed the continued colonial domination of Native peoples of Latin America and condemned religious missions and the profession of anthropology as perpetuations of the system of colonial rule. Dunbar-Ortiz, while recognizing the positive effects of the Declaration on the pan-Indian movement, nevertheless sees in the document evidence of the "combined power of the churches through their missions, and of anthropologists, through their field-work, over the lives of American Indians" (60). Bonfil-Batalla's participation in a symposium on Indigenous peoples that included little, if any, Indigenous participation, and the role he and other anthropologists played in defining the situation of Natives in Latin America and prescribing, to the extent that the Declaration does, solutions for redefining the relationships among Indigenous peoples, the state, the church, and the profession of anthropology, certainly leaves him open to the charge that he allied with dominant institutions of power, rather than with the Indigenous communities that they controlled.

These differing perspectives on indigenism draw attention to its various and competing definitions, considered by Bonfil-Batalla, Knight, and others in terms of public policy, by Dunbar-Ortiz to be "Indian advocacy," and by CRIC to be romanticized, exploitive, and reductive approaches to such advocacy. Prior to Churchill and Dunbar-Ortiz, Jack Forbes took up issues of Native history and social reality from a broad North American perspective. His 1973 study, *Aztecas del Norte: The Chicanos of Aztlán,* is an analysis of the place of Chicanas/os within the identity category of "Indian," providing reprints of selections of writings by and about Mexicans that help to advance Forbes' claim that the "Aztecas del norte . . . compose the largest single tribe or nation of Anishinabeg (Indians) in the United States today" (13). Like Churchill, Forbes advances a favorable conception of *indigenismo,* defining it as "placing emphasis upon the native heritage" (149). He writes that "Indigenismo has perhaps triumphed in some areas of thinking, but a so-called mestizo view of Mexico's heritage seems to be the basis for current Mexican national unity" (149). *Mestizaje,* according to Forbes, represents a privileging of the European components of the mixture that produced Mexicans and a disavowal of Mexican indigeneity. To claim mestizo identity, Forbes writes, is to "affirm white descent. A mestizo (according to the racist caste system) is, after all, not a lowly indio. He is at least part-white and, therefore, part-civilized, una persona de razón" (202). To affirm the Indigenous, according to Forbes, would be an indigenist act.

Forbes puts forth an intriguing option for the reclamation of indigeneity by mestizos, an option that draws its motivation from the historical transformations of Mexican communities in the United States, which include political acts of solidarity with Natives. An important example is his discussion of Analco, the 1680 union of "indios y chicanos" to resist Spanish oppression (72–76). What Forbes does not do is rely upon the mythic to relate the facts of Chicana/o indigeneity. Although he does often refer to Native spiritualities, particularly the commodification and consumption of those spiritual traditions by the non-Indigenous, and to the ways in which people practice those spiritual traditions, he does not attempt to inhabit or advance them within the pages of the text. When Forbes addresses ancient Mexican literature, his focus is on the Nahuatl language, the beauty of poetic Nahuatl, and the ease it lends to intellectual expression rather than its mythic elements (33–34). More compelling, however, is Forbes' claim to first use of the term "Aztlán" in 1962 to signify a Chicano homeland.[23]

Chicano Indigenism and the Symbol of Aztlán

Aztlán is perhaps the most enduring feature of Chicano indigenism, whether initially introduced into an activist lexicon by Jack Forbes or by Alurista, as is most often claimed by Chicana/o scholars. This symbolic ancestral home was a complex negotiation of identity because Aztlán encompassed not only the Mexican in Mexican-Americans, but an aspect of Mexicanness that had been particularly degraded: the Indian. A mythic symbol retrieved from Aztec codices and sixteenth-century Spanish accounts of the Conquest, Aztlán places Chicanas/os at the origins of the Mexican nation, in a pre-national moment that is distinctly and inarguably indigenous. Politically, Aztlán foregrounds the history of Mexican dispossession and occupation at the hands of Anglo-Americans and reconfigures the U.S. Southwest as a "homeland denied." Chicanas/os also took up a term that scholars argue is closer to what the people who in the nineteenth century became known as "Aztecs" probably called themselves: Mexica.

Early writings by Alurista and Armando Rendon, among others, argue that Indigenous cultural and racial ancestry had been denigrated in people of Mexican descent in the United States. These writers and artists looked to an Indian past to instill cultural and racial pride as they recovered a history that existed *before* Spanish and Anglo conquests. Chicanas/os were elevated from their positions as conquered people, "illegal aliens," and perpetual foreigners and found new identities as descendants of the original inhabitants of the region. We might locate the "official" emergence of indigenism in the preamble to "El Plan de Aztlán," presented at the National Chicano Youth Liberation Conference in 1969. Through various outlets, Chicana/o indigenism has promoted pride in Indigenous ancestry, recovered cultural traditions of language and spirituality, and disseminated historical narratives of dispossession and conquest. It has brought all of this to bear upon the Chicana/o claim to historical primacy in the United States. The poet Alurista conceptualized the indigenist agenda in the poem that later became the preamble to "El Plan." He pursued this agenda in poetic work that followed the conference, such as in the collections *Nationchild Plumaroja* (1972) and *Floricanto en Aztlán* (1976).

Alurista, whether motivated by the example of Jack Forbes or not, imported the term "Aztlán" (the ancient Mexica site of origin) from Conquest-era codices and immediate post-Conquest era accounts of the Spanish occupation and colonization of Mesoamerica. Following Alurista's lead, many activists, indigenist or not, adopted this usage. Luis Leal has laid out the contours:

> As a Chicano symbol, Aztlán has two meanings: first, it represents the geographic region known as the Southwestern part of the United States, composed of the territory that Mexico ceded in 1848 with the Treaty of

Guadalupe Hidalgo; second, and more important, Aztlán symbolized
the spiritual union of the Chicanos, something that is carried within
the heart, no matter where they may live or where they may find themselves. (8)

The metaphysical connotation of Aztlán is preeminent, according to
Leal's definitions. However disputed the geographic claim might be, the
homeland as a spiritual concept elides challenges to historical primacy and
recasts Aztlán as a sentiment that creates community.

Most scholars of the Mexica believe Aztlán, if an actual geographic
space, was located in Mesoamerica, somewhere north of Mexico City,
as Matos suggested to Carrasco.[24] For many others, the term has more
mythical than geographic significance and is understood as symbol or
metaphor, as an Edenic—to use a familiar Judeo-Christian term—place of
origins. For Chicanas/os, however, establishing location has at times been
paramount. Seizing upon the idea of "north of Mexico," early Chicano indigenists placed Aztlán north of the contemporary U.S.-Mexico border in
the southwestern United States. Aztlán is a valuable concept in a history
of migration that establishes a pre-Conquest Indigenous "Aztec" presence
in the western and southern border regions of the United States. In asserting that the ancestors of the Aztecs originated in what is now Arizona,
California, Colorado, New Mexico, and Texas, Chicanas/os claimed their
place in a pre-Conquest, pre-settler, pre-Columbian Mesoamerica. They
were thus to reposition themselves in a dual manner, gaining legitimacy
as not only having preceded Anglo-American settlement of the United
States, but also as having been present, in an ancestral sense, at the founding of the Mexican nation.

Rafael Pérez-Torres writes that "[t]he idea of a Chicano mythic 'memory' manifested in ethnopoetic expression represents less an unproblematic recuperation of indigenous culture than a complex cultural construction of self-identity" (*Movements* 176). True, Chicano indigenism, which
I take as the referent of the first part of Pérez-Torres' sentence, is indeed
complex, cultural, and constructed. What is more interesting about the
quotation, however, is the ambivalence it manifests even as the writer
privileges the more generous reading of indigenist practices. The structure of the sentence directs our attention to its latter half and the characterization of indigenism in positive terms. What may escape notice, however, is that Pérez-Torres does define indigenism also (and perhaps, after
all) as "an unproblematic recuperation of indigenous culture." Although
he emphasizes the second half of the sentence by diminishing the descrip-

tive force of the first (the use of "less . . . than"), indigenism nevertheless *is*, according to the grammar of the sentence, the "unproblematic recuperation" and *also* the "complex cultural construction." Being "less" of something does not obviate the characteristic altogether. But we might not want to dwell too long upon the problematics of practices that are taken to be "unproblematic," and so we might be inclined, following Pérez-Torres' lead, to deny, even as we affirm, the full range of the complexity of Chicana/o indigenism.

Conquest Histories and Indigeneity

Ambivalence is also at the core of Chicana/o claims to historical primacy in the U.S. Southwest. In addition to the argument that issues from indigeneity, Chicanas/os also assert rights to the region through the Treaty of Guadalupe Hidalgo and its provisions guaranteeing land grants assigned by the Spanish crown: "[I]n the nineteenth century, Texas courts regularly considered the Treaty of Guadalupe Hidalgo as it applied to Spanish and Mexican grants made before March 2, 1836" (Griswold del Castillo 85). Because Mexican titles were often not honored, many mestizas/os lost their land to Anglo-American settlers in local campaigns of removal that effectively completed the Anglo conquest of Greater Mexico.[25] The treaty is thus viewed as part of an illegal expansion of the borders of the United States that submerged the historical precedence of mestizas/os in the area. But the two claims to the Southwest, rather than complementing each other, contradict and compete, despite the idea of historical primacy that lies at the foundation of each. On the one hand, Aztlán is an assertion of land rights based on an Indigenous myth, and, on the other, the treaty rights afforded by the Treaty of Guadalupe Hidalgo are mestizo claims based upon a Mexican national identity and the settler privilege bestowed by Spanish and Mexican land grants. Chicano oppositional discourse uses both of these narratives.

In the charting of a Chicana/o politics of oppression, Indigenous heritage has been foregrounded as the defining feature of Chicana/o racial identity. Within most political communities and among individuals that would self-define as "Chicana/o," ancestral ties to the Spanish conquistador are consciously rejected to oppose a dominant U.S. Eurocentrism. Chicanas/os are marked by Indigenous ancestry, which at times announces itself through phenotypic and other physical markers. Yet, Indian ancestral lines exist alongside and are combined with Spanish and

Anglo-European lineages, not to mention those that emerge from Africa and Asia.[26] Yet, Chicanas/os conceptualize their otherness through other cultural markers as well. Spanish linguistic identity is at once the sign of otherness in relation to a dominant Anglo power base, even as it also reminds of a history of assimilation. Although many Chicanas/os identify as Spanish speakers, this identification is complicated by the fact that a good portion of Chicanas/os are not fluent in Spanish, are passive-fluent, or are at best uneasy with their knowledge of the language. Furthermore, the centralization of a Spanish linguistic identity has failed to account for, on one hand, the fact that many Chicanas/os are alienated from the Spanish language and, on the other, that virtually all Chicanas/os are alienated from the Indigenous languages of their ancestors. Each of these lines of identification is made the more complex because they rely upon necessary disavowals.

These markers of otherness, Indigenous ancestry and an affiliation with the Spanish language, exist in tension with one another. At the same time that they are able to represent cultural phenomena of *mestizaje,* they also allude to histories of conflict, domination, and subjugation. It is the Spanish domination of a Native indigenous population that has prompted the rejection of Spanish ancestry within Chicana/o critical discourses dating back to the movement period of the 1970s. Interestingly, however, it is the Anglo conquest of the U.S. Southwest in the nineteenth century that has figured most powerfully in positioning Chicanas/os politically as conquered and dispossessed.

There are ample and legitimate reasons for this privileging of the Anglo conquest over that of the Spanish during the Chicano movement. Lorena Oropeza interprets the rejection of Spanish ancestry as a rejection of the standards of whiteness in favor of ideals of cultural sophistication and physical beauty that better reflected the ethnic pride of Chicanas/os (83–85). This abandonment of the claim to European ancestry enabled solidarity with Third World peoples under assault by United States and European military power, such as the Vietnamese, along racial and ideological lines. The perceived supremacy of European civilization was overtly challenged as Chicanas/os organized politically as a vanquished group that had been dispossessed by the Spanish and now sought to revitalize a suppressed cultural patrimony.

The effects of the Anglo conquest were, and continue to be, visible in the Chicana/o present, as evidenced by the stark facts of segregation apparent in virtually all avenues of social life in the United States. This segregation is expressed socially and economically in a racialized division of labor that persists even as Chicanas/os become more educated and upwardly mobile. It is evident in political power structures as, in 2005, we witnessed the inauguration of the first "Hispanic" senators in U.S. history, and we had to make sense of the appointment of a Mexican-American from South Texas to the position of U.S. Attorney General under the Bush administration and the ongoing command of another Mexican-American from South Texas over the ground troops occupying Iraq. The persistence of ideologies of segregation also emerge in educational curricula throughout the country, although perhaps most astonishingly in South Texas where predominantly Mexican school administrations and faculty continue to impose Eurocentric course materials upon their predominantly Mexican-descent student populations.

The Anglo conquest, therefore, holds a central position as the defining moment of mestiza/o dispossession in Chicana/o academic and literary discourse. Quite simply, mestizas/os did not exist as a people prior to the Spanish conquest, owing their very emergence to that historical fact. It would be difficult, if not impossible, to position Chicanas/os as the people conquered by the Spanish even though Chicana/o Indigenous ancestry is easily and definitively traceable back through post-Conquest history, with some asserting that Chicanas/os are actually more racially Indian than Spanish.[27] Yet another fact is that cultural indigeneity has been largely either relinquished or deracinated through the politics and policies of colonization, and that history is much harder to delineate.[28] Nevertheless, the focus on Anglo settlement and subsequent removal of Indians and mestizas/os forges a productive connection between present-day Chicanas/os and Conquest-era Indigenous peoples of Mesoamerica. And, on the first day of the year 1994, yet another avenue of Indigenous reclamation was made available to U.S. Mexicans.

Indigenous Resistance at the Century's End

When the Ejército Zapatista de Liberación Nacional (EZLN) rebelled against the Mexican state on January 1, 1994, it brought Mexican Indians into the forefront of the U.S. activist consciousness. Indians again became symbols of contemporary resistance at a defining moment. The North American Free Trade Agreement took effect at the beginning of 1994, officially inaugurating the era of globalization and transnationalism, although by some accounts, that era began with conquest and colonialism during the Age of Exploration. Recognizing a potential for affiliation, the EZLN named and called upon Chicanos specifically in their communiqués, extending a cross-border summons to join the movement and begin organizing. The editorial of the first edition of the EZLN newspaper *El Despertador Mexicano,* published on December 31, 1993, for example, is addressed to "Mexicans: workers, campesinos, students, honest professionals, Chicanos, and progressives of other countries" (36–36). Indeed, it is easy to locate in Zapatista rhetoric a powerful elaboration of Chicana/o critiques of U.S. economic and political domination. This recognition of a Mexicanada on the U.S. side of the divide invites identification with the Zapatista uprising that rests upon shared social and political objectives and shared history.

María Jimenez, a board member of the National Commission for Democracy in Mexico, reported that the Zapatistas "have a special bond with Chicanos/Mexicanos living in the United States" (Gonzáles and Rodríguez). Upon returning from the First International Forum for Humanity and Against Neoliberalism in the Lacandón jungle in the summer of 1996, Jimenez reported that the Zapatistas held a separate meeting with a delegation of Chicanos/Mexicanos from the United States. The Zapatistas, she said to journalists Roberto Rodríguez and Patrisia Gonzáles, considered the interactions with Chicanos and U.S. Mexicans a "priority relationship" and "recognize that Chicanos/Mexicanos in the United States live parallel lives—of exclusion and discrimination in their own homelands" (Gonzáles and Rodríguez). By acknowledging the U.S. Southwest as Chicana/o homeland, Zapatista rhetoric provided a contemporary referent for the indigenism that long characterized Chicana/o discourse, even as the Zapatistas themselves engaged in the continued mythification of the non-Indian revolutionary hero Emiliano Zapata.[29] The cross-border alliance is an example of the potential linkages between contemporary Indian politics and Chicana/o activism. Considering the geographic location of U.S. Mexicans, solidarity with the EZLN could be viewed as a transnational Indigenous struggle, another episode in the history of Indian resistance.

The Zapatista hailing of Chicanas/os also strengthens and, in some cases, activates an oppositional indigeneity that asserts its origins in the pre-contact Mesoamerican civilizations from which the rank and file of the Zapatista Army are also descended. Hector Carreon, writing for *La Voz de Aztlan* about Chicana/o participation in the Zapatista march into the Zócalo in 2001, notes that its significance lies, in part, in a reverse migration, "a re-return from Aztlan to the 'Heart of Mexico' where around 1325 AD the Mexicas founded Tenochtitlan. To have made this entrance into El Zócalo in the company of the Zapatistas and hundreds of thousands [of] indigenous brothers and sisters made the event particularly dramatic. It was as if we were recapturing Tenochtitlan after 'La Conquista'" (www.aztlan.net/zocalo.htm).[30] Carreon invokes the ancient Aztec peregrination narrative that in a Chicana/o context establishes mestizas/os as Native both in the U.S. Southwest and in Mexico. Because the myth details a Mexica/Aztec migration from a place to the north of Mexico City/Tenochtitlan, Carreon recasts the Chicana/o accompaniment of the Zapatistas to the Zócalo as a repetition of that original migration. When he calls the journey into the Zócalo a "re-return," however, Carreon perhaps confuses his signifiers, misrepresenting Tenochtitlan as the original homeland. The march into the Zócalo, according to the logic of the Chicano Aztlán narrative, is, in fact, a "re-migration," a reproduction of the original ancient Mexica journey. The importance of locating the source of Chicana/o indigeneity in the Mexica capital of Tenochtitlan, however, is to activate claims to Indigenous origins that emanate from Mexico, which are more available to Chicanos, on one hand, because of their perceived status as immigrants, and, on the other, because of the more recognized claim to indigeneity in the United States made by American Indians. Chicana/o indigenist narratives, such as Carreon's, directly address the historical processes of ethnocide that weakened identifications with Indigenous communities and disengaged processes of cultural transmission.

From Modern Primitivism to Chicana Radical Feminism

In presenting themselves as the inheritors of Indigenous cultural patrimonies, Chicanas/os reconstitute social structures that have defined them as immigrants in the modern era, establishing their historical presence in North America as Native. Yet, Chicana/o indigenism is contained by the European and Anglo-American "regimes of representation" that provide the structure in which Chicana/o indigeneity is assembled. The attempt at authenticity through Indianness cannot help but interlock with authority and the "circuits of knowledge and power" (Spivak, "Subaltern" 274) represented by the textual histories I sketched broadly earlier. *Blood Lines* seeks to illuminate the links between Chicana/o indigenist writing and other literary traditions that also represent Indians. These include, for example, anthropological and archeological research, art history, modernist primitivism, and Mexican state indigenism. The literary strategies used by Chicana/o indigenists and modern primitivists rewrite European archeology and anthropology and reconceive Mesoamerican ancient history. Anzaldúa, as I will show, rewrites Burland and Forman to accommodate a feminized Aztec mythos that succeeds the indigenist nationalism represented by Alurista, Valdez, and Rendon. D. H. Lawrence answers William H. Prescott's conflicted response to Aztec culture—his horror at the gruesomeness of blood sacrifice and simultaneous romantic fascination with the *"golden age* of Anahuac"—by reviving the pre-Columbian pantheon of a vanished race. Similarities that may surprise us exist between the discourses of modernist primitivism, as evidenced by Lawrence, Chicano indigenist nationalism, and the Chicana indigenist feminism consolidated by Gloria Anzaldúa, and make clear the fact that these discourses drew from and were even propelled by a fascination with pre-Conquest Mesoamerica. This fascination began with the looting of Indigenous material objects—the plastic arts and cultural patrimonies of Conquest-era societies—at the moment of European arrival in the Americas.

Chicana/o interest in Mesoamerica is made possible in part because of this complex history of "discovering," excavating, collecting, cataloging, preserving, and stealing. The textual readings that follow explicate examples of Chicana/o indigenism found in nationalist and feminist writings, attempting to place Chicana/o literature within this history and yet resist the conflation of the multiple contexts and motives. Although the relationship between Chicana/o indigenism and European primitivism does not lessen the reality of an Indigenous history, in considering that relationship we are confronted with the broad range of discourses that represent Indians, a persistent feature of which is the reliance on myth.

A primary goal of *Blood Lines* is to highlight the intertextualities that exist between Chicana/o formulations of indigenism and these other artistic and textual traditions. Proceeding in a chronological manner, I begin with an analysis of the "Mexican period" of the British novelist, D. H. Lawrence. A major literary figure who produced a significant body of work on Mexico, the most familiar example being his novel *The Plumed Serpent* (1929), this well-known and widely-read modernist writer pursued actively his interest in myth and the Aztec pantheon, also significant themes in Chicana/o indigenism. Chapter One, "Mexican Myth and Modern Primitivism," takes his work as an example, situating Lawrence within the context of broader trends in modernist primitivism, the expatriate presence in Mexico in the 1920s, and Mexican state *indigenismo*. Bringing together biographers' accounts with Lawrence's correspondence and fiction, this chapter engages an analysis of *The Plumed Serpent* that focuses on the novel's privileging of European subjectivity and authority as the main characters pursue cultural revitalization, spiritual advancement, and political resistance through the emergent Cult of Quetzalcoatl and its revived Aztec pantheon.

Chapter Two, "The Mesoamerican in the Mexican-American Imagination," addresses male-centered Chicano movement politics and the use of indigenist themes. Armando Rendon's *Chicano Manifesto* (1971) offers a straightforward appropriation of Mesoamerican mythology in his adoption and redeployment of the Aztec peregrination narrative and the cycle of the Fifth Sun to establish the Chicano claim to the U.S. Southwest. More inventive are the indigenist writings of Luis Valdez and Alurista. Valdez's 1967 play *The Dark Root of a Scream* is unique in its emphasis on, rather than omission of, ritual human sacrifice as he reinvents the practice as an act of barrio empowerment. His 1973 *Pensamiento Serpentino,* a long poem presented as an indigenist treatise, offers additional examples of Valdez's manipulation of Mesoamerican mythic symbols and themes. Finally, I take up published and unpublished work of Alurista, looking in particular at his use of indigenism to challenge economic as well as racial forms of oppression. I examine the alterations made to his original preamble to "El Plan de Aztlán," his unpublished platforms for the development of Chicano Studies, and a 1974 play entitled *Dawn*. Alurista adopts Mesoamerican symbols and mythic figures as teaching tools to communicate to audiences the degenerative influences of corporatism, capitalism, and consumer greed, all of which are attributed to Anglo America. Despite the constructive uses of myth, transformative potential is held in check by each author's ultimate inability to imagine women beyond the confines of the very ideological strictures he attempts to expose and disassemble.

Chapter Three, "From La Malinche to Coatlicue: Chicana Indigenist Feminism and Mythic Native Women," describes how the Chicano (male) version of the Indian was transformed by feminists into a figure of women's resistance. This section assesses the trope of "'the' Native woman" in Chicana feminist discourse, beginning with the revision of La Malinche in the context of nationalism and charting her development into the theoretical "Native woman" of 1980s Chicana feminism. Focusing on two foundational texts, Adelaida del Castillo's originary essay on La Malinche and Gloria Anzaldúa's *Borderlands/La Frontera: The New Mestiza,* I show how the Indian is feminized and redeployed in the critique of racism, sexism, and homophobia. This chapter situates Gloria Anzaldúa's mestiza-indigenist constructions in the context of and in conversation with modernist primitivism and its critically underacknowledged fascination with Mexico and culminates my argument that the characteristic form of Chicana/o indigenism is myth.

Chapter Four arrives at what I call the "contra-mythic," texts that operate in ways that reject, resist, and deconstruct the mythic. "The Contra-mythic: Refashioning Indigeneity in Acosta, Cervantes, Gaspar de Alba, and Villanueva" calls attention to texts that pronounce the ambiguity of Chicana/o ancestry and demonstrate analytical methods that challenge the naturalization of identity. Such texts refuse to essentialize Indigenous origins, instead deploying self-conscious, unsettled performances of conflicted mestiza/o identities. The works of Teresa Palomo Acosta, Lorna Dee Cervantes, Alicia Gaspar de Alba, and Alma Luz Villanueva enable alternative ways to read and write the Indian into the Chicana/o past and present. Ultimately, these texts make clear that, rather than being mere birthright, Chicana/o indigeneity is the result of purposeful and political acts of self-creation and critique.

Calling upon the history of a glorious Indigenous past, Chicano movement discourse introduced the Indian as a symbol of Mexican-American disenfranchisement and resistance. The use of the Indian has continued to the present as Chicana/o activists, artists, and authors have recovered a variety of Indigenous cultural traditions to elaborate political agendas and identity formations. The particular challenges I see with regard to Chicana/o Indigenous history are as follows: to acknowledge the contemporary realities of Native peoples in the United States, as well as in Mexico; to recognize the centrality of land rights in American Indian politics; to reconsider the historical and social erasure of the Indian in the mestizo and yet recognize the ways, rhetorical and material, in which mestizos obliged that erasure.[31] As I have shown, there is history of appropriation and redefinition of *indigenismo* within a U.S. North America outside of Chicana/o critical discourse, as the examples of Churchill and Forbes demonstrate. Chicana/o indigenism similarly does not acknowledge critiques of that tradition within a Latin American, particularly Mexican, context.

This study is about the complications and paradoxes of Chicana/o literary indigenism, most especially the reliance on mythic pre-Columbian pantheons to advance claims of ancestry and land rights. My argument is that Chicana/o indigenism creates cultural narratives of Indianness that rely most prominently on mythic accounts drawn from anthropology and archaeology, and, as it most often does, myth here supplants history. Nevertheless, through indigenism, Chicanas/os have been able to place themselves in an oppositional historical context and to generate discourses of social change because of that positioning.

A Word About Terms

Readers might notice that, beyond initial uses, I have not used quotation marks to call attention to my ideological position on the concepts "primitive," "civilized," "other," "savage," "tribal," and "Indian." I do want to make clear that I consider these to be just that, *concepts,* and not references to actual groups of people. I have used quotations marks initially to make clear my distance from the terms and my awareness of their status as constructs rather than legitimate designations. Using the convention of "scare quotes" would rightly imply my sense of irony, suspicion, disapproval, mistrust, and probably much more depending upon the context. But the continued use of that tactic throughout the essays that follow would very quickly, I am sure, become tiresome, distracting, even annoying. Instead, I choose to trust the interpretative skills of readers, who, I believe, are easily capable of perceiving the multiple valences of such terms. The capacities of these terms to refract multiply, I fear, would only be dulled by the excesses of the punctuation tactic.

Additionally, I have chosen to use "Indian" to refer to the Western *idea* of Indigenous cultures and peoples and "Indigenous" and "Native" to refer to the actual groups of people or individuals. At times, I have chosen "American Indian" when the context seems appropriate—for example, when discussing movement activities of the 1970s—and also with an understanding that many Natives in the United States choose that designation over others. I am similarly aware that "Indian" is also used in communities, its viability indicated in the title of one of the most widely-read of Indigenous periodicals, *Indian Country Today.* I have chosen, however, not to use it to designate people.

CHAPTER 1

Mexican Myth and Modern Primitivism: D. H. Lawrence's *The Plumed Serpent*

Henry Moore's British Museum holds as part of its permanent Mexican Gallery Collection a pre-Columbian stone sculpture of a serpent, the heavy figure coiled around itself, flitting tongue frozen on the verge of striking, a gripping representation of both ancient and contemporary Mexico available to Europeans who might not ever travel to the Americas. Archaeological convention argues that pre-Columbian figures of serpents or snakes symbolically represent Quetzalcoatl, a god of ancient origins.[1] Also known as the plumed serpent, its prominence in pre-Conquest Mesoamerica is displayed on artifacts from various cultural contexts dating from the "middle pre-Classic" Olmecas to the "late post-Classic" Aztecas.[2] Its importance to contemporary archeologists, anthropologists, and travel writers is displayed in titles such as *Feathered Serpent and Smoking Mirror* by C. A. Burland and Werner Forman (1975) and *Legends of the Plumed Serpent* by Neil Baldwin (1998).

To Moore's contemporary, the British traveler and novelist D. H. Lawrence, the serpent signified all that was frightening, seductive, and even inspiring about Mexico. Most biographies point to Bernal Díaz del Castillo's *The Discovery and Conquest of Mexico* and Lewis Spence's *Gods of Mexico* as sources for Lawrence's knowledge of Mexican history and pre-Columbian mythology.[3] Drawing from these accounts, as well as from archeologists and from scholars of comparative mythology like Zelia Nuttall, he set his "American novel" in Mexico and titled it *The Plumed Serpent* (1926).[4] His interest in this Mesoamerican figure merged with his fascination with the uroborus, a symbol that appears in ancient Egypt, among the Phoenicians, but is predominantly associated with the Gnostics and Western alchemy. Carl Jung designated this figure of a snake consuming its own tail as an archetype. In *Mysterium Coniunctionis,* his study of the links between the symbols of alchemy and developments in theories of the unconscious, Jung writes, "[I]n the age-old image of the uroborus lies the thought of devouring oneself and turning oneself into a circulatory process . . . the uroborus is a dramatic symbol for the integration and assimilation of the opposite, i.e., of the shadow . . . he slays himself and brings himself to life, fertilizes himself and gives birth to himself" (365).[5] The snake, depicting both self-destruction and self-origination, suggests an unending cycle of energy transference and perpetual motion. Lawrence brought these distinct contexts together—ancient Mesoamerican religion and modern psychoanalytic theory—when he chose the self-consuming snake as the emblem of the masculinist Quetzalcoatl Cult in *The Plumed Serpent,* borrowing from an archaeological record, as well as from emerging psychoanalytic theories of the unconscious. In Lawrence, the serpent is made to represent Mexico, which itself stands for the primitive, a convenient trope of the modern unconscious that was his real object of interest.

American and European writers have repeatedly used the serpent to advance their own understandings of Mexico. The snake, however, is also a dominant image in a Mexican context. For example, Diego Rivera chose to frame his series of mural panels in Mexico City's Ministry of Public Education with figures of feathered serpents. Mexican scholar Enrique Florescano devoted a book-length study to the serpent, titled *The Myth of Quetzalcoatl,* published in Spanish in 1993 and translated into English in 1999. Furthermore, one of the most prominent displays of national identity, the Mexican flag, combines modern nationalist sentiments with the fetishization of pre-Columbian history, using the serpent to establish the symbolic origins of the nation.

The flag stages a scene from the first page of the *Codex Mendoza,* commissioned in approximately 1525 by Don Antonio de Mendoza, the first Spanish viceroy, for the purposes of gathering information about the Aztec Empire. The names of the actual authors of the text, a Native artist and a Spanish scribe, are unknown.[6] Reiterating the Indigenous account of the founding of Tenochtitlan, the flag depicts the god Huitzilopochtli, in the form of an eagle holding a serpent in its mouth, landing on a nopal (cactus). According to the *Codex Mendoza,* this was the sign indicating to the Mexica/Aztecas the site of their future empire, Tenochtitlan. This visual on the Mexican flag, selected in 1821 after independence from the Spanish, asserts the beginnings of the Mexican nation, claiming the heritage of a Native, rather than European, past and creating an associative link between contemporary mestiza/o society and the pre-Conquest inhabitants of Mexico. After defeating the colonial power, the new Mexican state foregrounded these Indigenous origins as a further expression of its resistance to European dominance. In the attempt to oppose colonialism, however, the state reinscribes a hegemonic order in which Indians are present only as part of the ancient past. Indigenous historical subjects and their descendants are banished to the margins of popular consciousness even as the nation announces itself through Indigenous iconography.[7]

Class, Travel, and the "Escape" into Primitive Imaginings

Lawrence certainly did not idealize the Mexican Indians of his imagination, and his characterizations exemplify what Terry Eagleton has called "'spontaneous-creative life' . . . happily co-exist[ing] with the most virulent sexism, racism and authoritarianism" (42). The contradictions in Lawrence's writing and thinking—contradictions that have prompted a variety of responses to his work—are not to be resolved. That Lawrence held racist ideas about Mexicans and Indians, sexist ideas about women, and elitist ideas regarding just about everyone is indisputable. But it is also difficult to dispute his prominence both as a modernist writer and as one who wrote about Indian Mexico.

In 1960, Raymond Williams said that "[i]t is easy to be aware of Lawrence's great effect on our thinking about social values, but it is difficult, for a number of reasons, to give any exact account of his actual contribution" (*Culture and Society* 199). Lawrence's Mexico period, culminating with the publication of "The Woman Who Rode Away" in 1929, indulges a primitivist sensibility that was latent in much of his earlier work but found easy expression in the Americas. Lawrence's work should be understood not as an exercise in chronological primitivism, but, rather, as a studied use of primitive imagery. In Lawrence's New Mexico and Mexico writings, he uses his ideas about Indians to devise alternatives to early twentieth-century industrialism while at the same time rejecting the viability of pre-industrial, pre-capitalist primitive society.

Although D. H. Lawrence was certainly no Socialist, his background as the son of a coal miner growing up in Eastwood, Nottinghamshire, England, left him with an acute sense of class segmentation, even as his writing career made possible the privileges of bourgeois leisure.[8] When he made the decision to seek publication with private presses that produced high-priced limited editions of his work, he was very much aware that these texts would probably not be read by the working class from which he emerged. Nevertheless, as John Worthen writes, "his last four years would see his work divided between the two forms," that is, popular and limited press editions (136). Lawrence's politics around this issue were inconsistent. At best, he vacillated between disdaining what the "tupenny public" (*Letters V* 387, quoted in Worthen 135) would do with his novels and claiming that "on principle I believe in cheap books,"(*Letters V* 626, quoted in Worthen 135); between commenting that "[s]mall private editions are really *much* more to my taste" (*Letters V* 387, quoted in Worthen 135) and viewing "these private editions as a swindle" (*Letters V* 415, quoted in Worthen 135). Speaking of the publications of *Lady Chatterley's Lover,* Worthen observes that

> [t]he two types of publication, like the expensive Florentine and cheap Paris editions of *Lady Chatterley's Lover,* perfectly corresponded to the kind of writer he had finally become: the esoteric writer who made his money from the expensive purchase, by well-off people, of signed and limited editions; and the working-class, ordinary writer who wrote for popular newspapers and who would have liked his books sold cheaply. (157)

The contradiction that Worthen notes represents but a glimpse of other, more profound discrepancies that fuel much critical animosity toward Lawrence's work.

Certainly, however, to intellectuals associated with the British New Left and *New Left Review*—Raymond Williams, E. P. Thompson, Stuart Hall—D. H. Lawrence's singular achievement as not only "the most gifted English novelist of his time" (Williams, *The English Novel* 170), but also as the first major English novelist to come from the industrial working class, was not lost. Lawrence's unrelenting critique of the industrial system issued from the perspective of one who was desperately trying to break free from it. Furthermore, the suppression of *Lady Chatterley's Lover* made Lawrence an icon in the battle against censorship and capitalism.[9] For example, in a 1960 issue of *New Left Review,* Thompson prefaces his essay with a quotation from *Women in Love* and Hall contributed an article entitled "*Lady Chatterley's Lover.* The Novel and its Contribution to Lawrence's Work."[10] Again, in *Culture and Society,* Williams speaks with great respect of the struggles that Lawrence undertook to realize his "escape":

> But the real importance of Lawrence's origins is not and cannot be a matter of retrospect from the adult life. It is, rather, that his first social responses were those, not of a man observing the processes of industrial-

ism, but of one caught in them, at an exposed point, and destined, in the normal course, to be enlisted in their regiments. That he escaped enlistment is now so well known to us that it is difficult to realize the thing as it happened, in its living sequence. It is only by hard fighting, and, further, by the fortune of fighting on a favourable front, that anyone born into the industrial working class escapes his function of replacement. (203)

We see in Williams' comments an emphasis on Lawrence's emergence from the industrial working class, a biographical fact that the novelist shared with the sculptor Moore, also from a Northern coal mining town. In fact, throughout his life, Lawrence was constantly on the move, always searching—for new sources of creative material, material accommodations, and new sources of income—always escaping, to "America," Italy, Mexico. That his peregrinations eventually led him to the Southwestern United States and then to Mexico is not surprising, considering a developing interest in the "New World" that he began to document in 1920 with the publication of the essay, "America, Listen to Your Own" in the *New Republic.*

It was Mabel Dodge Luhan who succeeded in bringing Lawrence to North America for the first time in 1922. "She says she can give us a *house* there, and everything we need. And I think it is there I should like to go" (*Letters IV* 112), Lawrence wrote to Robert Mountsier, his U.S. literary agent, in November 1921. The correspondence with Luhan over the year before the Lawrences finally arrived at her home in Taos whetted Lawrence's desire to visit North America, particularly to learn more about its "old races." But in April 1922, Lawrence wrote to Luhan that he felt apprehensive about the artists he was sure to meet in Taos, and also "the dark races," which he similarly mistrusted: "I find all dark people have a fixed desire to jeer at us: these people here [Ceylon/Sri Lanka]—they jeer behind your back" (Luhan 19, *Letters IV* 225). Although the quotation refers to Sri Lankans specifically, we can find the sentiment expressed to Luhan replicated throughout Lawrence's Mexico writings. On the one hand, he finds non-white people threatening and malicious, predisposed to a hatred of white travelers. On the other hand, he finds in the *idea* of Indians some sort of hope or challenge to the crushing effects of Western culture, even as he wrote with ridicule, scorn, and paternalism about his interactions with Native people.[11]

In his memoir of their 1923 trip to Mexico together, *Journey With Genius,* Witter Bynner wrote that "Lawrence had already indicated his sense of the 'Red Indian' spell by the runes of his mimic Indian troupe in *The Lost Girl*. He was now actually present in the neighborhood of the noble savage" (7). In another section of *Journey With Genius,* Bynner quotes his own Mexico diary entry from Cuernavaca: "Lawrence tells me that he has better hope for them [the "peons" of Cuernavaca] than for any of the dark-skinned races; but I more than suspect him of fitting them into a prearranged edifice" (69). These quotations, along with Lawrence's writing to Luhan, suggest the contours of both Bynner's and Lawrence's imagistic and ideological introduction to non-Europeans. Bynner assumes the position of the critic, calling attention to Lawrence's entrancement by the idea of "the Indian," which Bynner then attaches to the term "noble savage." This is clearly a disparagement of D. H. Lawrence, as Bynner charges that the writer actually creates nothing new in his "American" writings. Lawrence arrives in the Americas with a conceptual scaffolding and uses his observations about Natives as mere content. Bynner attributes this "prearranged edifice" not to Lawrence's unique creativity, but instead marks it as an already familiar and historically persistent concept—the Noble Savage.

Admittedly, years passed between their time with Lawrence and Luhan's and Bynner's penning of memoirs. Furthermore, one cannot overlook the wide-ranging reactions to Lawrence and the conflicting readings of his personality, even from the perspective of a single observer. Lawrence biographer David Ellis has said of Bynner's *Journey With Genius,* which was not published until 1951, that it was written at a time "by which . . . he had grown increasingly hostile and malicious. He was nevertheless an intelligent man whose observations are always worth attending to" (61). But Lois Rudnick seems to corroborate Bynner's observations in her study of Mabel Dodge Luhan. She reminds us that Lawrence wrote and published "America, Listen to your Own" *before* he made his trip to the United States, in the December 15, 1920, issue of the *New Republic*.[12] The essay, which Mark Kinkead-Weekes tells us was criticized for its primitivism by Walter Lippman, is notable for its discussion of America's "lack of tradition." It also, however, reveals Lawrence's pointed interest in pre-Conquest Mexico.[13] This interest was to be unknowingly encouraged by Luhan through her invitations to New Mexico.[14] For although Luhan long expected that Lawrence would write about the Pueblo of Taos, in retrospect, it does appear that Lawrence always intended to write about Indian Mexico in his American novel.

Many have cited Lawrence's exhortation in the essay that "Americans must take up life where the Red Indian, the Aztec, the Maya, the Incas left it off" (90). Although the "Red Indian" refers to Native peoples of what is now known as the United States, Lawrence's gaze was always turned toward Mexico. In a November 16, 1921, letter to the painter Earl Brewster, shortly after Luhan extended her invitation, Lawrence fielded his own version of Taos-based mythology: "Taos has a tribe of Indians, there since the Flood. It is a centre of Sun worship. They say the sun was born there."[15] Quickly, however, the emphasis shifts to Mexico: "The Indian, the Aztec, old Mexico—all that fascinates me and has fascinated me for years. *There* is glamour and magic for me" (*Letters IV* 125). Lawrence's impressions of pre-Conquest Mesoamerica were sure to find ready support in Mexico, where post-Revolutionary Minister of Education José Vasconcelos expounded not only on the promise of *mestizaje,* but also on the superiority of Indigenous Mexico when compared to the Native populations of the United States. In a lecture titled "The Race Problem in Latin America" delivered at the University of Chicago in 1926, he stated, "Our Indians then are not primitive as was the Red Indian, but old, century-tried souls who have known victory and defeat, life and death, and all the moods of history" (79). The fact that nationalist perspectives such as Vasconcelos' were channeled toward elevating the status of Mexico's ruling mestizo population on the world stage may well have been lost on Lawrence. At any rate, in a December 1921 letter to painter Jan Juta, he suggests, "*Let us meet in Taos.* It is only about one day's journey from real Mexico" (*Letters IV* 138). And although he indicated that he might like to write a novel from Taos, an "American novel" (*Letters IV* 257), when he does finally travel to Mexico, he turns to the pre-Conquest mythology of that region for inspiration.[16]

Lawrence's resentment toward Luhan's status as his "padrona" may well have influenced his creative decisions (*Letters IV* 305). Shortly after his arrival, references to his discomfort at "living under anybody's wing" (*Letters IV* 306) begin to appear regularly in his correspondence. He obviously resented Luhan's attempts to guide his American novel toward her own purposes, and this may explain in part why only a few of the prose pieces he produced out of his "American journey" were directly related to Taos, such as "Hopi Snake Dance," "Indians and an Englishman," "Taos," and "New Mexico."[17] We detect his disdain toward Luhan in a letter he wrote to her after arriving in Mexico: "*This* is really a land of Indians: not merely a pueblo" (Luhan 120, emphasis added). Luhan's disappointment with and even annoyance at Lawrence's refusal to be enlisted in her attempt to "save" the Pueblo and "give voice to this speechless land" (280) is a consistent preoccupation throughout her own memoir:

In brief, though he and Frieda joined Bynner and Spud in Old Mexico
and spent the spring and summer there, I know little of his life during
those months but that he wrote *The Plumed Serpent* then, and all he knew
of Indians and the drum he had learned from Tony [her husband]. He
simply transposed Taos and took it down there to Old Mexico. What
I had wanted him to do for Taos, he did do, but he gave it away to the
mother country of Montezuma. (114)

In November 1923, writing from México, D.F., Lawrence intimates the
reasons for which he forewent the Pueblo and Apache in favor of the
Aztec and Maya: "This is the Indian source: this Aztec and Maya" (*Letters IV* 541). Finding, or inventing rather, the "source" was the mission
Lawrence chose for his "Mexican-American" journey, rather than the political action that Luhan so desired from his work.[18]

Reading *The Plumed Serpent*

Virtually any treatment of European representations of Mexico locates
Lawrence at the forefront of literary renderings of the country. Benjamin
Keen's 1971 *The Aztec Image in Western Thought* culminates in a chapter
titled "The Plumed Serpent," which analyzes Lawrence's novel of the same
name. Drewey Wayne Gunn, who wrote the first study of Anglo writers in
Mexico, claims that "Lawrence remains the most important author in the
British-American literary world to have used Mexico as a setting" (123).
John Britton credits D. H. Lawrence as being "a more profound critic of
the cultural potential of the Indian" and argues that his writing influenced
the U.S. expatriate community in Mexico in the 1920s (60). More recently,
Daniel Cooper Alarcón has placed *The Plumed Serpent* within the context
of "Mexico in the Modern Imagination," a project in which he includes
Chicana and Chicano self-representation.[19]

Furthermore, the specter of Lawrence in the work of other authors
who discuss Indians of North America is curious. Luhan dedicated her
memoir, *Lorenzo in Taos,* "To Tony and All Indians," implying that Lawrence's words, deeds, and life resonated somehow with Native struggles
for sovereignty and self-determination. Leslie Fiedler, in his study of the
rhetorical figure of the Indian in American literature, *The Return of the
Vanishing American,* opens with a quotation from Lawrence's *Studies in
Classic American Literature:* ". . . within the present generation the surviving Red Indians are due to merge in the great white swamp. Then the Dai-

mon of America will work overtly, and we shall see real changes" (quoted in Fiedler 11). The quotation advances Lawrence's idea that the influence of Native belief systems will effect some sort of transformation for the "white race." This idea, however, is not to be confused with chronological primitivism; Lawrence in no way advocated a return to Native dominance of any kind. He calls for a "merge," and one that ultimately serves to benefit white civilization.

The 1920s, during which Lawrence traveled in North America, were characterized both by the establishment of foreign artistic and political communities in Mexico and by the flourishing of cultural and political versions of Mexican *indigenismo*. Lawrence was influenced by both of these trends, drawn to Mexico as so many Anglo-Americans and Europeans had been and finding when he arrived the full artistic expression of many of his own nascent ideas about indigeneity, spirituality, and revolution. Bynner wrote that the novelist was "interested in the Indian revival which was being encouraged by the Minister of Education, with men like Dr. Atl renouncing their Spanish names in favor of Aztec" (26).[20] Mestizos such as Dr. Atl and Diego Rivera and criollos like José Vasconcelos, who was responsible for commissioning public murals during his tenure as minister of education (1921–24), promoted a recognizably primitivist cultural indigenism. An existing discursive network of American and European primitivism enabled Lawrence's interest in Mesoamerican myth; however, his literary fetish was also encouraged by the Mexican artistic renaissance that Bynner refers to above as "the Indian revival."[21]

In his history and analysis of the mural movement, *Mexican Mural Renaissance, 1920–1925*, Jean Charlot avers that "Indian archaeological remains stand in relation to Mexican art as Greco-Roman ruins and fragments did to Renaissance Italy" (2). Mexico was in the process of reviving its artistic traditions, which served the dual purpose of invigorating contemporary art and providing an ancient backdrop that would grant to the country the historical maturity necessary to command international respect. Yet Lawrence made public his disdain for what he perceived as the fetishism of the muralist movement in an essay, "Indians and Entertainment," collected in *Mornings in Mexico*. His character Kate Leslie's response to a mural in *The Plumed Serpent* offers an additional critique of Mexican artistic indigenism, particularly as the mural described has been linked to an existing mural by José Clemente Orozco. Ronald Walker has claimed, however, that "while he was contemptuous of their work for the most part, there is much evidence in *The Plumed Serpent* that he grasped some of the implications of their epic theme" (5). Orozco, incidentally, publicly distanced himself from the indigenism movement, although he trained under Dr. Atl, whom he greatly respected, and continued to work on projects with indigenist artists.[22]

Despite his criticisms, Lawrence also sought to manipulate the Indian as a trope to serve his own literary goals. In an article on Lawrence, Kingsley Widmer has drawn a distinction between "primitivism" and "primitivistic," characterizing the latter as an aesthetic endeavor distinct from the values and motivations of the former, which include the elevation of "nature," simplicity, and the pre-historical. This division is at odds with other versions of primitivism, such as Rubin's, yet the significance of Widmer's essay lies in how he applies these definitions to Lawrence, rather than in the definitions themselves. Lawrence, Widmer argues appreciatively, uses "primitivism's moral concepts (the rejection of industrial life and mass civilization and the longing for a more simple and virile life) to lead his characters towards a primitive landscape where they reveal not their moral transformation but their own repulsions and self-destruction" (345). Although it is true that the "primitive" context of a novel like *The Plumed Serpent* is no exercise in championing chronological primitivism, the fact remains that Lawrence drew from a general rubric of primitivist thinking to lament "mind-consciousness" and to expose the spiritual destitution of Western civilization. Ultimately, as Widmer's quotation suggests, primitivistic themes reveal little more than the particular experiences of particular Western subjects.

D. H. Lawrence developed his negative social critiques in various literary attempts to explain "blood-consciousness," which he opposes to "mind consciousness." Blood-consciousness was for Lawrence the experience of the pre-rational, instinctual, and primal forces of human connection. Very often, as in *Women in Love,* as well as in *The Plumed Serpent,* Lawrence demonstrated its potentiality through depictions of sexual intercourse. In its emphasis on instinct and sexuality, blood-consciousness quite neatly and logically presents itself as a primitivist notion. This association is made stronger by Lawrence's obvious goal of exposing the vacuity of the Western condition and the alienation of the modern individual.

His endeavor resonates with what Lionel Trilling saw in 1965 as "one of the shaping and controlling ideas of our epoch . . . the disenchantment of our culture with culture itself" (3). In "On the Teaching of Modern Literature," Trilling identifies a central thematic or "characteristic element" of modern literature as "the bitter line of hostility to civilization which runs through it" (3). His thesis reflects the conventional wisdom within literary studies of modernism that identify it with disjuncture, rupture, and fragmentation. In the concepts that Trilling employs and that Lawrence exemplifies, the breakage occurs with the rejection of accepted notions of civilization. In *The Plumed Serpent,* specifically, this rejection is directed toward Victorian mandates of sexual containment as well as toward social institutions of control such as the Catholic Church.

All is not settled, however, as terminological debates over the meanings of "modern," "modernity," and "modernism" attest. Susan Stanford Friedman has dwelt upon these discussions, calling our attention not only to the differences among accounts of modern/modernism/modernity, but to the coexistence of opposing meanings, and not simply across disciplinary boundaries, but within disciplinary provinces themselves (501). Therefore, although some assessments of Lawrence's Quetzalcoatl Cult in *The Plumed Serpent* might consider it quintessentially modernist in its break from past histories and traditions of Catholicism and Eurocentrism, to other critics the Cult promotes equally modernist enterprises of absolutism, order, and centralization that are nothing less than fascistic. Cornelia Nixon, for example, has called it Lawrence's "most authoritarian novel" (205) and, like others, places it within what many critics refer to as his "leadership phase," a term that again alludes to this latter definition of modernism.[23]

The crucial point to be taken from debates about the meanings of modernism is not that the search finds a more convincing answer in one argument rather than another, but that, like primitivism, theories of modernism are conflicted, holding oppositional tension at their very core. Lawrence's writings, particularly on Mexico, embody such contradictions, most specifically, the simultaneous attraction to and recoiling from perceived "real" primitives, an anxiety that moors the very foundations of primitivist thinking.

The Plumed Serpent lays out these embattled impulses in its opening chapter, "Beginnings of a Bull-fight." The novel was written during two trips to Mexico, with the first draft, originally called *Quetzalcoatl,* produced in Chapala in 1923. The revision was completed in Oaxaca in 1924.[24] Referred to as Lawrence's attempt at an "Aztec revival," the novel, according to F. R. Leavis, fails where the novella "The Woman Who Rode Away" succeeds because the latter "imagines the old pagan Mexican religion as something real and living; living enough for its devotees to entertain the confident hope of reconquering Mexico" (273). Leavis identifies an important aspect of Lawrence's Mexico writings, and that is the author's attempt to fashion movements of Indian resistance. Primitivist thinking marks Indians as quintessential figures of resistance to Western civilization; therefore, sympathy—even if guarded, as in the case of Lawrence—and fascination with Native rebellion conforms to a broader logic of primitivism. Leavis' qualitative judgment of Lawrence's literary attempts in the two texts places more validity in the presentation of a persistent Chilchui Indian way of life in contrast to the depiction of cultural revitalization through the Cult of Quetzalcoatl. In either case, however, we should think more about what Lawrence's novel reveals about Western conceptions of Native America, rather than dwelling upon the believability of such depictions.

The Plumed Serpent chronicles the relationship of Kate Leslie, the forty-year-old widowed Irish protagonist, to the Quetzalcoatl Cult and her gradual initiation into it as Malintzi, wife of the Aztec "war-god" Huitzilopochtli. The character is often read as representative of the voice of Lawrence the writer and also as a composite of both the writer's and his wife's subjective responses to Mexico. Rudnick, for example, sees Kate as "an amalgam of Mabel, Frieda [Lawrence's wife], and Lawrence at the points where they were most congenial" (223). Kate sojourns in Mexico City with two Americans, Owen and Villiers, characters based on Witter Bynner and his lover, Spud Johnson, with whom Lawrence made his first visit to Mexico. Kate quickly rejects their company, however, feeling "a red pang of hatred against this Americanism which is coldly and unscrupulously sensational" (16). She retreats to Lake Sayula, a thinly disguised version of Lake Chapala, in the state of Jalisco, Mexico.[25] The remainder of the novel details Kate's interactions with the Cult of Quetzalcoatl, facilitated by Juana, her domestic servant, Don Ramón Carrasco, "an eminent historian and archaeologist," (58) and General Cipriano Viedma, an Indigenous counter-revolutionary working on behalf of the Mexican state.[26]

The bullfight scene of the first chapter installs the social context in which the novel takes place, and in which Lawrence wrote it. Jeffrey Meyers convincingly argues that the writer's fear of Mexico was informed by "revolutionary violence, tempered by a fascination with primitive power" (59). Set in immediate post-Revolutionary Mexico, the novel situates Kate Leslie, Owen, and Villiers within an Anglo-American and British history of travel to Mexico. Foreign journalists, anthropologists, novelists, cultural workers, and political organizers were a noticeable presence at the time the novel was written. The chapter also hints at Lawrence's critique of the Revolutionary State, one which, he seems to suggest, serves the military rather than the people, who remain hopelessly degenerate.

In "Beginnings of a Bull-fight," Kate attends with Owen a spectacle that she feels compelled to observe simply because she has never seen one. She is excited and curious and at the same time filled with dread at the thought of the event (7). The chapter introduces major images and thematics, all of which are to some degree narratively transformed as Kate gains knowledge of the Cult. Most pronounced is the association of Mexico with destructive energy, visualized through the figure of the snake, and this first chapter is emblematic of Lawrence's vision of Mexico as preoccupied with death and negative reptilian energy. He had used the serpent imagery in previous writings, and while in New Mexico, decorated Luhan's outhouse door with a huge serpent.[27] In *The Plumed Serpent,* the snake appears in conjunction with Cipriano, a concatenation underwritten by contemporary archeological knowledge.

After her first meeting with the almost "pure Indian" Army General Cipriano, during which she imagines a "heavy, black Mexican fatality" about him, Kate's impressions of the general fuse with more ambient feelings about her host country. Her sensations find conceptual expressions that rely upon her previous responses to archaeological artifacts housed in the National Museum in Mexico City, that is, stone figures that fill her with "depression and dread. Snakes coiled like excrement, snakes fanged and feathered beyond all dreams of dread" (79). Reception of such artifacts is guided by non-Indigenous archaeologists and museum directors who select and contextualize objects like stone serpents for their viewing publics. Kate's thoughts mirror Lawrence's nonfictional characterizations of one of Mexico's most famous mythic symbols and indicate the extent to which the author and his character are unable to comprehend Indigenous material existence apart from the signifiers of an ancient past.

The bullfight also functions as a repository for Eurocentric sentiments about Mexico and for Lawrence's own ideas about America more generally, focalized through the character of Kate. The same force that Lawrence saw devastating the English countryside through industrialization and that he wrote of as "the great negative will . . . turned against all spontaneous life" (*Letters IV* 310), he saw quite starkly in the "death-continent," America. He writes in a letter to Else Jaffe, his sister-in-law, about the lack of feeling he observes in the United States, "superimposing the individual, egoistic will over the real genuine sacred life" (*Letters IV* 311). Ironically, this "genuine sacred life" was represented by Lawrence, once he arrived in the Americas, through images of Indigenous cultural practices and his own notions about Indigenous spirituality. The bullfight opposes the sacred life that Lawrence envisions and is, rather, proof of the corruption of the Indian "old vision," its vulgar spectacle evidence of the decimation of "the ancient centers of life" ("Certain Americans" 243). As Kate pulls back in disgust, the majority mestizo audience, and her American traveling companions, crane to view the horror.[28]

Lawrence's entire novel indulges a widespread representation of Mexico that fixates upon a presumed death fetish. This assumption arises, in part, from non-Mexican fascination with ritual celebrations of Día de los Muertos (Day of the Dead). In Lawrence's writing, the negative energy and "death-pull" of the North American continent are at times linked to capitalist greed and mechanization and at others attributed to the mixing of European blood with that of the Indigenous (*Plumed Serpent* 64). Still yet, Lawrence also ascribes the underlying threat to a resistant Indigenous presence that he understands solely through the archaeological ordering of Aztec civilization and its association with ritual violence. He writes in the essay "Au Revoir, U.S.A." that "[i]t's a queer continent — as much as I've seen of it. It's a fanged continent. It's got a rattlesnake coiled in its heart . . . the stone coiled rattlesnake of Aztec eternity" (104–105). Thus, his discomfort and apprehensions about contemporary Mexico and Mexicans are attached to historical and archaeological conventions that emphasize the Aztec Empire, serpent imagery, and the practice of ritual human sacrifice. At the end of the piece, he proclaims that the difference between the United States and Mexico is that "here in Mexico the fangs are still obvious. Everybody knows the gods are going to bite within the next five minutes. While in the United States, the gods have had their teeth pulled, and their claws cut, and their tails docked, till they seem mild lambs. Yet all the time, inside, it's the same old dragon's blood" (106). The hold on society, particularly through the controlling influences of Christianity, seems much more tenuous to Lawrence in Mexico, where Indigenous cultural expression in a variety of forms is persistently visible, in contrast to the touristic packaging of the Apache and Hopi ceremonies he attended, along with masses of other "palefaces," in New Mexico.

Lawrence portrays this "spirit" of the American continent in terms of an oppressive heaviness, as in Kate's image of the snake unable to hoist itself. Mexican people are perceived as resigned to a negative fate and the doom of death, such as that which awaits the bull when he enters the ring. Although spectators want to see a bull that resists, according to Owen, the bull is essentially Mexican and, as such, will never fight hard enough. Instead, because it knows that a violent and horrible death awaits, the bull does little to defend itself. When, at a tea party hosted by Mrs. Norris, a character modeled after the very real Zelia Nuttall, Don Ramón Carrasco proclaims, "The famous revolutions . . . began with *Viva!* But ended always with *Muera!* Death to this, Death to the other, it was all death! death! death! As insistent as the Aztec sacrifices. Something forever gruesome and macabre" (50), Kate's impressions seemed to be confirmed by one who is both authentic—an actual Mexican, even if "mostly Spaniard"—and expert. In other words, Mexico is unable to escape the violent precursor of the Aztec Empire and, knowing this, submits itself to a predetermined and ugly end.

Kate's feelings about Mexico, however, are transformed in significant degrees after she reads on her fortieth birthday the newspaper account of the return of Quetzalcoatl. It describes "an incident of almost comic nature," in which women washing their clothes on the shores of Lake Sayula were witness to a supernatural event: "A man of great stature rise[s] naked from the lake and wade[s] towards the shore. His face, they said was dark and bearded, but his body shone like gold" (56). He reports to the women that "I have come from out of the lake to tell you, the gods are coming back to Mexico, they are ready to return to their own home" (57). The article also mentions that Don Ramón Carrasco will be leading an investigation into the incident. Spellbound by the account, Kate ponders the myth of Quetzalcoatl, reflecting on the scant amount she has read about the "fair-faced, bearded god" with "eyes that see and are unseen, like the stars by day" (58) who left Mexico to go eastward.

The scene presages the very similar reaction of a Western female subject in Lawrence's 1929 short story, "The Woman Who Rode Away." The unnamed "Woman" hears a snippet of information about an ancient tribe of Indians living in a high valley south of her home in the Sierra Madre, a tribe that continues to live "with their own savage customs and religion" (549). She responds to the account with a fascination for their "old, old religions and mysteries," imagining that "it must be wonderful, surely it must" (549). Despite the admonishments of her husband and the visitor who introduces the subject, the Woman fixates her imagination on the idea of the Chilchui as the antidote to her bored, soulless way of life and decides to set off alone to find them and submit herself to them. Kate, similarly, upon encountering a small piece of information about the return of the god at Lake Sayula, decides she must go there. In each case, Lawrence creates alienated, disenchanted Western female characters who seek out Native religion in order to transform their own deprived existences.

As Kate embarks on her journey toward initiation into the Cult, the initial negative presentations of the North American continent, Aztec snakes, and Natives are redeemed and redeployed as vital tools for her own deliverance. Cipriano, however, who becomes Kate's husband as they are both inducted into the Quetzalcoatl pantheon, remains an ambiguous figure as she wavers between desire and disdain for him. This vacillation arises from her inability to separate Cipriano from the residues of initial, fearful impressions of Native Mexico engendered by museum trips and her own ethnocentrism. In addition, however, Kate is never quite able to overcome the experience of being rejected by the European Ramón, whom she favors, when he chooses a Mexican wife.

It is the criollo Don Ramón, rather than the Indian Cipriano, upon whom Lawrence bestows the title of "living Quetzalcoatl." The character of Cipriano, on the other hand, assumes the identity of Huitzilopochtli, god of war and blood sacrifice, a transparent commentary on Cipirano's blood quantum — "biologically" he is more Indian than any of the other characters in the novel and therefore closer both historically and temperamentally, in Lawrence's understanding, to ancient Mesoamerican ritual violence. Don Ramón Carrasco is identified early in the narrative as distinctly non-Indian when Kate first meets him at the tea party in Tlacolula at Mrs. Norris' house, after she has read the article in the newspaper.[29] Later that same afternoon at Ramón's house, guests have a lively dinner discussion about "mixed-blood" Mexicans and "pure blooded" Indians, the conversation punctuated by hints from the other guests — Mirabal, Julio Toussaint, and García — that something greater is brewing, a miracle perhaps. As Kate gushes, "I love the *word* Quetzalcoatl" (60), Mirabal asks if it would not "be wonderful if the gods came back to Mexico: our own gods?" (61).

Toussaint's contributions to the conversation consist of his own theories about the tragedy of the "mixed-blood." The tragedy, he claims, is the hopelessness of the mixed race, a hopelessness borne of the violence that brought about the "moment of coition": "In what spirit have the Spanish and other foreign fathers gotten children of the Indian women? . . . And then, what sort of race do you expect?" (64). Toussaint's comment is an oblique reference to the history of sexual violence as a tool of war and conquest, as well as to the metaphoric representation of the conquest of the Americas as a rape. In 1926, Manuel Gamio had the following to say about post-Conquest "racial contact" between Spaniards and Natives: "The white man possessed the native woman wherever and whenever he saw fit. Therefore the offspring of these inharmonious and forced unions had none of the advantages of a normal origin" ("Incorporating" 108). In such configurations, Indigenous subjects are rendered as female victims and conquerors as male aggressors. As much as such narratives operate to expose a submerged history of conquest violence, they also reinscribe and attribute a lack of agency to women and feminize victimization. Indigenous male subjects become "like women" in that they are subjugated as women are forever consigned to a state of powerlessness.[30]

Toussaint is the only one present who attributes a state of hopelessness to mestizos; everyone else understands Indians as those with truly no hope. Mexicans "prostitute themselves . . . and so they can never *do* anything," Mirabal claims, "[and] the Indians can never do anything either, because they haven't got hope in anything" (66). The conversation ends with his somber, yet earnest imperative: "We must make the miracle come. The miracle is superior even to the moment of coition" (66). Kate responds to Toussaint's ideas about the "calamity" of the half-breed who "is divided against himself. His blood of one race tells him one thing, his blood of another race tells him another" (64). "Some people believe in the mixed blood . . . . some of your serious-minded men," answers Kate, in what appears to be a clear reference to Vasconcelos' prevailing ideas at the time (66).

"Don Ramón is almost pure Spaniard, but most probably he has the blood of Tlaxcalan Indians in his veins as well" (64), says Toussaint at one point in the conversation. Ramón's mixed-blood status is explained through reference to Tlaxcaltecas, an intriguing choice on Lawrence's part. Historically, the Tlaxcaltecas were one of many Indigenous groups who allied with the Spaniards against the Aztec Empire. The ancestral lineage of "betrayal" is on one hand reversed by Ramón's role in the Quetzalcoatl movement, but also helps to position him as a character that may be associated with Europe. Technically, Ramón *could* be read as mestizo, but the narrative voice seems to suggest otherwise: "Kate looked round. Don Ramón was flashing his knowing, brown Spanish eyes, and a little sardonic smile lurked under his moustache. Instantly Kate and he, Europeans in essence, understood one another" (41). Because Ramón's racial composition is primarily Spanish, his defining racial character is European, according to the dominant theories of racial essence at the time, which we can attribute not only to Lawrence, but also to Mexican intellectuals such as Vasconcelos, who expounded his racial philosophy in his 1925 book, *La Raza Cósmica*.

Vasconcelos' work has been interpreted as a progressive proclamation about the value of racial mixture, an answer to centuries of legislation, pseudo-science, and popular world-views that labeled "miscegenation" as degenerative. In the past, Vasconcelos' term *"la raza cósmica"* was appropriated by Chicanas/os to invigorate mestiza/o pride. In effect, however, Vasconcelos advocates racial composition more along the lines of a Ramón, in whom the tiniest amount of Indian blood is all that is necessary to achieve the status of new world prototype. Contrary to popular conceptions that saw in Vasconcelos' support for *mestizaje* a belief that Native culture and society were equal to Spanish, his theories promoted racial mixture for the purpose of elevating Indigenous people, raising them "to the higher standards of life, where reproduction becomes regulated and quality predominates over numbers" ("The Race Problem" 101).[31] Too much mixture, conversely, and as Toussaint and Mirabal suggest, has only disastrous consequences.

Although not "pure" Spaniard, Ramón is not mixed enough to be degraded by his "Indian blood." The apparent ease with which he is able to inhabit both his European racial identity and retrieved Aztec spirituality is striking in comparison to how the novel judges the ability of Indians to negotiate this same terrain. He has been educated in the United States, at Columbia, although this cultivation of "the white man's Dead Sea consciousness" (65) seems not to produce culture confusion in this 99 percent Spaniard character.[32] In Toussaint's argument that the "homogenous blood" of European races makes "consciousness automatically unroll in continuity" (65), he uses the figure of Benito Juárez as counterexample:

> Take a man like Benito Juarez, a pure Indian. He floods his old consciousness with the new white ideas, and there springs up a whole forest of verbiage, new laws, new constitutions and all the rest. But it is a sudden weed. It grows like a weed on the surface, saps the strength of the Indian soil underneath, and helps the process of ruin. No, madam! There is no hope for Mexico short of a miracle. (65)

In other words, Lawrence's version of "Indian consciousness" is unable to negotiate effectively the infiltration of white forms of knowledge and is, in fact, diminished by them. This may in part explain why it is Ramón, rather than the "pure and simple" Indian Cipriano, who is designated as leader of the Cult. Although Ramón's racial essence is European, his smattering of Tlaxcalan blood provides an avenue through which he can access his own "Indian consciousness." This residual consciousness exists in a small enough portion that it does not threaten his continued status as "civilized" in opposition to the "intensity and crudity of the semi-savage" Cipriano (67). Ultimately, it takes a European to lead Indians back to their gods and their own forms of spiritual and other knowledges. Ramón, like other Europeans (Lawrence, for example), recognizes the value of Indian spirituality whereas the "real" primitives, the simple peons, do not. Indians do not lead their own movements of resistance here; they are simply followers.

Gamio communicated a similar lack of confidence in the prospect of Indigenous leadership, claiming that "the Indian . . . has the right to expect the white [mestizos] to understand his peculiar way of thinking since he cannot be expected to ascend mentally, rapidly, miraculously, to the plane of the difficult ideological and material mechanism which characterizes the modern civilization of the white minorities" ("Incorporating" 126). We are thus able to see certain symmetry in the assessments of Indigenous capabilities among Gamio, Lawrence, and Vasconcelos. There is little to no documentation to suggest that Lawrence was well acquainted with the writings of Gamio and Vasconcelos, but it is not difficult to imagine him coming into contact with their ideas about Indian glory and Indian abjection. It is unlikely that Lawrence was introduced to this pattern of thinking while in Mexico; rather, his own assumptions about the degraded status of Indians were reinforced in Mexico as was his fetishistic urge to capture something of their past greatness to serve his own artistic purposes.

Cipriano Viedma is vitally important in this regard, although he has been treated with little interest by Lawrence scholars. He functions for Kate as an emblem of the continuing presence of "this all-enwreathing dragon of the horror of Mexico" (79) and her interactions with him crystallize in the last lines of that first chapter with the figure of the serpent. It is a phallic image that is at once impotent and latently powerful: "She felt again, as she had felt before, that Mexico lay in her destiny almost as a doom. Something so heavy, so oppressive, like the folds of some huge serpent that seemed as if it could hardly raise itself" (24). Cipriano enters the narrative during the bullfight as the terrorized protagonist attempts to make her way through the tunnel entrance, desperately wanting to escape the horror of not only the inhumane killing of the animals, but also the glee with which most observers appear to respond. As she tries to push her way through the crowd toward the exit, Cipriano comes to her rescue. An army general who travels the countryside putting down "bandit attacks," he is the primitive of the novel. Adopted as a child by a wealthy and influential bishop, he is now in the business of protecting the landowning class. When they gather later at Ramón's, he tells Kate of the Bishop who became his godfather, that he had a hacienda and a "fine library" expropriated during the Revolution. Cipriano did not fulfill his godfather's wish that he become a priest and instead became a soldier, refusing to take his place within the ranks of the clerical hierarchy. He is a military man, which establishes his identity in the novel as a modernized primitive. As a soldier, he may be linked with the forces of modernization and "civilization" implemented through conquest and containment. In spite of his refined background and elite education, however, Cipriano's primitive Indian status remains barely masked by his Oxford education and Catholic socialization, as Kate's frequent association of him with serpent imagery makes clear. He is a partially, not completely, civilized primitive.

Early critics of the novel easily dismissed the characters of Ramón and Cipriano. Leavis, for example, claimed "that Cipriano is not himself the supreme world-saviour; he is second in command to Don Ramón, the living Quetzalcoatl, who we certainly do not take for Lawrence, and in whom we are not very much interested (nor, in fact, are we in Cipriano himself)" (67–68). Meyers calls them "unattractive heroes" (62 n.25), and Walker finds Cipriano "repulsive" (91). Yet, the characterization of Cipriano, in particular, is compelling and the relationship between the two men significant. Kate marvels that Ramón is not intimidated by the Indian Cipriano, who "looked at Ramón with a curious intimacy, glittering, steady, warrior-like, and at the same time betraying an almost menacing trust in the other man" (67). Always we find Cipriano evoking Aztec violence, through references either to the threatening power of snake imagery or to the militarization of society under the Aztecs, for example, in his "steady, warrior-like" gaze. Yet it is the quality of "trust" rather than the threat of usurpation that prevails in Lawrence's rendering of interactions between the men as their relationship becomes the "successful" example of *mestizaje* in the novel. The physically adept, yet intellectually awkward Indian gives himself over to the enlightened European leader.

Cipriano unabashedly recognizes Ramón's leadership. He acts with deference toward Ramón and at times seems almost to worship him. The novel does not reveal the basis of such authority, although Lawrence writes the character of Ramón as one who naturally commands the respect and attention of the Indian acolytes he leads in the movement. And, although the two characters are often presented in opposing terms, no evidence of competitive tension exists between them. Cipriano's relationship with Ramón actually parallels his relationship with the Bishop, Cipriano's superior and mentor throughout his childhood and young adulthood.

Like the Bishop, Ramón is a highly educated and genteel criollo, or European, who takes Cipriano under his wing and provides him with tutelage. And although Cipriano was unwilling, as mentioned earlier, to take his place in the Catholic clerical pantheon of which his beloved Bishop was a part, he is more than eager to occupy the role of living Huitzilopochtli as second in command to Ramón's Quetzalcoatl. As the narrative unfolds, Lawrence foregrounds the emotional and physical intimacy between the two men. After their participation in the Quetzalcoatl movement is revealed, they are often depicted in close physical contact: "The two men embraced, breast to breast, and for a moment Cipriano laid his little blackish hands on the naked shoulders of the bigger man, and for a moment was perfectly still on his breast. Then very softly, he stood back and looked at him, saying not a word" (182). The description of Cipriano with his head on Ramón's breast is both paternal and erotic. And although Cipriano is childlike compared to Ramón's manliness, it is the former who exhibits the exotic and sensual masculine sexuality in "his small but strong and assertive body, with its black currents and storms of desire" (310). In this "new" example of symbolic racial fusion, Lawrence retains elements of the older model that emerges from the historical realities of conquest: Spanish domination of Native people extends to the realm of sexual relations. Lawrence's version keeps the responsibility for intellectual and social transformation in European hands, but also depicts it as a process with physical components enacted "between men," to use Eve Kosofsky Sedgwick's phrase. Kate can never participate fully in the Quetzalcoatl revival, not only because she is not Mexican, but also because of her gender, as the example of Ramón's wife, Teresa, makes clear. Rather than producing biological offspring, the physical and emotional contact between Ramón and Cipriano produces a new social and racial consciousness.

After this embrace, as Cipriano backs away from Ramón, Lawrence deepens our understanding of the powerful loyalty and deference that Cipriano exhibits to Ramón:

> "*Bien! Muy bien!*" said Cipriano, still gazing into the other man's face with black, wondering, childlike eyes, as if he, Cipriano, were searching for *himself* in Ramón's face. Ramón looked back into Cipriano's black, Indian eyes with a faint, kind smile of recognition, and Cipriano hung his head as if to hide his face, the black hair, which he wore rather long and brushed sideways, dropping over his forehead. (182)

The Indian looks to find himself in the European. Ramón's "faint, kind smile" suggests not only sympathy, but also superiority as Cipriano finds himself embarrassed by his own relative deficiencies. Cipriano's "wondering, childlike" eyes and his behavior, which could very well be called demure, reinforce our understanding of the line of authority within the Quetzalcoatl Cult and between these two men—the Spaniard and the Indian.[33] Cipriano turns to Ramón for guidance, to find the way back to the Indian roots that they share marginally. According to the race theory that Lawrence expounded in the novel and in other writings about Mexico, the European overlay of consciousness is too powerful for an Indian such as Cipriano to negotiate alone. A Spaniard like Ramón is able to chart a path toward redemption and find his own way, but Cipriano must rely, ironically, on Ramón to lead him out of the "whole forest of verbiage" (65) that diminishes Indian consciousness.

This consciousness, or Kate's idea of it, prompts her to look to non-European spirituality as a source of transcendence, even as she continues to feel threatened by Cipriano's Indianness:

> She wanted to go to Sayula. She wanted to see the big lake where the gods had once lived, and whence they were due to emerge. Amid all the bitterness that Mexico produced in her spirit, there was still a strange beam of wonder and mystery, almost like hope. A strange darkly-iridescent beam of wonder, of magic.
>
> The name Quetzalcoatl too fascinated her. She had read bits about the god. Quetzal is the name of a bird that lives high in the mists of tropical mountains, and has very beautiful tail-feathers, precious to the Aztecs. Coatl is a serpent. Quetzalcoatl is the Plumed Serpent, so hideous in the fanged, feathered, writhing stone of the National Museum.
>
> But Quetzalcoatl was, she vaguely remembered, a sort of fair-faced, bearded god; the wind, the breath of life, the eyes that see and are unseen, like the stars by day. (58)

Kate is thus able to latch onto, amid all her negative impressions of Mexico, mestizos, and Indians, this "strange beam of wonder and mystery, almost like hope." As Lawrence describes in "Au Revoir, U.S.A." and as Kate notices in her observations, Mexico here is the location of a regenerative spiritual power that is at times diminished in the menacing imagery of snakes and "dragon's blood," but at others redeployed as the residual and persistent force of centuries-old ways of life that more deeply connect individuals to each other and to spiritual realms of existence. Kate's ability to see beyond or through the "bitterness" of Mexico is further testament to the novel's premise that it is Europeans who are best able to recognize the recuperative value of Indigenous knowledge. Like Ramón, Kate is able to overcome on her own the oppressive dampening control of European ideology, whereas the Indian Cipriano cannot. One of the ways she navigates this terrain is by reimagining the serpent-god Quetzalcoatl as the "fair-faced, bearded god," a less threatening and more familiar image, which certain archaeological and Conquest-era accounts promote.

This linking of Mexican Indians with the serpent is based upon archaeological interpretations of the Mesoamerican god Quetzalcoatl, as mentioned earlier. The name is often translated as either "plumed serpent" or "precious twin," although the god is sometimes represented in Nahuatl codices as emerging from the mouth of a plumed serpent, rather than as the plumed serpent itself. According to modern interpretations of codices, such as the *Codex Chimalpopoca,* Quetzalcoatl is believed to have once been a great Toltec king who ruled the empire appropriated by the Aztecs as their ancestor civilization. Successive Toltec rulers took the name Quetzalcoatl, but the original Quetzalcoatl, represented as both man and god, was eventually banished for angering the gods, and retreated toward the east, promising to return.[34]

Furthermore, Quetzalcoatl is associated with Venus, the Morning Star, and wind. He is a mild, gentle god of agriculture, the arts, and civilization in general. Most importantly, Quetzalcoatl is disassociated from ritual sacrifice in most studies of ancient Mesoamerica. William H. Prescott, whose 1843 *A History of the Conquest of Mexico* provided source material for Lawrence, advances a highly romanticized version of the god, as "a far more interesting personage . . . god of the air, a divinity who, during his residence on earth, instructed the natives in the use of metals, in agriculture, and in the arts of government. . . . Under him, the earth teemed with fruits and flowers, without the pains of culture. . . . It was the *golden age* of Anahuac" (23). But the Aztecs, according to scholars, eventually came to revere Huitzilopochtli, translated as "hummingbird," as their supreme deity, the god of war and the sun. In contradistinction to Quetzalcoatl, Huitzilopochtli is believed to have originated with the Aztecs. As a "war-god," he demanded human sacrifice and, according to Prescott, loathsome amounts of blood.[35]

Like Prescott, Lawrence also seems to have found Quetzalcoatl to be more interesting. But perhaps the most fantastic aspect of Quetzalcoatl recruitment manifests itself in the responses of Ramón and Cipriano to the European Kate. For some reason, this Irish woman is viewed as a valuable potential participant in the Cult of Quetzalcoatl by the two supreme living gods. Kate's relationship to them remains ambivalent through the end of the novel, although she actually does consent to a great deal in spite of her aversion to certain aspects of Quetzalcoatl ideology. Her racial identity, in Lawrence's imagined schemata, appears to render her a unique addition and somewhat of a precious conquest for the two men.

But it is the Indian Cipriano who exhibits the most passionate adoration of the non-Indian acolyte:

> The wonder, the mystery, the magic that used to flood over him as a boy and a youth, when he kneeled before the babyish figure of the Santa María de la Soledad, flooded him again. He was in the presence of the goddess, white-handed, mysterious, gleaming with a moon-like power and intense potency of grief. (71)

The Indian is in awe of the white goddess even as he rejects European Catholicism for the reinvented spiritual practices of the Quetzalcoatl Cult. Cipriano is lured by Kate as the white version of an Indian goddess; her presence facilitates his movement toward spiritual redemption the Indian way. When we recall the Spanish clerical use of the Virgin of Guadalupe, an indigenized version of a European goddess-figure, the centrality of the European woman in a recovered Aztec pantheon becomes part of a curious reverse conversion account. Cipriano is led to transfer his adoration of the Christian goddess to the pseudo-Indigenous goddess, a process aided by the manifestation of the latter as racially European. Thus, Kate's European physiognomy presents Cipriano with a familiar and beloved object of devotion that intensifies the emotional fervor of his transition. The scene implies that Europeans still need a conversion mechanism to seduce Natives to a "new" religion, with Ramón Carrasco as the clerical authority presiding over it all. From this position of superiority, the European Ramón is able to remain above Kate's seductive power, recognizing without the aid of conversion techniques the value of a "return" to Quetzalcoatl. He chooses Teresa, a mestiza, as his own wife, although he acknowledges Kate's usefulness and incorporates her as the goddess Malintzi, a name invented by Lawrence although probably a deformation of "La Malinche." Ultimately, Kate's place in the pantheon, even as the wife of the lesser god, is much more prominent than that of Teresa, who is presented as stoic, enduring, accepting, loyal, and, above all, submissive.

It is Cipriano, however, who encourages the "native" Quetzalcoatl dances "with curious passion" (364).[36] And it is Cipriano, the "semi-savage," who performs what comes closest to a modern rendition of blood sacrifice when he kills three of the people who plot to murder Ramón, including a woman, with a "bright, thin dagger" and "three swift, heavy stabs" (380).[37] Cipriano performs the executions in a rapid, impersonal manner, carrying out his new duties as second-in-command to and protector of Ramón/Quetzalcoatl. Lawrence's characterization of the army general in terms that call forth an Aztec warrior figure make him the obvious choice to wield the dagger, an object that evokes the obsidian knives believed to have been the tools used to carve out the hearts of the Aztecs' sacrificial victims.

Writing about primitivism in museum culture, Sally Price observes that "[t]he imagery used to convey Primitive Artists' otherness employs a standard rhetoric of fear, darkness, pagan spirits, and eroticism" (37). Lawrence's Cipriano offers a classic example of the figure of the primitive in narrative form. Kate's subjective accounts of his menacing appearance, the constant references to his dark features and secretive personality, the raw sexual energy that Kate responds to in spite of herself, all of this positions Cipriano as the primitive of *The Plumed Serpent* more so than the "refined," "cultured," and almost 100 percent Spaniard, Ramón. The popularization of pre-Columbian artifacts, and the accepted association of Aztec civilization with ritual human sacrifice and militaristic dominance, makes this pre-Conquest Indigenous society, personified in Cipriano, readily available to the divergent cultural expressions of modernist primitivism more than has perhaps been recognized.

As she wrestles with the question of "to stay or not to stay," it is the image of the Indian that lures Kate back toward Mexico. It is not, however, the Indian Mexico that Cipriano represents, but, rather, passive, mute figures of suffering:

> Those pale-faced Mexicans of the Capital, politicians, artists, professionals, and business people, they did not interest her. Neither did the hacendados and the ranch-owners, in their tight trousers and weak, soft sensuality, pale victims of their own emotional undiscipline. Mexico still meant the mass of silent peons to her. (75)

Kate rejects a de-masculinized, effeminate, modern Mexico for premodern, pre-Conquest Mexico, the vestiges of which she sees, or thinks she sees, in materially dispossessed Indian subjects who nevertheless hold the wealth of untapped spiritual traditions and insights. Similarly, it was not Mexico the modern country that interested Lawrence, but Mexico before the Conquest, aspects of which he thought he could see and identify as the residue of a conquered "vanished" culture in contemporary Mexico. It is this sense of Mexico and its people that also provides, in some instances of Chicana/o indigenism, the incentive for and basis of resistance.

Yet, the Cult of Quetzalcoatl is a *representation* of primitivism within a modern primitivist text. It is never suggested that this is an Indigenous movement; rather, it is one in which the European Ramón appropriates pre-Conquest symbols to fuel a rhetoric and seduce new recruits. It is not one that is distinctly Native in terms of leadership and only marginally so in terms of participants, variously identified as "peons," "peasants," "mere natives," terms that can operate as code words for "Indians." Furthermore, Cipriano's professional identity as a counter-insurgent drastically mitigates the degree to which one can indulge a reading of the Quetzalcoatl Cult as resistance from "the bottom up." And Ramón's failure to reject his own wealth—to commit class suicide—places him within the ranks of the nationalist petite bourgeoisie that even Lawrence recognized as betraying the revolutionary causes of Villa and Zapata.

Through the invocation of an ancient Mexican past that is as much associated with the religiosity of ritual human sacrifice as it is with the formal complexity of its art and the technological sophistication of its society, Lawrence creates a version of Mexico that is by no means his alone to claim. Ronald Walker's study of Mexico in the modern English novel makes the point that other English writers—Malcolm Lowry, Graham Greene, Aldous Huxley—also perpetuated the idea of Mexico as "infernal paradise." Although Walker gives credit to Lawrence for initiating this "daemonic/paradisal rendering of Mexico" and directly influencing the perceptions of later novelists, it remains crucial to recognize that Lawrence himself was led by extant images of Mexico and Aztec culture—for example, those that arise from Prescott and other writing in English about Mexico that began to appear in the nineteenth century.[38] In any case, the profound link between Aztec culture and ritual violence that exists in the popular imagination cannot be underestimated as we attempt to understand novelistic representations of the country.

At the end of the novel, Kate finds herself again in the conflicted position with which her story began. In spite of an apparent reconciliation of her fear of Cipriano, the snake, and the Mexican death-wish, Kate remains ambivalent about her role in the Quetzalcoatl pantheon and her prospects for a satisfying life in Mexico. In the last line of the novel Kate admonishes the confounded Cipriano, "You won't let me go!" (444). Despite his and Ramón's attempts to convince Kate of her value to them, ultimately she feels that she remains an "intruder" (443), destined to be forever on the outside. Her sense of isolation most probably stems from the fact that she is a woman; the Quetzalcoatl Cult is clearly masculinist in its privileging of male leadership and relegation of women to no more significant positions that that of "wife" to a reborn god. The mestiza Teresa is content with this supplemental role, but Kate's own sensibilities rail against it. Perhaps this is where the novel reveals its position on the restorative potential of "primitive" spirituality for the modern Western subject. Kate's doubts, fears, and anxieties redound upon her, rendering the Quetzalcoatl Cult bankrupt as an option for her spiritual and psychic restoration and, by extension, for the rejuvenation of Western culture itself.

CHAPTER 2

The Mesoamerican in the Mexican-American Imagination: Chicano Movement Indigenism

C hicana/o poetics encompasses a range of textual expressions, including fiction, drama, poetry, and political manifestos. The movement period of this literary history is marked by the thematic recurrence of particular iconic images. For example, student and off-campus activist participation in the farmworker unionization movement helped create public awareness of the material conditions under which many agricultural workers labored.[1] This movement was also popularized through the work of El Teatro Campesino, an organizing tool founded in 1965 to stage performances in the fields and recruit workers for the union.[2] Characterizing farmworkers as "the least acculturated and most economically exploited members of Mexican-American society," José Limón considers them "an ideal resolving symbol" for movement discourse (*Mexican Ballads* 83). Within the farmworker movement itself, however, it was the image of la Virgin de Guadalupe that graced the march banners, a unifying image from the shared culture of Catholicism.

In addition to migrant agricultural laboring forces, literary attention focused on the urban conditions of Chicana/o communities and politicized the figure of the pachuco. Long considered by both Mexican-American and Anglo-American societies as little more than a gangster or hoodlum, the pachuco was reclaimed by movement poetics as a counter-cultural figure of resistance. José Montoya's 1972 poem "El Louie" has received significant attention in Chicano literary criticism and is perhaps the most highly regarded treatment of the theme of urban pachuco life.[3]

The language of indigenism and the theme of Chicana/o indigenous ancestry are thus but one set of iconic signifiers deployed within movement rhetoric. Articulated within a matrix of recovered Mesoamerican mythology, Chicana/o indigenism mobilizes the story of the Aztec migration from the ancestral homeland of Aztlán, the cosmogonic narrative of *el Quinto Sol*/the Fifth Sun, and the cross-culturally significant figure of the plumed serpent, also known as the god-king Quetzalcoatl. Indigenism found outlets in fiction and poetry, in public mural art of the period, and in the drama productions of El Teatro Campesino.[4]

Aztlán and Chicano Indigenism

Very often, indigenism elaborated the mythic beginnings of Chicanas/os through the Aztlán myth, which has figured prominently in some writings. Analyses of the poetics of movement indigenism have been characterized both by an acknowledgment of its positive force, as well as by a dismissal of its political value, with a few exceptions. Even as they critique the homogenizing effects of movement discourse, for example, Rosa Linda Fregoso and Angie Chabram-Dernersesian recognize it as "a space where an alternative cultural production and identity could flourish" (204). They present Aztlán as a case in point in that it "provided a basis for a return to our roots, for a return to an identity before domination and subjugation—a voyage back to pre-Columbian times" (204–205). And Genaro Padilla writes that myth was a strategy to "maintain group cohesion . . . and a heroized national past distinct from that of the United States" ("Myth" 116). More recently, Pérez-Torres has contended that "[i]dentification with the Indian gave birth to a Chicano/a critical subaltern identity in solidarity with other indigenous groups throughout the Americas" (*Mestizaje* 9).

Gustavo Segade, in his introduction to the 1976 *Festival de Flor y Canto: An Anthology of Chicano Literature,* characterized Aztlán as a "mythic timespace," (3) and, indeed, it is a term that cements myth, history, and geography in a continuum that enables nationalist consciousness. Both Alurista and Armando Rendon were committed to the idea of Aztlán, with Alurista retaining credit for having imported the term into an emergent Chicano nationalism. Alurista also explicitly rewrote the Aztec migration story as a Chicano narrative of origin that linked ancient Indigenous travelers to present-day mestizo communities in the United States.[5] He presented a poem to attendees at the 1969 Denver Youth Conference, which eventually became the preamble to "El Plan de Aztlán." According to the poet's account, documented in an interview collected in the first installment of the PBS series *Chicano!,* he was startled at how quickly people seized upon the idea of Aztlán and how readily the poem was incorporated into a founding document of the Chicano movement.[6] The tale of southward migration became the basis for claiming that Chicanas/os in the United States were not immigrants, but had returned to or resided historically in a long-forgotten homeland. The narrative also operated as a statement of unified opposition to Anglo domination and an announcement of filial loyalty and pride. In the early 1970s, however, Aztlán quickly became a hegemonic theme within Chicana/o discourse.

But recent years have seen a critical reevaluation of Aztlán that draws attention to its conceptual shifts and breaking points. Daniel Cooper Alarcón makes a compelling argument for understanding Aztlán as a palimpsest, a paradigm that allows for multiple layers of meaning that conflict, contest, overlap, and reinforce one another. Moreover, the palimpsest model invites readers to consider the discursive presence of Aztlán in sources outside of Chicano nationalism, a heuristic strategy that parallels my own interests in Chicana/o indigenism.[7] Cooper Alarcón sketches a textual history of Aztlán that takes into account Conquest-era source material as he argues that Aztlán "obscure[s] and elide[s] important issues surrounding Chicano identity." At the same time, he also argues for the potential for Aztlán to be "remade into . . . [a] multidimensional model" that will be able to "examine precisely the issues that [it] has been used to evade in the past" (8). Similarly, Rafael Pérez-Torres sees Aztlán as emblematic of "the discontinuities and ruptures that characterize the presence of Chicanos in history" ("Refiguring" 217).[8] Davíd Carrasco has of late entered the conversation, calling for a reappraisal of the enabling aspects of Aztlán and bringing his deep knowledge of Mesoamerican religion to a heuristic that acknowledges previous critical insights, such as Pérez-Torres' argument that Aztlán has been marginalized in Chicana/o discourse. Basing his "reestablishment" of Aztlán on the account from Diego Durán's *Historia de las Indias de Nueva España e Isles de la Tierra Firme* (1581), Carrasco adds to Pérez-Torres' understanding, pointing out that "Aztlan was always a borderland and a *nepantla*," a passageway of sorts (196). He concludes, "Aztlan was not only the place of creation or the hearth from which the ancestors departed. It signified, in the Durán account at least, a series of sacred actions designed to regenerate the paradigmatic *altepetl,* the sacred hill of water, and the granary of creative hearts" (196).

But the dominance of Aztlán and the larger context of indigenist activity in which it was consolidated were never universally accepted, as mentioned earlier. Rosaura Sánchez has written of indigenism as the "decontextualized and dehistoricized manipulation of indigenous narratives" ("Reconstructing" 358), and Limón calls attention to the hegemonic status of Aztec and Mayan societies "that practiced no small amount of domination" (*Mexican Ballads* 109–110). Generally, the critiques target the spiritual aspects of indigenism, which Limón characterizes as a focus on "inwardness, indigenous purity and metaphysical transcendence" (109–110), as unable, or even unwilling, to engage with the hard work of social transformation. The "romantic idealism" of "El Plan de Aztlán," according to Juan Gómez-Quiñones, "strips" the document of its radical potential, whereby it becomes nothing more than "reformism" (*Chicano Politics* 124). Most critics acknowledge the lack of ideological coherence in movement indigenism, agreeing that such confusion only limits political potential. And Gustavo Segade contends that a "new analysis" in the period 1969–1970, the language of Marxism influenced by Third World liberation movements, displaced "the complicated Nahuatl symbology [that] did little to address the enormous economic and political questions of poverty . . ." ("Identity and Power" 90). Thus, debates are characterized in terms of a simple conflict between "politics" and "culture," or "materialism" and "spiritualism."[9]

If we recognize, however, the multiple motivations of indigenists in the Chicana/o movement, that division is not so clear-cut. The glorification of indigenous ancestry initiated narratives that established the historical precedence of Chicanas/os in the U.S. Southwest who could then "ontologically" identify, as Jorge Klor de Alva asserts, as "primordial Americans" ("Invention" 58).[10] The connection to the Aztecs redeemed racial identity as well. Identifying Aztecs as ancestors set in motion an empowering explanation of racial identity in which Chicanas'/os' non-white status became evidence of an indigenous lineage that made them heirs to a cultural patrimony rivaling anything claimed by Europeans. Furthermore, by associating their racial identity with Native people more generally, Chicanas/os were able to articulate the racism they experienced and their history within the more established, if romanticized, narratives of dispossession in the United States. Thus, while the charge against indigenists of retreating from pressing political and social challenges into the realm of metaphysics was not without basis, we should not overlook that indigenism served important political purposes that engaged both cultural revitalization efforts and the struggle for land.

Writing of the creation of "new ethnic origins" among Chicanos and Puerto Ricans, Klor de Alva contends that identification with ancient Mexico provided to young Chicanos "symbolic weapons," or "fetishes," with which to protect themselves from Anglo society. Additionally, "pre-Columbian tropes" addressed the "symbolic importance of narrating a new founding myth" and helped to instill a "new corporate identity" in which cultural characteristics associated with indigeneity were promoted as positive in contrast to the negative markers of capitalism assigned to Anglo culture ("Invention" 57).[11] There occurred, then, a process by which cultural traits such as communal ownership and collective production, viewed as primitive in a Western context, were transvalued and redeployed as markers of a superior and originary status. Indigenism offered a wealth of alternative, positive imagery that could oppose the generally negative stereotypes of Mexicans circulating in mainstream U.S. culture. These stereotypes can be traced to an era when European and Euro-American settlers first began to encounter mestiza/o populations. Armed with preconceived ideas about the savagery of both Indians and Spaniards, settlers and military personnel legitimated expansionist ideology by documenting their judgment of the primitive state of mestiza/o culture, which included a propensity for violence, indolence, and sexual licentiousness.[12]

These negative assumptions were strengthened in no small part by popular accounts like Prescott's *History of the Conquest of Mexico,* long considered authoritative. Prescott indulged in graphic descriptions of human sacrifice, helping to solidify, in the minds of the nineteenth-century reading public, a lasting association between the Aztecs and ritual violence. The effects of Prescott's narrative are evident even one hundred years later in the texts of law enforcement and the courts. In 1942, Los Angeles police lieutenant Edward Duran Ayres testified in the trial of seventeen young Mexican-American men accused of an assault that resulted in the death of José Díaz near Sleepy Lagoon, a Los Angeles reservoir. The "Sleepy Lagoon trial" was followed by a series of physical confrontations between military personnel and Chicano civilians. In the most sustained, the June 1943 "Zoot Suit riots," U.S. Naval personnel targeted young men and boys of color, particularly those wearing "zoot suits."[13] Anthologized by Matt Meier and Feliciano Rivera in *Readings on La Raza,* the "Edward Duran Ayres Report" was designed to convince a grand jury of the natural proclivity for violence among Mexican-descent youth. The report argued that these youth were responsible for high rates of juvenile crime in their neighborhoods and was presented as evidence in the prosecution of the defendants. In George I. Sánchez's 1943 response, he quotes from the Report:[14]

When the Spaniards conquered Mexico, they found an organized society composed of many tribes of Indians ruled by the Aztecs, who were given over to human sacrifice. Historians record that as many as thirty thousand Indians were sacrificed on their heathen altars in one day, their bodies being opened by stone knives and their hearts being torn out while still beating. This total disregard for human life has always been universal throughout the Americas among the Indian population, which of course is well known to everyone. (129)

The references to Indian blood-lust might have been lifted straight out of Prescott's chronicle of the Conquest, which is full of sensationally violent, yet also oddly romantic, depictions of the Aztecs. Even in twentieth-century scholarly accounts of the Conquest and colonization, ideas about racial personality continued to be proffered as historical explanation. Antonia Castañeda has argued that the assessment of the racially degenerate state of mestizas/os is evident in scholarship on the conquest of California in that researchers attributed the sexually violent conduct of mission soldiers to their mixed-blood status, rather than to the ideologically-conflicted policies of conquest.[15] And Holly Barnet-Sánchez, in a brief discussion of the Sleepy Lagoon trial, insightfully observes that the "historical irony of bringing Pre-Columbian art into the modern world as a source of or inspiration for contemporary U.S. artists in the 1940s lay in the contradiction between presenting Pre-Columbian art as the creation of great civilizations . . . while the courts and press in the United States were positioning contemporary Mexicans and Mexican Americans as descendants of 'blood savages'" (189–190).

Additionally, the dominant historical narratives in U.S. education systems still do little to inform student-citizens about the history of mestiza/o presence in the United States, one that, as we know, precedes Anglo colonization of the Southwest and the West. The great irony is that, historically, legislative barriers to citizenship for Mexican immigrants were based upon presumptions about their racial status and its containment within a Mexican national context. Martha Menchaca's fascinating chapter on racial segregation and the courts in *Recovering History, Constructing Race* documents the disempowering effects of these Anglo assumptions as "Mexicans" were reclassified as "Indians" and thus denied the opportunity to apply for U.S. citizenship. In her treatment of *In re Rodriguez* (1897), a petition for citizenship originally filed in Bexar County, Texas, Menchaca quotes the representative of the naturalization board:

[The] applicant is a native-born person of Mexico, 38 years old, and of pure Aztec or Indian race. . . . The population of Mexico comprises about six million Indians of unmixed blood, nearly one-half of whom are nomadic savage tribes. . . . Now it is clear . . . from the appearance of the applicant, that is one of the 6,000,000 Indians of unmixed blood. . . . If an Indian, he cannot be naturalized. (quoted in *Recovering History* 283)

The quotation is made the more pertinent here because of its reference to the "pure Aztec" race, a late nineteenth-century assertion of the Aztec connection that obviously predates the nationalist rallying call. The political implications of the Chicana/o valorization of Aztec origins become more forceful when placed in the context of an Anglo-American discourse of racism that denied rights to Mexicans because of a presumed Aztec Indian racial identity.

The central objective of Aztec cultural revitalization was to transform self-image. Chicanas/os accepted the association with the Aztecs and revised conventional depictions by emphasizing technological achievement, cultural sophistication, and spiritual advancement, generally diminishing the role of human sacrifice. This tactic addressed the anti-Indian racism that exists outside Mexican communities, as well as within them. People recognized the degrading treatment of Indigenous people and chose to distinguish and distance themselves in ways that challenged associations between biology and identity, or physical features and cultural affiliation. An anecdote a student once told in class sums it up brilliantly: After being the last one in the family served dinner, her father asks with indignation, *"Qué soy, indio o qué?"*

Chicanas/os confronted negative accounts of their racial identity that had a history even older than the conquest of the U.S. Southwest—in fact, going back to the European conquests of the Americas and the representations of Indigenous populations that were launched into circulation to justify removal and subjugation. Chicanas/os faced the institutionalization of anti-Mexican racism in virtually every area of public life: health care, education, law enforcement, and even religion. And because it is precisely the racial status of "mixed," with a negative emphasis on the Indian part of the mixture, that has historically motivated racism against Mexicans in the United States, attempts to elevate the Indian features of Chicano culture and physiognomy make real political sense.

Finally, the spiritual dimensions of indigenism, although the target of harsh critique, were nevertheless attempts to develop Chicana/o political discourse, expanding it to address the psychic and spiritual components of domination, subjugation, and resistance. Virtually all expressions of indigenism contain spiritual elements in the form of recovered mythic narratives and reclaimed deities. The story of Aztlán and the mytho-calendric cycle of the Fifth Sun afford to Chicanas/os opportunities to conceptualize and narrate their origins and subsequent evolution to a contemporary moment. Figures such as Quetzalcoatl and Coatlicue, and the material documentation of their significance in pre- and immediate post-Conquest Mesoamerica, make available spiritual and religious systems that came before and therefore disrupt the hegemony of European Judeo-Christianity.[16]

Armando Rendon's Narrative of Chicano Beginnings

The year 1971 brought the publication of two vastly distinct, yet oddly resonant texts: Benjamin Keen's *The Aztec Image in Western Thought* and Armando Rendon's *The Chicano Manifesto*. While Keen charted the centuries-old fascination of "Western man" with Aztec civilization, Rendon represented a people that he and others identified as the inheritors of that civilization. Keen's work, which he describes as a "sociology of knowledge" (xiii), is marked throughout by Aztec iconography and mythic references and in these features mirrors the primitivist modes of expression set out in the book. What Keen's text also does for us, then, is both to outline and to exemplify Western treatments of the image of the Aztec, helping to define traditions of expression that also shape the forms of Chicano indigenism.

The first chapter of *The Aztec Image in Western Thought*, "The People of the Sun," provides a brief chronicle of the history of the Aztecs prior to and following their arrival in the Valley of Mexico. Although the chapter title evokes the Aztec cosmogonic narrative of the Fifth Sun, overall it does little to address the spiritual systems of the Aztecs, focusing on their migration to and conquest of the Valley, social institutions—including the military, education, kinship, arts and crafts production—and, briefly, the Aztec system of tribute to the gods. But it has been the complex mythic systems of Mesoamerica that have captured the interests of "the West," an enthrallment evident in the texts of archaeology, fiction, and the literatures of tourism and travel. Keen continues this convention by placing his own references to the Fifth Sun and Quetzalcoatl in places of overpowering significance. The chapter moves toward closure with allusions to the forebodings and bad omens that, convention holds, warned the Aztecs of an impending doom. "The year 1519, Ce Acatl, One Reed, approached," writes Keen in an ominous tone, "[t]he god-king Quetzalcóatl might return to reclaim his lost realm" (29).[17] The author thus introduces to readers the myth of Quetzalcoatl, his exile from power and expected homecoming in the year One Reed during the time of the Fifth Sun, and ends his chapter-length treatment of Aztec history at the moment of conquest. The text eventually comes full circle from its cover visual of the mask of Quetzalcoatl to the final chapter titled "The Plumed Serpent," a survey of the influence of Aztec culture in twentieth-century art and a clear reference to D. H. Lawrence's novel of the same name.

Indigenous accounts of the conquest of Mexico, such as those collected in the mid- to late-sixteenth century by Bernardino de Sahagún and known now as *The Florentine Codex,* have claimed that Moctezuma mistook the Spaniards for gods and Cortés for Quetzalcoatl, specifically. This confusion is offered as explanation for the apparent ease with which the Spaniards established dominance in the region and has been incorporated into popular accounts of the Conquest. Keen perpetuates this narrative when he writes that the arrival of the Spaniards in 1519 followed frightening omens that appeared to the Aztecs and that the encounter also coincided with the predicted return of Quetzalcoatl.[18] He uses the markers of the Fifth Sun and the Plumed Serpent as bookends, an indication of their conceptual significance in the representation of pre-Conquest Mesoamerica. The prominent placement of mythic signifiers to launch and conclude this far-reaching study attests not only to the deep interest in Mesoamerican religious systems, but also to the extent to which ideas about Aztec myth structure thinking and writing about every other facet of Aztec civilization.

It is precisely these mythic systems that also organize Rendon's approach to the indigenization of Chicana/o history. Quetzalcoatl and the Fifth Sun are brought together explicitly by Rendon as he informs readers of the central role that the god plays in the Aztec creation myth. He writes that Quetzalcoatl gave birth to and is "creator of the epoch and its spirit" (8), which corresponds with the treatment of the Fifth Sun narrative in archaeological and historical scholarship.[19] Although anthropologists, cultural critics, and historians have claimed that the Aztec empire was made vulnerable by the misidentification of Hernán Cortés as the returned god, Chicanos who would insist on a filial relationship to that empire recuperate the image of Quetzalcoatl as a symbol of resistance rather than acquiescence.

The texts by Keen and Rendon are bound by their initial invocations of Aztec cosmology encapsulated in the idea of the Fifth Sun. This fact makes Rendon's own beginning to *The Chicano Manifesto,* "The People of Aztlan," notable as an act of appropriation that remains contained within the grand narrative of ancient Mesoamerica. This strange congruence between the mythic features of "Western" writing about the Aztecs, which includes Keen, and the manner in which other Chicanas/os, such as Valdez and Alurista, have chosen to chart the paths of cultural and political resistance is sometimes startling. Yet, this unwitting reinscription of dominant modes of representing Aztecs has nevertheless been an effective enterprise. Mexican-American appropriations and revisions of Mesoamerican myth launch stories of beginnings that precede historical data. Chicana/o origins therefore become mythologized and, to a certain degree, unquestionable.

The Chicano homeland is central to Rendon's nationalist agenda in *Chicano Manifesto*. A freelance journalist whose work Carlos Muñoz Jr. has called a "polemic," Rendon relies heavily on myth to assert non-immigrant status and to pursue an argument that characterizes Chicanos as inheritors of a unique spiritual disposition. An intriguing mixture of recovered Aztec mythology, sociology, legal analysis, racial theory, and cultural nationalism, *Chicano Manifesto* was reissued in 1997 by Ollin and Associates. It has received the critical attention of feminists, such as Angie Chabram-Dernersesian, who have challenged Rendon's negative portrayal of Chicanas as race betrayers and his glorification of "machismo" as a unifying principle of Chicanismo, features of *Chicano Manifesto* that I will address in the next chapter.[20] Rendon's elaboration of Aztlán borrows much from Alurista, but differs in its sustained attempt to transfer the structure of that myth onto contemporary Chicano culture. In doing this, he draws from a number of sources, which include Prescott's *History of the Conquest of Mexico* and Alvin Josephy Jr.'s *The Indian Heritage of America* (1968).

Although most of the book consists of sociological and historical arguments to advance the idea of a Chicano nation, the opening section, "People of Aztlán," mobilizes the myths of Aztlán and the Fifth Sun as a basis from which Rendon is able to elaborate the Chicano claim to territory. Rendon builds upon Aztlán as both material and metaphysical entity by using the myth of the Aztec homeland and the cosmogonic narrative of *el Quinto Sol*/the Fifth Sun to establish a foundation for Chicano resistance. The legends of Aztlán and the cosmic cycle of the Fifth Sun enable, for Rendon in particular, a historical narrative that antedates Spanish and Anglo colonization of the U.S. Southwest. He opens his treatise with a more formal, yet also more intimate, invocation of Aztec myth than we find in Keen: "We are the people of Aztlan, true descendents of the Fifth Sun, el Quinto Sol" (7). These first lines encapsulate the ideas of homeland, patrimony, and myth as Rendon asserts the legitimacy of Chicanos against false claims to the land base of the U.S. Southwest. Most importantly, this act of naming asserts a pre-contact presence that relies more heavily on the forces of myth than on those of history. This first chapter, in effect, is Rendon's statement of national consciousness, drawing its critical force and galvanizing power from narratives of the ancient past.

Rendon retells the story of the Aztec migration to the Valley of Mexico, where the travelers received the sign to found their future empire, Tenochtitlan. He notes that the Aztecs were latecomers to the region, having assimilated the culture and technology of various other groups that they encountered during the journey and after their arrival in the Valley. He nevertheless locates the origins of Mesoamerican greatness in Aztlán, the northern homeland that the Aztecs left behind and that has long been assumed to be mythic. Rendon writes: "[M]y people began walking toward the south in the hope of founding a new world. Among the earliest of my ancestors were the Nahúas, from whom sprang the most advanced and sophisticated peoples of the North American continent" (7). "Nahua" as a term designates Nahuatl-speaking people, of which the Aztecs were but one group. The terms "Nahua," "Mexica," and "Tenocha/Mexica" are but a few applied to the migrants who journeyed south and eventually became known as the Aztecs. The *Codex Boturini,* a text whose historical origins in either pre- or post-Conquest Mexico remain under debate, documents this pilgrimage and its beginnings in a place called Aztlán. And because Aztlán is an Aztec myth, when Rendon calls the ancient homeland the "the seed ground of the great civilizations of Anáhuac" (10), he appears to claim that the Aztecs are fundamentally responsible for the accomplishments of a civilization that was in reality a conglomerate of diverse cultural influences and achievements. When the conquered Aztecs are isolated as the "forebears" of Chicanas/os, however, U.S. Mexicans gain access not only to a cultural patrimony, but also to the Aztecs' status as a conquered people.

The association of the Fifth Sun with movement makes it for Rendon a period of dynamism, change, and progression: "The Fifth Sun is born out of man's sacrifice. At its center is the spirit; its mode is movement" (9). The myth of the Fifth Sun is a story of cosmogony, one that tells of the origins of the world. The Fifth Sun, the period that the Aztecs considered to be their own, was the last in a cycle of suns conceptualized through astronomy, calendrics, and mythology. The cosmogony narrates an understanding of time that is cyclical, in which chaos is transformed into order, which is itself ultimately ruined by the destructive power of natural catastrophe. The cycle thus begins anew five times, with the Fifth Sun as the epoch that has not yet ended. The four previous suns correspond to the earth and its elements, wind, fire, and water, while the Fifth Sun is known as the "movement" sun, for it was to be destroyed by earthquakes. The gods Quetzalcoatl and Tezcatlipoca together create the world of the Fifth Sun, constraining the waters and the sky so that humans would be able to walk the earth. Tezcatlipoca brings fire and Quetzalcoatl recreates the human race and, ultimately, all the gods sacrifice themselves so that the sun and moon will move through the sky and sustain life.[21]

The placement of Chicanos at the outer edge of the epoch positions them at the forefront of this movement; they are the agents of change and prototypes of new world citizens. Unlike Keen, Rendon relies upon the details of the story of the Fifth Sun/*el Quinto Sol*, as it, along with the tale of the migration from Aztlán, becomes a structuring device for his own first chapter. It is Chicanos' special relationship to the Fifth Sun that is the source of Rendon's claim to a "profound" spirituality (9). Taking his cue from Octavio Paz, who notes both the palimpsestic quality of Aztec religion and what he terms the "genuine" relationship of modern Mexico to the divine (Rendon 9), Rendon creates a teleology that begins at the Fifth Sun and ends with contemporary Chicano culture. For example, the elemental characterization of the first four suns in terms of earth, air, wind, and fire suggest to Rendon the broad encompassing range of Chicano spiritual life. He writes that "the Chicano's religious experience embodies all of nature" (9), an assertion that suggests a religiosity that is earth-centered, as well as metaphysical.

Another significant component of Rendon's interpretation of the creation myth is that it "destroyed and subsumed" the four suns that preceded it (8). The Fifth Sun's cannibalization of the previous four suns means that the last epoch contains within itself the preceding epochs.

> It is the unity, cohesion, synthesis of all that has come before, bound into the human soul. Thus, the Fifth Sun is the very foundation of life, of spirituality, not in the restricted sense of an organized religion but in the nature of a common bond among all soul creatures. We can speak, therefore, of a union with the cosmos, of a cosmic sense of spirit, of an alma Chicana. (Rendon 9)

According to a common indigenist refrain, Chicanos are "children of the Fifth Sun," a moniker that assigns to them a cultural patrimony that has long been thought of as destroyed or "lost." Rendon conceives of this Aztec cosmogony, essentially a mytho-history, as also imparting an

internal dimension to Chicanos. The connection to the Fifth Sun uni-
fies mestizos with each other, as well as with the "cosmos," as Rendon
calls it. As "*hijos del quinto sol*," Chicanos can organize around their shared
identity as descendants of the civilization that formulated this account
of the creation. The ancestral ties that Rendon charts also impart to Chicanos, he asserts, an inheritance of knowledge. He suggests that every
Chicano is born already hardwired to plug into not only the greater Chicano community, but into the cosmos itself. Chicanos become unique as
a people because of this privileged connection and the enhanced spiritual
experiences to which they have access. Furthermore, as inheritors of the
Fifth Sun, they also represent the continuation of a monumental civilization. The Aztec creation myth, apart from offering an account of the
origins of the world, thus lays a foundation for establishing a nationalist
spirituality.

There is a biological element to this argument as well. Rendon's initial
claim is one of descent that entitles Chicanos to a particular inheritance.
His argument is made by locating the Aztec homeland in a geographic
space that contemporary Chicanos occupy in large numbers, or where
they are, in fact, the majority: the U.S. Southwest. But a profound connection is established in the powerful, yet subtle manner in which Rendon asserts that although history has been erased in the landscape and repressed in the historiographical record, it asserts itself in physiognomy.

> Where they came from originally is hidden in the sands and riverbeds
> and only hinted at by the cast of eye and skin which we, their sons, now
> bear. (7)

Geography and biology collapse in the concept "indigenous," which signifies origins in terms of place, as well as in terms of race. Rendon mobilizes a link to Aztec civilization based on a presumed parallel between ancient and contemporary "homelands," as well as upon facial features and
phenotypes that are coded as Indian. Chicano faces are thus able to tell a
story not only of ancestry, but also of a relationship to territory.

Luis Valdez, Snakes, and Sacrifice

Following the Delano grape strike, Luis Valdez wrote in *Bronze* that
"[m]ost of us know we are not European simply by looking in a mirror—
the shape of the eyes, the curve of the nose, the color of skin, the texture
of hair, these things belong to another time, another people" (2). As he

reads history in the faces of Chicanos, Valdez advances another common, although often unrecognized, perception of indigeneity in this brief statement: it does not belong to the present. The time of the indigenous is past, and so far in the past that one might think of it as a time before history, as *pre*-historic, as mythic.

The spiritual dimensions of nationalist politics that interested Rendon were also pursued vigorously in the work of Valdez and El Teatro Campesino. Valdez came to prominence as a playwright and director with El Teatro Campesino in the late 1960s. Credited by many with founding the troupe and as sole author of many of its productions, he has been positioned as the leading creative influence not only within El Teatro, but also in the context of Chicano theater more generally.[22] This centrality, however, has been ably challenged by Yolanda Broyles-González in her book-length study of El Teatro. She presents a critical alternative that calls attention to a history of collective production, rejecting "the great-man ideological construction of history" (4) that, she argues, has misrepresented Valdez's role and virtually erased the significant contributions of women and other members of the troupe.

Questions of authorship aside, Valdez has had a successful and productive career in theater, transferring that success to mainstream venues, for example, with his big-screen production *La Bamba* (1987). The feature film version of *Zoot Suit*, from a play written by Valdez and originally staged in 1979 by El Teatro Campesino, was released in 1982 before *La Bamba*. Although it received negative reviews when staged on Broadway in New York, *Zoot Suit* was hugely popular in Los Angeles. But despite the critical attention the film version continues to draw, it did not have even the limited commercial success of the later film.[23] *Zoot Suit* attempts to bring together two important sites of representation in Chicana/o critical discourse: the urban barrio and the mythic past. The play and the film can be seen as expressions of El Teatro Campesino's commitment to the exploration of Indigenous forms and icons of spirituality in the representation of Chicana/o realities.

The troupe developed their indigenist theory and practice, known as "Theater of the Sphere," with an emphasis on Mayan systems of thought and as a challenge to the conventions of theater and the narrowly conceived language of Chicano nationalism.[24] Chicanos had access to a pre-Christian tradition that provided them, in Valdez's view, with the necessary tools for community empowerment. That pre-Christian tradition is Indigenous and mythic and available to supplant Judeo-Christian and Eurocentric cultural forms. These concerns began to be addressed much earlier than the production of *Zoot Suit*. Here, I take up two early indigenist Valdez texts: the play *The Dark Root of a Scream* and *Pensamiento Serpentino (Serpentine Thought): A Chicano Approach to the Theater of Reality*.[25] The play, according to Jorge Huerta, was originally produced in 1967 by El Teatro Campesino in Fresno, California, and directed by Valdez (38). It was later collected in the anthology *From the Barrio: A Chicano Anthology*, edited by Luis Omar Salinas and Lillian Faderman. The epic poem, *Pensamiento Serpentino* was first published by El Teatro Campesino's publishing arm, Cucaracha Publications, in 1973, and later included in Valdez's *Early Works* released by Arte Público in 1990. Despite its appearance at a later date than the play, *Pensamiento Serpentino* lays out the ideological lessons that *Dark Root* attempts to teach: the revolution depends upon a return to the source and the recapturing of Indigenous myth both to understand and to transform Chicano conditions.

Pensamiento Serpentino brings together Christian and Mesoamerican religious symbolism in a challenge to the strict materialism of Chicana/o revolutionary politics. Broyles-González views the text as the philosophical basis of El Teatro's Theater of the Sphere, an integration of performance, theories of performance, spirituality, and political action developed in the 1970s. Attempting to rescue Theater of the Sphere from charges of escapism or an excessive religiosity that detracts attention from social issues of the day, she argues that "the Theater of the Sphere must be conceptualized in part as an oppositional or alternative social *practice* and long-term educational process intertwined with a larger system of social practices and power relations" (82).[26] *Pensamiento Serpentino* gives narrative form to Theater of the Sphere as a "model of human liberation" (123) and an example of "countercultural education" (124). Valdez expounds upon the teachings of Mayan, and, to a lesser extent, Aztec philosophy and mythology, suggesting an alternative conception of liberation struggles that is based upon knowledge of ancient cultural patrimonies and the assimilation of the spiritual and philosophical lessons of those intellectual traditions, accessed in large part through Mayan scholar Domingo Martínez Paredez.[27] Broyles-González credits the written and oral teachings of Martínez, Ignacio Magaloni Duarte, and Virgilio Valadares Aldaco—which, she points out, "take issue with and refute many of the findings of the Mesoamerican studies establishment"—as having great influence on the development of the Theater of the Sphere. Additionally, the writings of Nezahualcoyotl, the monotheistic "poet-king," codices, and, especially, the Mayan *Popul Vuh* were foundational.[28]

This reclamation of "indigenous knowledge," to use Broyles-González's term, services Valdez's critiques of racism and imperialism, particularly the condemnation of the Vietnam War. In noting that El Teatro's sources challenge the theories and conclusions of academic Mesoamerican studies, Broyles-González takes care to position El Teatro's development of Indigenous themes as oppositional within the context of mainstream discourses on pre-Columbian art, civilization, religion, and society. In *Pensamiento Serpentino,* as in *The Dark Root of a Scream,* Judeo-Christian mythological traditions are supplanted by Indigenous signifiers, although Valdez's critique of Catholicism is here less strident. His treatise calls for a return to Indigenous spirituality to revitalize ancient cultural practices that could enable Chicanas/os to resist more successfully the debilitating effects of Anglo-American hegemony. In connecting Chicanas/os to the Maya, Valdez helps to develop in readers the nationalist consciousness fundamental to male movement poetics. Yet, this national membership exists on at least two levels as he calls upon Chicanos to honor their filial relationship to Mexico and to claim the Maya as source community:

> pero
> MEEX-KIN-CO
> (Co means serpiente also)
> eventually gives us
> MEXICO
> which means
> serpiente emplumada
> and according to the
> mathematical interpretation
> of the Mayas
> refers to the
> espiritual-material duality/of all things (*Pensamiento* 11)

Nationalist allegiance to a present-day nation state is redirected toward the Indigenous as Valdez reminds the reader of pre-Conquest Mesoamerican philosophical traditions that encapsulated both the physical and the metaphysical. That the symbolism of the feathered serpent is able to be explained by the Maya in the language of science exemplifies the union between spirituality and materiality that is often hailed as the mark of intellectual sophistication in non-Western traditions. It stands as a counterpoint to the binary splits of post-Cartesian thought that provide the scaffolding upon which "the West" judges and assigns cultural and other forms of value. Valdez advocates an education in ancient Mayan teaching as a means for Chicanos to liberate themselves from the oppressive forces of foreign ideologies that constrain thinking and retard action. Chicanos can only truly be motivated, he argues, through the teachings of their own ancestors. "El Chicano" must be "LIBERATED FIRST BY/HIS PROPIO PUEBLO" (*Pensamiento* 3).

Quetzalcoatl appears in this text as an important signifier of ancestral tradition, as is immediately evident in Valdez's title, *Pensamiento Serpentino: A Chicano Approach to the Theater of Reality.* Drawing from both Aztec and Maya traditions, Valdez uses the snake's cyclical shedding of skin as a dominant motif to represent the rebirth and renewal of spiritual and material forces. The undulating movement of the snake connotes the eternal presence and circulation of energy throughout the physical world, including humanity. Because of its association with energy, Quetzalcoatl, Broyles-González writes, "stands as a symbol of the creation, of the life process" (91), which is consistent with translations of the *Popul Vuh* that place Quetzalcoatl at the creation of the world. According to archaeological interpretations, the history of the Quetzalcoatl image in Mesoamerican systems of thought is complex, revealing both unity and great differences as it appears in the material culture of different groups.[29] The emphasis on the Maya makes the appropriation of Quetzalcoatl less complicated for Valdez, and when he does refer to Nahua uses, such references are incorporated seamlessly — for example, when he brings in the concepts of the Fifth Sun/Nahui Ollin and the Aztec god who opposes Quetzalcoatl, Tezcatlipoca.

The feature of Chicano movement poetics that stands out most strongly in *Pensamiento Serpentino* is the idea of revolutionary action grounded in a spirituality based upon pre-Conquest teachings. Appealing to the Christian sentiments of his audience, Valdez constantly draws comparisons between the wisdom of Mayan texts and Christian principles such as "love thy neighbor" (4), echoing Octavio Paz's earlier work in *Labyrinth of Solitude* and presaging Armando Rendon's later *Chicano Manifesto* when he writes that "above all/to be CHICANO is to LOVE GOD" (6). The innate religiosity of Chicanos positions them to re-identify with the "Cosmic Center" of Mayan spirituality (7), providing revolutionary action a more substantial basis in the synchronization of human action with astronomy, calendrics, and the philosophical systems in which they are embedded. In this "Cosmic Center," knowledge of the material and metaphysical and devotion to a divine being simultaneously inform all thought and action and produce, in Valdez's estimation, a more complete and sustainable path to community liberation. Telling Chicanos that "[w]e must all must become NEO-MAYAS" (*Pensamiento* 3), Valdez suggests that underlying Christian iconography and maxims of behavior are Indigenous principles that are more appropriate to a Chicano context and become present when one peels back the layers of Conquest ideology.

> JesuChristo is Quetzalcóatl
> The colonization is over.
> La Virgen de Guadalupe is Tonantzin
> The suffering is over.
> The Universe is Aztlan
> The revolution is now. (7)

Valdez presents the return to the pre-Christian and pre-Columbian as a revolutionary act that has the potential to end the misery of the present. Effective resistance would throw off the ideological yokes of European Catholicism and reclaim the Indigenous gods and goddesses displaced by Judeo-Christian monotheism.

Like others, Valdez tried to provide for his Chicana/o audiences the tools with which they could transform thinking about themselves and the place of Mexicans in the Americas and beyond. As much as his text is about matters of spirituality, it is also an indictment of the politics and policies of U.S. war making that waged violence on communities both at home and abroad. *The Dark Root of a Scream* and *Pensamiento Serpentino* each articulate condemnations of the Vietnam War as they also offer invitations to reconceptualize Chicana/o religious traditions and spiritual expressions.

The drama, *The Dark Root of a Scream,* is also an exploration of the Quetzalcoatl theme, and Valdez here puts a decidedly Aztec spin on the narrative. Quetzalcoatl is not associated with ritual human sacrifice, as is the war-mongering Huitzilopochtli, considered the dominant deity in the militaristic Aztec society and the god responsible for leading them into the Valley of Mexico. Although Rendon seems to acknowledge a history of human sacrifice when he writes that the "Fifth Sun is born out of man's sacrifice" (9), he places emphasis on spirituality as the particular legacy of the Aztec Fifth Sun. But in *The Dark Root of a Scream,* Valdez brings the spiritual transformation and human sacrifice together in an early attempt to introduce *mito* (myth) to Chicana/o audiences.[30]

The action takes place in a living room, on a street corner, and at the top of a pyramid and centers around a wake for a soldier killed in combat in Vietnam, Quetzalcóatl Gonzáles, also called Indio.[31] The characters are the dead soldier's mother, Madre; his girlfriend, Dahlia, who is also

Conejo's sister; three *vatos* from the barrio, Conejo, Lizard, and Gato; and the parish priest. The play sets up a battle between ideologies, European Catholicism versus Mesoamerican spirituality, as the Anglo priest works to convince Indio's girlfriend and his mother of the futility of Indio's indigenist teachings, handed down to him in part by his indigenist father, Mixcóatl, who gave Indio his name. Indio's father, Mixcóatl/Cloud-serpent, had been a teacher in Mexico, but "over here he was a wetback, a farm laborer just like everybody else" (85–86), Lizard contends at one point.

Indigenist knowledge is carried on by a few of the characters, who deploy it against the priest. Dahlia, Conejo, and Lizard understand the value of connecting barrio communities to a historical legacy that would instill pride and delegitimate the treatment received in the United States. In the context of Mixcóatl's experience of immigration to the United States, the rhetorical force of Lizard's claim that "we got Aztec blood" (85–86) derives from a recognition of the diminished status awaiting many Mexican immigrants when they arrive and are stripped of academic and professional credentials. Lizard's statement, made during a conversation with the priest, makes clear the significance of indigenism as a strategy intended to challenge the degradation of Mexicans in the United States.

Indio tried both to teach others in the barrio about their rich history in the Americas and to transform an alienated spiritual existence that relied on the teachings of Western Catholicism doled out by white Spanish-speaking priests. That Indio was killed in Vietnam speaks metaphorically, on the one hand, to the draining of barrio human resources in the interests of protecting a capitalist military-industrial complex and, on the other, to the destruction of Indigenous cultural systems by the colonizing forces of the West. Indio's mother has now sacrificed three sons to the U.S. military and its foreign wars: Cuahtemoc, killed in France; Nezahualcoyotl, killed in Korea; and, Quetzalcóatl, killed in Vietnam.[32]

The priest uses his institutional power in an attempt to coerce both Dahlia and Madre into rejecting the alternative knowledge represented by Indio. The religious authority figure tells Dahlia that Indio was "politically naïve" and that it was community members who refused to loan the church hall for Indio's meetings (89). To Indio's mother, he denies what her own eyes tell her, that her son's coffin is leaking blood, a sign to her of his life. Instead, he tries to appease her with platitudes that diminish the significance of her observations. He argues vehemently against Indio's attempts both to politicize and to spiritualize the barrio community through the rhetorics of Indigenous heritage and class politics.

Yet, the priest's disadvantage is revealed when he cannot comprehend the names of Madre's three sons, Cuahtemoc and Nezahualcoyotl and Quetzalcóatl:

PRIEST: My Spanish isn't bad but that—
DAHLIA: It isn't Spanish, father. Those are the Indian names of her three
    sons. (85)

The priest's use of Spanish is a strategy for developing more intimate relationships with his parishioners, but it is also an exertion of control. When he initially speaks to Dahlia in Spanish and she responds blankly, he asks if he should instead use English. Dahlia continues to speak to the priest in English throughout the play, despite his consistent use of Spanish when addressing her. Her resistance to conversing with the priest in the language of the parishioners is a deliberate rejection of the Church's intrusion into a private community space. Although Madre is represented as a dominant Spanish speaker, Dahlia and those of her generation have clear facility with English. For them, Spanish is used among community members, and the priest is not one. His use of Spanish indicates the arrogance that clouds his ability to understand the fundamental issues facing those in the barrio and that Indio wanted to change. Dahlia's correction of the priest asserts an older, more powerful knowledge that displaces the European linguistic traditions of Spanish. Furthermore, the priest's misinterpretation also reveals how fully the Church has erased its own history of collusion with the practices of conquest and deracination.

When the priest labels Indio a racist, Dahlia confronts him with the argument that Indio "taught Chicanos to be proud of what they have—their culture, their heritage . . ." (86). The priest counters with an assertion embedded within a question: "What heritage is that—human sacrifice?" (86). For the priest, this is the most enduring image of Aztec culture, and not worthy of glorifying. But the play suggests a critique of both the European and Indigenous priestly classes, as when Indio's acolyte Conejo advises the other characters that it was the Aztec priests who "got rid of" Quetzalcoatl as "they wanted war and human sacrifice" (88), which Quetzalcoatl rejected. In the indigenist celebration of Aztec society, sacrifice is not often a prominent topic; Valdez presents a compelling exception.[33]

At a certain point in the play, the conversations between the *vatos* and between the priest and the women begin to merge into one conversation as other binaries also begin to unify. The text works hard to establish parallels between the Aztec priests, who diminished the importance of Quetzalcoatl in favor of Huitzilopochtli, and the Catholic priest, who preaches rejection of Indio's work: "Why were you against Indio, father?" asks Dahlia (88). Furthermore, the parallel between Quetzalcoatl the god and Quetzalcóatl the man becomes more entrenched as we learn that Indio launched a drunken binge after receiving his draft notice, embarrassing himself at community events and alienating himself from his closest relationships.[34] He stays drunk for two weeks, breaks up with his girlfriend, and leaves the community in disgrace. Indio's story resonates with the mythic example of the god-king Quetzalcoatl, who falls prey to the altering effects of pulque and engages in forbidden sexual relations with a woman sometimes said to be his sister. The series of events, all part of a ruse orchestrated by his brother Tezcatlipoca, lead to Quetzalcoatl's self-imposed exile. When he leaves his community, he vows to come back one day.

An apotheosis of sorts takes place as the *vatos* proceed to alter the ritual of the wake, overwriting the Judeo-Christian dictate of servitude with a Mesoamerican homage to Quetzalcoatl. The liturgical call and response, which relies upon community knowledge of and compliance with the codes of the ritual, undergoes a subtle, yet radical, transformation. Where the *vatos* are expected to intone "your humble servant," following the priest's lead, they at first "clumsily," and then later, with more confidence, begin to shout "your humble serpent" (94). The priest, incensed by this incident of sacrilege, becomes doubly enraged by the sight of Gato's physical harassment of Dahlia during the ceremony. He threatens to call the police and rushes from the room, with Lizard chasing after him.

After having "defrocked" the priest, Lizard later returns to Madre's living room wearing the cassock. The blood begins to drip from Indio's coffin more intensely, apparently in response to Gato's ridiculing of the dead hero and his commitment to community empowerment: "Heh, Indio, it's me man—Gato! I'm calling you out, ese! I say you're a liar! The Raza's full of shit!" (96). As Madre becomes increasingly traumatized by the events—the humiliation of her son, the blood pouring from the box that holds his body—the group decides to open the coffin. Inside, they find "a brilliant headdress of green feathers and a cloak of Aztec design" (97). Lizard takes off the robes of the Catholic priest, puts on the Aztec headdress and cloak, and is transformed, at least visually, into the Aztec priest. Drums begin to sound, suggesting the beating of Indio's heart, which Lizard then pulls out of the coffin and holds before him in the final scene, screaming, "Indio's heart!" (98).

The final image, in which Lizard as priest appears to offer up Indio's heart as sacrificial object, invites a reading that the priests, Catholic and

Aztec, have, once again, destroyed the gods. It is important to remember, however, that Lizard does not know what is in the coffin. It is interesting that Valdez chose to give the character of Lizard the role of priest at the conclusion of the play, when it is Conejo who is Indio's strongest male advocate throughout. When Lizard discovers Indio's heart, he is as surprised and shocked as the others, as evidenced by his scream that ends the play. Depending upon the manner in which this scene is performed, Lizard's "offering" of Indio's heart could well be read as one made to the community, rather than to the gods. And rather than an "offering," per se, perhaps we should view Lizard's handling of the heart as an attempt to "show" the others, not only the damage done to Indio by the U.S. military, but also the survival of the knowledge that Indio tried to disseminate, the return of the god Quetzalcoatl, so to speak. Thus, this final scene can also suggest that the heart of the god is recovered and given to the community to strengthen and revive it. The man Indio is still dead, but the priesthood has been recuperated and revived by Chicanos. Lizard has defeated the Catholic priest, who is the agent of oppression and exploitation, and stands before his community. As he holds up the heart, he embodies the reclaimed Aztec priesthood. This final "offering" becomes an act of resistance to the ideology represented by the Church, which paved the way for conquest throughout the Americas.

Lizard's marginal status in relation to the indigenist leadership in his community may, however, diminish the revolutionary value of the final scene. The oppositional force of the Aztec priestly figure and his displacement of the Catholic priest depends upon a certain awareness that Lizard does not definitively possess, although as a "lizard," he is most closely related to the serpent-god. If we choose not to grant to Lizard's character the degree of consciousness and motivation necessary to transform the final act from being solely confused, to being confused and also resistant, the offering loses its ideological value. Lizard appears inauthentic and uncertain, swept up by the events of the moment, incapable as a character of resolving the divisions that have permeated the play. We are left, in this reading, with little hope that this revival will bring community empowerment.[35]

The heart has obvious and significant Catholic iconographic connotations. Valdez merges Catholic and Aztec religious imagery with a bleeding heart that evokes an object of devotion for many Catholics, the sacred heart, which represents Jesus Christ, his love for humanity, his sacrifice, his wounds, and his grief at humanity's failure to abide by his teachings. Furthermore, the blood dripping from Indio's flag-draped casket mimics reports of weeping and bleeding stone sculptures or pictorial images of the Virgin and Jesus Christ. In this case, the miracle of the blood relates directly to the resurgence of Indigenous spirituality. When, in the final scene, Indio's still-beating heart is pulled out of the casket by Lizard, who is dressed in the supposed garb of an Aztec priest, the implication is that Quetzalcoatl lives. Quetzalcoatl, however, has moved beyond its individual association with the man called Indio and instead may be read as a signifier for pre-Columbian mythology and spirituality more generally, which Valdez saw as a means to revive Chicana/o existence and to contend with the oppressive forces of U.S. racist capitalism. Yet, the play also uses the structures and icons of Catholicism as tools of conversion—in reverse.

In the final analysis, Indigenous spirituality has won out over European Catholicism as the final image of the priest, relayed by Lizard, is of the man running though the streets in his shorts seeking the police and fleeing the *vatos* who have taken over the ritual space. The reclamation of sacred space and rejection of European institutional power, however, is constrained by the homophobia and sexism that we must assume remain intact, even if the transformative potential of the final scene becomes a reality.

The *vatos* serve as the foil to their dead *carnal* and their sexist, homophobic bickering and constant diminishment of each other suggest some of the barrio realities that Indio tried to rectify through his teachings. The combative, if also familiar and petty, interactions among them highlight a misdirection of critical energy that would be better spent on improving the material conditions of barrio life. The initial teasing of Conejo suggests a sexual relationship between him and Indio that becomes a target of ridicule by the other two *vatos*. The exchanges between Gato and Lizard eventually deteriorate to the point where they threaten each other with knives. Gato pins Lizard, who concedes defeat before the three exit to attend the mass being held in Indio's honor. The relationship among Gato, Lizard, and Conejo is also a metonym for the destructive, internal warring actions of the gods that destroyed each sun cycle before the fifth.

Furthermore, Gato's harassment of Dahlia is left untroubled by the narrative. His desire for her is expressed in a crude and offensive manner that demeans Dahlia and rejects the codes of respect that, ideally, would characterize *familia* and *carnalismo*. Dahlia manages to fight off Gato, but the event quickly retreats from the narrative to allow for the focus on Quetzalcoatl, the man and the myth, and the move toward the pivotal final moment. The narrative does not even seem to judge Gato's behavior too negatively as Dahlia is left to fend for herself, although she finally asks for her brother Conejo's help, who provides an ineffectual "Cut it out,

Gato" (95). That a *carnala* would be assaulted in the midst of her community by one of that community is perhaps a less invigorating image to ponder than that of the male priest holding the beating heart of the man-god while poised on the cusp of community revitalization.

Finally, the title itself is another site of mitigated success. *The Dark Root of a Scream* operates as a reference to Lizard's final scream, and the title implies that the play offers a revelation about the sources, or origins, of that scream. If the scream is symbolic of a community recognition of, and perhaps even recoiling from, a lost cultural heritage then the title also plays into the binary drawn between the goodness and "light" of Christianity and the savagery and "darkness" of "primitive" religion. We can only assume that Valdez intends a transvaluation of that binary, in which the "dark root" of the scream is hidden knowledge that becomes now worthy of recuperation.

Valdez makes significant changes to typical understandings of the myth of Quetzalcoatl, one of the most popular Mesoamerican mythic references within, as well as outside of, Chicano indigenist discourse. He associates the god with the practice of human sacrifice and also makes the god a sacrificial victim. The myth of the Fifth Sun, according to Enrique Florescano's interpretation, does portray a final and ultimate sacrifice by the gods for the survival of humans.[36] In order to initiate and maintain the movement of the sun, the gods sacrifice their own blood so that the humans may live. Indio's death may be seen as a sacrifice, in which he goes to Vietnam so that another Chicano will not. But it also may be interpreted mythically in the context of the cosmogonic narrative of the Fifth Sun, which would suggest that Indio dies so that the Chicano community might renew itself and thrive. Quetzalcóatl, in this sense, again represents the cultural patrimony that Chicanas/os can access through pre-Columbian myth, an action that they are able to legitimate through their Indigenous ancestry. Like Rendon's use of the Fifth Sun narrative, Valdez's manipulation of Quetzalcoatl motivates a nationalist consciousness that is cemented through narrative access to the mythic resources of an ancient past.

Alurista and the Critique of Imperialism

Although Valdez wrote *Dark Root* in 1967, it is Alurista's later venture into Aztec myth that has captured the most attention, primarily because of the significance of "El Plan de Aztlán." Alurista's knowledge of Mesoamerican religion, culture, and myth came from a variety of sources, including anthropology, art history, and poetic meditations. According to a reading list attached to the typewritten manuscript of "Aztlan: Reality or Myth" (1971), Alurista had read and recommended several works by historian Miguel León-Portilla and archaeologist Laurette Séjourné, among others.[37] The poet made it a project to incorporate Nahuatl concepts, symbols, and language into his poetic and theoretical writings, and his 1972 poetry collection, *Nationchild Plumaroja* is an instructive example of how he tailored "recovered" knowledge into a vehicle for anti-imperialist critique. The collection is divided into sections that are marked as indigenist less by content than by the visual framing of that content. The five sections are "Nopal" (Cactus); "Xochitl" (Flower); "Serpiente" (Serpent); "Conejo" (Rabbit); and "Venado" (Stag). These section names correspond, with one exception, to day signs in the Aztec calendrical system. Xochitl, conejo, serpiente, and venado are taken directly from this system and then translated into Spanish. The translation of "coatl" into "serpiente," "tochtli" into "conejo," and "mazatl" into "venado" are purposeful iterations of cultural *mestizaje* as Nahua calendrics and Spanish lexicon are combined and transformed to produce a numeric register. The apparent deviation of the first section "Nopal"—it is not an Aztec day sign—is resolved by the Aztec peregrination narrative. The *Codex Mendoza* represents the culmination of the Aztec journey on its frontispiece: an eagle clutching a serpent in its mouth lands on a cactus (*un nopal*). This is also the image emblazoned on the modern Mexican flag and in both cases reproduces the divine sign indicating to the Aztecs the site of their future empire, Tenochtitlan. The "Nopal" section is therefore a reclamation of the territory of Aztlán in all its forms: mythic, national, historic, and geographic.

At the time of these movement writings, Alurista was pursuing a curiosity about religion and spirituality in tandem with his readings on Mesoamerica and liberation struggles. The reading list mentioned earlier contains works on subjects ranging from Zen Buddhism to psychoanalysis and religion. But it is significant that the poetry itself does not attempt to superimpose Aztec religious or mythic systems onto Chicano realities. Alurista's appropriation and alteration of the Nahuatl glyphs—the day signs are used to represent numbers, for instance—seems to refrain from the spiritual emphases that are central in Rendon's and Valdez's forms of indigenism. In the case of *Nationchild Plumaroja,* Alurista's appropriation of this Indigenous writing system might even seem to work more effectively toward an assertion of Native status in the United States specifically and in the Americas more generally, since the work is less encumbered by the mythological.

Alurista's poetics is for the most part focused on the material aspects of contemporary Chicano life and conditioned by its acknowledgment of Chicano participation in and benefit from a social system that rewards individual effort and stigmatizes collective action. Reclaiming indigenous values becomes, for Alurista, a potent form of resistance to privatization, consumerism, and Anglo-American hegemony. In unpublished essay material, such as *Chicano Studies: A Future?*, Alurista stresses the importance of Indigenous forms of knowledge to the success of Chicano Studies and to the overall empowerment of Chicano people. The Quetzalcoatl-Tezcatlipoca binary is a dominant structuring device in his writing, in which Quetzalcoatl represents "the Source of Life, Creator, Preserver, Joy, Love, Peace, Power, Fertility and Wisdom" and Tezcatlipoca is "the Source of Death, Idleness, Spoiler, Emptiness, Hatred, Weakness, Barrenness, Violence and Ignorance" ("Chicano Studies" 4). This opposition seems to stand outside dominant Judeo-Christian conventions for conceptualizing universal forces of good and evil and provides an alternative signifying model for a discourse of opposition. The forces of Tezcatlipoca "rule the United States of Northamerikkka" (Chicano Studies 7), and it is up to Chicanos "to strengthen the forces of Quetzalcóatl" and rectify the widespread economic, moral, and spiritual degradation of the "Amerikkkan way of life."

"The way of Tezcatlipoca," Alurista writes in "Aztlán: Reality or Myth," "is driven by fear, dollars and war" (2). Edmond S. Bordeaux's *The Soul of Ancient Mexico* may have provided some guidance for Alurista in these characterizations of Quetzalcoatl and Tezcatlipoca. The poet's familiarity with Bordeaux's text is suggested by its inclusion on the reading list mentioned earlier, part of Alurista's papers at the Benson Latin American Collection, University of Texas at Austin. The inside cover to *The Soul of Ancient Mexico* lists more than forty publications by Bordeaux, on subjects ranging from Beethoven to the Dead Sea Scrolls to yoga. He also was responsible for a series of "Long Playing Phonograph Records of Ancient Cultures" from across the globe. In *The Soul of Ancient Mexico,* which he dedicates to "the spirit of King Nezahualcoyotl, Poet, Philosopher & Law-Giver, The King Solomon of Pre-Columbian America," Bordeaux defines his work as "archeosophy . . . the science of applying philosophical methods to archeology" (9). He finds value in ancient Mesoamerica as a "foundation of human civilization" that can "help to show [man] a way out of his present chaos" (9). His discussion of the Toltecs is punctuated by the binary of Quetzalcoatl and Tezcatlipoca, the first "considered to be the source of all good, of all things belonging to life," and the second, representing "hatred, destruction and war" (10). Alurista's formulation of the Quetzalcoatl/Tezcatlipoca binary echoes Bordeaux's work, even as Alurista manipulates the idea to serve the specific context of Chicana/o empowerment.

Alurista's constant references to Nahuatl mythic deities, however, serves to propel a critique of U.S. society that is marked boldly by attempts to demystify consumerism and the quest for instant gratification in the quick-fixes of television, fast food, and the beauty industry. He insists upon the global effects of the U.S. military-industrial complex, which finds its human resources in poor communities of color and the markets for its war machinery in Third World counter-insurgency campaigns. The significance of Third World liberation movements is underscored time and again in Alurista's essay on Aztlán, and, like many Chicana/o intellectuals, he takes inspiration from and sees parallels with international liberation struggles: "Quetzalcóatl emerges in China, Vietnam, Cambodia, Cuba, Chile and Aztlán; all these members of earth community of National Liberation Struggles, burst with Life (Creativity) and Brightness (wisdom) which heralds an end to the Northamerikan Way of Death, Neocolonialism" ("Aztlán: Reality" 2). We know that Alurista consulted Frantz Fanon's *The Wretched of the Earth* and Lee Lockwood's *Castro's Cuba, Cuba's Fidel*, as well as texts by Malcolm X (*Malcolm X Speaks*) and Stokely Carmichael and Charles Hamilton (*Black Power*) ("Aztlán: Reality" n.p.). In much of his work—for example, the play, *Dawn*—we are able to recognize the connections implied between the forces of multinationalism and neo-imperialism.

In *Dawn*, published in the 1974 "Chicano Drama" issue of *El Grito,* Alurista stages a tribunal in which corporate greed and military industrialism are personified and tried for their sins against the people. The play employs Aztec deities as the major characters, pitting two families against each other. Representing fertility, indigeneity, and community perseverance are Quetzalcóatl and Cihuacóatl, or Snake-Woman. Both descend from the deities Mixcóatl and Chimalma, and together created humanity, according to the interpretation of Nahuatl myth that Alurista follows in the play.[38] On trial are Pepsicóatl and Cocacóatl, "lord of imperial racism, lady of blood monies . . . master of destruction, mistress of detergent" (*Dawn* 65), who are born of Coatlicue and schooled by Huitzilopochtli, god of war, and Tezcatlipoca, the smoking mirror, also Quetzalcoatl's brother and nemesis. Alurista's playful naming of the two defendants does not diminish his incisive critique. They are the post-Aztec future generation of gods, the worship of which is driven not by the human desire to influence the forces of nature and maintain social power over rival communities, but by the desire to consume and to dominate economically through the creation of the commodity fetish. Pepsicóatl and Cocacóatl appear as the latest manifestations of the quest for power and control embarked upon by the Aztecs and embodied in the figures of Huitzilopochitli and Tezcatlipoca. Pepsicóatl and Cocacóatl are, obviously, the creations of Alurista, and designed both to ridicule the hedonism of consumer culture as well as to indigenize the contemporary struggles of Chicana/o activists.

Alurista imports terms from Aztec belief structures to advance his analysis of contemporary global politics and Chicano nationalism. His recovery of mythic symbols repeats the privileging of Quetzalcoatl as the central entity, much as Rendon and Valdez do. Perhaps more significant, however, is Alurista's representation of Coatlicue as the mother of imperialism and, by extension, evil itself. It is a less creative deployment of this particular goddess figure, certainly, than we see in the later work of Gloria Anzaldúa. Additionally, Alurista's representation reproduces "Western" conceptions of a complicated deity whose association with destructive processes overpowers her concomitant creative roles as earth goddess and fertility figure. Granted, Alurista does position her as mother in his play, but a mother who can give life only to aberrations. In the end, it is the transformed Cocacóatl who gives birth to twins of the new dawn. This new age of the divine offers the potential for a changed civilization rejecting militarism, individualism, and capitalism in favor of reciprocity and collectivity. But Cocacóatl must pay with her life and dies amidst the celebratory dancing.

Elsewhere, Alurista's indigenism takes a different path. The inaugural announcement of Chicano nationalism, "El Plan de Aztlán," uses the mytho-historical homeland of Aztlán as the conceptual center of its political platform. In subsequent years, Alurista revised his original preamble to that text, a version of which introduces *Nationchild Plumaroja*. The epigraph, titled "the red spirit of Aztlán: a plan of National Liberation," is now easily recognized as an altered form of the preamble to "El Plan." There are significant differences from the version that has been collected and published as "El Plan de Aztlán" in, for example, *Documents of the Chicano Struggle* (1971) and *Aztlán: Essays on the Chicano Homeland* (1989).[39] These changes, on the whole, signal Alurista's more inclusive political consciousness with regard to gender and ethnic affiliation. The original reads as follows:

> In the spirit of a new people that is conscious not only of its proud historical heritage but also of the brutal "gringo" invasion of our territories, we, the Chicano inhabitants and civilizers of the northern land of Aztlan

from whence came our forefathers, reclaiming the land of their birth and consecrating the determination of our people of the sun, declare that the call of our blood is our power, our responsibility, and our inevitable destiny.

We are free and sovereign to determine those tasks which are justly called for by our house, our land, the sweat of our brows, and by our hearts. Aztlan belongs to those who plant the seeds, water the fields, and gather the crops and not to the foreign Europeans. We do not recognize capricious frontiers on the bronze continent.

Brotherhood unites us, and love for our brothers makes us a people whose time has come and who struggles against the foreigner "gabacho" who exploits our riches and destroys our culture. With our heart in our hands and our hands in the soil, we declare the independence of our mestizo nation. We are a bronze people with a bronze culture. Before the world, before all of North America, before all our brothers in the bronze continent, we are a nation, we are a union of free pueblos, we are *Aztlán*. ("El Plan" 1)

The decidedly male-centered references to "brotherhood" and "brothers" are expanded in the later version to include "sisterhood" and "sisters," surely a response to the feminist critiques of movement patriarchy that were circulating by the time of *Nationchild's* publication. And two major changes that appear in the 1972 version of the preamble imply a strategic move from a Mesoamerican-centered indigenist politics, to a U.S.-based indigenist politics that calls out to the American Indian Movement (AIM).

THE RED SPIRIT OF AZTLÁN: A PLAN OF NATIONAL LIBERATION
in the Spirit of a new people that is conscious not only of its proud historical heritage but also of the brutal yankee invasion of our territories, we, the chicano inhabitants and guardians of our motherland, Aztlán, from whence came our forefathers, reclaiming the land of their birth and consecrating the determination of our people of the sun, declare that the call of our blood is our power, our responsibility, and our inevitable destiny.

we are free and sovereign to determine those tasks which are justly called for by our house, our land, the sweat of our brows, and by our hearts. Aztlán belongs to the Creator who brings nourishment to the seeds, and brings rain and sun to the fields to give people crops for food, and not to the yankee empire. we do not recognize capricious borders on the Red Continent.

brotherhood and sisterhood unites us, and love for our brothers and sisters makes us a rising people whose sun has come and who struggles against the alien yankee who exploits our riches and destroys our culture. with our hearts in our hands and our roots in the soil, we declare the independence of our Red Mestizo nation. we are a Red People with a Red Culture. before the world, before all of north Amerikkka, before our brothers and our sisters in Amerindia, we are a Nation, we are a Union of Free Pueblos, we are *Aztlán*.

end the genocide and biocide
   of the yankee empire
        humanize
        conscience
        organize
for National Chicano Liberation
   build
   a
   Red Nation
(*NATIONCHILD* 3)

In all cases, the word "bronze" has been abandoned in favor of the more politically recognizable "Red," which evokes not pre-Columbian Meso-america, but contemporary U.S. Native America. "Bronze continent" becomes "Red Continent" and "mestizo nation" becomes "Red Mestizo Nation." A term that has its origins in the discourses of conquest, colo-nization, and expansion, "Red" entered the U.S. settler lexicon as a racist description of American Indian phenotypes. "Red Indian" and "Redskin" are phrases that continue to alienate and denigrate, yet remain extraordi-narily popular as names for contemporary sports teams and their mascots. In the 1970s, however, when Alurista published *Nationchild,* "Red" had been recently appropriated, transformed into a powerful tool of cultural and political opposition by American Indian activists.[40]

Alurista's choice to change his terminology is an acknowledgement of the American Indian Movement and inscribes Chicano nationalism as a parallel struggle for recognition and reparation. In what also seems to be a self-conscious move to distance Chicano nationalist rhetoric from the discourses of manifest destiny and expansion, Alurista deletes the term "civilizers" from the original phrase "civilizers of the northern land of Aztlán," revising it to "guardians of our motherland of Aztlán." He also removes the "frontiers" in the phrase "capricious frontiers" in favor of another version of a statement that reads, "We do not recognize capricious borders on the Red Continent." Evident, however, in the change from "civilizers" to "guardians" is also a rejection of the concept of ownership of land in favor of human stewardship and divine beneficence. Later in the text, the original "Aztlán belongs to those who plant the seeds, water the fields, and gather the crops and not to the foreign Europeans" becomes:

> Aztlán belongs to the Creator who brings nourishment to the seeds, and brings rain and sun to the fields to give people crops for food, and not to the yankee empire. (*Nationchild* 3)

The indirect reference to farmworkers is discarded in a negation of "Western" ideas about private ownership of land and a privileging of the experience of colonization shared with American Indians. The Anglo landgrab of the U.S. Southwest is presented as an act of empire that exploits labor and extracts wealth from the rightful inhabitants of the region, among whom Chicanas/os may be counted. Although the original version appeared to make a connection between the nineteenth-century dispossession of the Spanish-speaking mestizo population and the twentieth-century status of their descendants as landless laborers in the fields of Anglo agribusiness, the later version favors the rhetorical authority derived from articulating Chicana/o and American Indian resistance. Alurista stresses the anti-imperialist argument through this alignment while also making the Chicana/o indigenous assertion stronger.

The "call of our blood" that is sounded in the first version remains central in the later, laying the groundwork for relation to American Indians and establishing Indigenous descent. Biology and ancestry are crucial to the Aztlán narrative, for they are taken as the "history" that makes the myth real. It is important, nevertheless, that Alurista chose to modify the proclamation that Chicanas/os are "a people whose time has come" to "a rising people whose sun has come," a change that ultimately constructs a more coherent adaptation of the Aztec migration narrative to the Chicana/o context. In evoking the Fifth Sun stage of the Aztec cosmogonic cycle, the preamble becomes a more complete pre-Columbian mythic revival. Finally, however, Alurista's revisions to the text originally presented in 1969 at the Denver Youth Conference reveal an attempt to negotiate the space between American Indian resistance and Chicana/o indigenist nationalism, while at the same time drawing authority from the realms of contemporary politics and forgotten spiritualities.

Conclusion

Chicano indigenist nationalism is anti-imperialist and anti-colonialist, influenced by Third World liberation movements, civil rights activism, and Native struggles for land. Indigenism provided powerful tools for the elaboration of nationalist consciousness by motivating cultural pride and challenging the legitimacy of degrading dominant imagery. The writers examined here take different indigenist approaches to pursuing such goals. I focused on Armando Rendon's challenge to the immigrant status of Chicanos and insistence on land rights claims legitimated by Indigenous and mestizo ancestry. I highlighted Luis Valdez's emphasis on spirituality and his attempt to integrate Mesoamerican philosophical systems with political critique and revolutionary action. Valdez's work, particularly *Pensamiento Serpentino* and El Teatro Campesino's Theater of the Sphere, present themselves as supplements to the materialist critique of empire. In selections from Alurista's work, we see indigenist strategies deployed to critique consumerism and the quest for instant gratification, which are subtly linked to an emergent multinationalism proliferating through the pursuit of foreign markets and an interventionist U.S. foreign policy.

In all cases, however, it is the language of myth that propels these indigenist strategies. Myth enables Chicana/o indigenism in its reinscription of the ancient; it is a form of language that allows certain exigencies of history to be, at least temporarily, disabled. To dwell in the realm of myth is to be able to ignore the very problematic that Chicana/o indigenism produces. Even as they recognize their own difference from U.S. American Indians and simultaneously claim indigeneity through the cultural signifiers of pre- and post-Conquest Mesoamerica, Chicana/o indigenists fail to recognize the interruption of their mythic beginnings by American Indian anti-colonial discourse and activism. The movement writing addressed here expressed solidarity with AIM and yet persisted in presenting unique mestiza/o land claims as undisrupted by American Indian ancestral occupation of the land base known now as the United States and the treaty rights that institutionalized the recognition of that historic presence. The condition of Chicana/o indigeneity is instead traced from the south and established through emphases on the language, philosophy, science, and mythology of ancestral cultures for the most part unclaimed by American Indian rhetorics of resistance and liberation.[41]

Like Valdez and Rendon, Alurista imported pre-Columbian spiritual and philosophical concepts into a Chicano context, mobilizing them in service of a movement agenda to empower communities and provide the conceptual tools necessary to challenge an oppressive status quo. The borrowing from an archive of Mesoamerican studies that exists in spite of, and because of, the Conquest, is both resourceful and ingenious, especially in the work of Alurista and Valdez. The interest in pre-Conquest codices and their modern interpretations evince keen intellectual insights, especially when we see the fruits of that cognitive labor in the reorganization of Aztec and Maya mythology to address the material realities of struggles for liberation in the United States and in the Third World. The reliance on this archive is less overt than what we see, for example, in Adelaida del Castillo's historiographic revision of La Malinche, or Norma Alarcón's theoretical construction of "'the' Native woman." Feminist interventions like these also consciously and clearly took up the challenges posed by movement patriarchy, evidence of which we can see in Alurista, Valdez, and perhaps most explicitly, Rendon. Again drawing from an anthropological and archaeological archive, Chicana feminists assumed control of the discourse of indigenism, redeploying philosophical precepts and conceptual iconographies to narrate a new mytho-history made to oppose the male-centered imperatives of masculinist nationalism. This new indigenism, Chicana feminist indigenism, anchored itself in the realities of Chicana subjectivity and continued the search for a movement poetics and activism that would nourish the spiritual needs of a community.

Indigenism, finally, both establishes and expresses consciousness in many forms. Although it is most associated with nationalist consciousness because of the prominence of Aztlán as a political signifier, it also gave expression to religious and spiritual consciousness. But the internal patriarchal structure of movement communities legislated that, for a time at least, the language of indigenist movement poetics was itself masculinist, designed through the privileging of male gods, male ancestors, and male heirs to elevate the consciousness of contemporary Chicanos toward an understanding of identity that was fundamentally gendered.

We thus cannot overlook the features of Chicano indigenism that ally it with both heterosexism and patriarchy. Angie Chabram-Dernersesian has noted that nationalism "celebrat[ed] primarily masculine Mexican cultural symbols and national identities" ("Construction of Whiteness" 130). In the texts of three Chicano indigenists addressed here, the significance of women lies in their roles as mothers and girlfriends, as the bearers of children, and as sacrificed goddesses. In the most extreme example of movement sexism, Rendon's *Chicano Manifesto,* it is the Chicana who embodies race betrayal in her attempts to secure her own rights and privileges within and outside of movement communities, as I will discuss in the next chapter. Furthermore, representations of male relationships, like Valdez's depiction of the homophobic targeting of Conejo in the first scene of *The Dark Root of a Scream,* call attention to the exclusivism of Chicano nationalism. And despite Alurista's apparent attempts to assign to women the powers of the gods, ultimately his Coatlicue and Cocacóatl are sacrificed as the new age of Chicanos is born. These are restrictions that Chicanas would fundamentally challenge as they wrested control of the most prominent symbol of movement indigenism, the Indian.

CHAPTER 3

From La Malinche to Coatlicue: Chicana Indigenist Feminism and Mythic Native Women

C hicana feminists have used the motifs of indigenist nationalism to advance some of the earliest critiques of relations of power within the movement, eroding the cultural authority of patriarchy to sustain Chicano revolutionary thought. In her groundbreaking essay on Chicana feminism, Norma Alarcón writes that "the reappropriation of 'the' native woman on Chicana feminist terms marked one of the first assaults on male-centered nationalism on the one hand and patriarchal political economy on the other" ("Chicana Feminism" 251). In linking feminism and indigenism, Alarcón's text confirms the degree to which feminist analysis has been propelled by the symbols of nationalist indigenism, symbols that had to be recaptured from the discourses of masculinism and misogyny and reformulated to provide points of identification and sources of empowerment for Chicanas. Women have at times written from within nationalist spaces, voicing internal challenges that also glorify an indigenous ancestral past. And even when women write from outside a nationalist framework, their projects of indigenism resonate with earlier attempts to assert indigeneity and revitalize communities bound by shared cultural and racial characteristics.

Feminist indigenism follows two dominant paths in its relation to myth. Some mythmaking enterprises claim their beginnings in specific historical events while another mode invokes mythic figures who did not exist historically. The reclamation of La Malinche, the Nahua advisor and translator to Hernán Cortés, occurred during a formative stage of Chicana indigenist feminism and elevated a gendered racial subject, the Indigenous woman. In recovering some facts about her life, Chicana feminist writing also established a mythical matriarchal origin for *mestizaje*. Certain meditations on the Virgin of Guadalupe—written and visual emphases on her indigenous features and similarities to Mesoamerican goddesses—also fall within this feminist indigenist tradition of challenging patriarchy.[1] Chicana feminists use these Mesoamerican goddesses to symbolize both the limitations and potentials of Chicana material existence. Gloria Anzaldúa's work on the serpent goddess Coatlicue, around which she builds a complex indigenist schematic, is the best-known illustration. More recently, Cherríe Moraga has made another ancient Mesoamerican goddess, Coyolxauhqui, a central icon of her own cultural criticism. Thus, we can see that indigenist feminism, and its reliance on the languages of myth, continues to hold a vital position within Chicana/o critical discourse.[2]

This chapter outlines two critiques of nationalism mobilized through the languages of indigenism and primitivism. Adelaida del Castillo's early recuperation of La Malinche in "Malintzin Tenépal: A Preliminary Look into a New Perspective" recovers a Native ancestor and, in this sense, is indigenist. Del Castillo's motivation, however, is to reclaim La Malinche as a Christian who opposed a tyrannical and murderous Aztec priesthood. In the depiction of this priesthood and the emphasis on the Quetzalcoatl and Huizilopochtli narrative, del Castillo's text aligns with dominant representations of the Conquest that emphasize precisely this "barbarity." The second text I address, Gloria Anzaldúa's *Borderlands/La Frontera: The New Mestiza,* like del Castillo's work, draws from and reproduces certain conventions. Yet, Anzaldúa calls our attention to Quetzalcoatl and Huizilopochtli in a dramatic retrieval and revision of the Aztec pantheon. Her text mobilizes indigeneity by valorizing vilified Aztec symbols and practices, such as the "monstrous" snake goddess Coatlicue, the obsidian mirror, and ritual sacrifice, while del Castillo recovers the Indian mother by rejecting the Aztec pantheon claimed by Chicano nationalists and later feminists, like Anzaldúa. Both La Malinche and Coatlicue, however, are examples of "'the' native woman" that Alarcón identifies with challenges to Chicano nationalism, and each motivates an indigenist feminism that finds its ground through the processes of mythmaking.[3]

La Malinche, Indian Mother of Mestizas/os

"'The' native woman," as Alarcón says, "has many names" ("Chicana Feminism" 251). "La Malinche" was perhaps one of the first names bestowed by Chicana feminists; others would follow, for example, Coatlicue, Coyolxauhqui, Tonantzin. In some forms of Chicana indigenism, the icons of pre-Columbian myth are central, whereas the case of La Malinche derives from a process of mythmaking begun after, rather than before, the Conquest. An actual historical figure, Malinche, the Nahua woman who translated for and advised Hernán Cortés, was made into myth over five centuries of accounts of her life, which came to symbolize female treachery, unreliability, and victimization. Her status as a mythic object was recognized early in Chicana critical theory, as when Alarcón wrote that "[e]xpropriating Malintzin from the texts of others and filling her with the intentions, significances and desires of Chicanas has taken years. Mexican men had already effected the operation for their own ends; it was now women's turn" ("Traddutora" 72).

In 1980, Cordelia Candelaria presented La Malinche as a "Chicana feminist prototype."[4] A participant in the recovery of La Malinche that began in the mid-1970s, Candelaria made an incisive observation. Taking note of a "current reevaluation of pre-Columbian culture," she pointed out that "La Malinche remain[ed] one of the few indigenous figures in the Conquest of Mexico to be viewed with contempt" (1). The contempt is encouraged by the Mexican cultural representation of La Malinche as female betrayer. Because she acted as a translator for the Spanish and provided information that benefited military campaigns against the Aztecs and others, she has been marked in the Mexican popular consciousness as the embodiment of treachery. What distinguishes La Malinche, as Candelaria rightly notes, is the scorn that has been heaped upon her, even as her historical presence serves as the basis for myths of Mexican beginnings.

In addressing the continued denigration of a Conquest-era Indigenous woman in the midst of the revitalization of Indigenous origins, Candelaria's comment pinpoints one of the most limiting features of Chicano nationalism—its sexism. Feminist analyses of social relations within movement communities, according to Chicana critics, were easily diminished and marginalized as divisive ideological tactics originating from an Anglo/European power base, that is, the "enemy camp." This marginalization of Chicana movement feminists has been documented by scholars such as Ana Nieto-Gómez, Martha Cotera, and Mirta Vidal, among others.[5] Alfredo Mirandé and Evangelina Enríquez wrote in 1979 that many Chicanas identified with the figure of La Malinche as "a positive symbol because 'malinche' has become identified with 'vendido,' or traitor—labels which Chicana feminists have also endured" (242). Feminists who felt marginalized from decision making and spoke critically of the failure within movement communities to recognize and honor female leadership projected their situations onto a particular Native woman. La

Malinche began to function as an example of how misogynist nationalism asserted control over not only the bodies of women, but also their representation in the domain of the image.

The alignment of patriarchal and nationalist ideology is evident in Armando Rendon's *Chicano Manifesto,* discussed in the previous chapter. Its illustration of movement masculinism is made the more pertinent here because it rests upon the portrayal of La Malinche. In a chapter titled "Who is the Enemy?" Rendon tells La Malinche's story in one sentence. As he brings the Mexican narrative of her treachery into a Chicano nationalist context, he foregrounds La Malinche's roles as provider of sexual services, interpreter, and informant, respectively. He is uninterested in the circumstances of her decisions, the specifics of her life in enslavement, or the possibility that her actions were motivated by experiences of victimization. Rendon manipulates the concept of "malinche" to condemn internal divisions that result from what he views as assaults on the most profound aspect of Chicano community identity:

> We Chicanos have our own share of Malinches, which is what we call traitors to la raza who are of la raza, after the example of an Aztec woman of that name who became Cortez' concubine under the name of Doña Marina, and served him as an interpreter and informer against her own people. . . . In the service of the gringo, malinches attack their own brothers, betray our dignity and manhood, cause jealousies and misunderstandings among us, and actually seek to retard the advance of Chicanos, if it benefits themselves. (97)

Rendon highlights La Malinche's sexual relationship with Cortés, marking it as concubinage, a term with obvious negative implications. At the heart of this critique of "malinches," however, is the accusation of self-interest. Rendon does not charge Doña Marina with the responsibility of Aztec defeat, but he does use the history of her relationship with Cortés to speak of betrayal and misplaced allegiances. It is self-interest, he claims, that propels acts of race traitorship, in that such treachery is initiated in the quest for personal gain. Furthermore, by linking contemporary acts of "betrayal" to the disastrous consequences faced by the Aztecs after the arrival of the Spanish, Rendon attempts to transfer Mexican contempt for La Malinche onto Chicana/o subjects who do not conform to particular codes of behavior.

The pointed reference to betrayed "dignity and manhood" genders not only the Chicano community, but also acts of treachery. Pairing the idea of worth or inherent nobility with masculinity reinforces already accepted notions about the association of manliness with characteristics such as bravery, honor, and leadership. Womanhood's presence in the passage is contained in the figure of La Malinche who is accused of informing against "her own people" and providing tactical and sexual services to the enemy. As Rendon masculinizes Chicano communities, he conversely feminizes this idea of race betrayal. Although all "malinches" are presumably not female, the epithet is linked in his passage both to a historical woman and to the act of betrayal. The condemnation of the translator perpetuates already established cultural ideas about the inherent unreliability of women, in particular.

Angie Chabram-Dernersesian concludes that because "traitors to la raza" are a feminized group within Chicana/o communities, Chicanas in general are fundamentally associated with duplicity. Furthermore, Chabram-Dernersesian says, Chicanas are "targeted through the figure of La Malinche and a ranking of betrayal that favors the male gender" ("Construction of Whiteness" 131). Women who felt targeted as feminists within Chicana/o movement communities were able to identify with La Malinche based on their own experiences of being judged as "traitors to la raza." Rendon's pronouncements about malinches imply that any divergences from established nationalist strategies and goals could be judged negatively as reiterations of that first betrayal.[6] Implied in Rendon's glossing of malinche is the cultural belief that it is women who set their sights on individual advancement, as men embark on the quest for community empowerment.

In Mexican Spanish, over time the term "malinche" evolved into an insult signifying "traitor" or "sellout." Octavio Paz has defined "malinchista" as a term popularized by Mexican newspapers in the 1960s "to denounce all those who have been corrupted by foreign influences" (86). Paz's analysis refuses to grant agency to La Malinche or to credit her with the foresight and intelligence that Chicanas have emphasized. Her status as Native within a racialized sex-gender system positions her at the nexus of at least two discourses of disempowerment: she is multiply removed from institutional power as a woman of the conquered race. Many literary treatments of her existence, such as that of Paz, have been overwhelmed by the fact of her identity as an Indian woman in a European patriarchal order and for too long denied her power and her agency, even as she was assigned blame for the downfall of an empire.[7]

In "The Sons of La Malinche," published in Spanish in 1950 and reissued in English by Grove Press in 1961 and 1985, Paz contends that the

figure of La Malinche lies embedded within the Mexican nationalist rallying call of *"¡Que Viva México! Hijos de la chingada!"* In what Alarcón calls
the "third, modernistic stage" of the narrative trajectory of La Malinche,
Paz may be credited, she suggests, with observing "the metonymic link
between Malintzin and the epithet *La Chingada*" ("Traddutora" 63).[8] Paz
explicates the term *"chingada"* as "the Mother forcibly opened, violated
or deceived" (78), immortalizing La Malinche as mother of all Mexicans,
and also as a woman who suffered the humiliation of sexual violation and
emotional manipulation.[9] Her relationship with Cortés is made to symbolize the figurative as well as the literal rape of all of the Americas and its
original inhabitants. It is an association that, according to Paz, degrades
contemporary Mexicans: "The hijo de la Chingada is the offspring of violation, abduction or deceit . . . the fruit of a violation" (79–80).

Paz's essay circulated in early Chicano Studies anthologies, influencing
an emerging discourse of opposition.[10] Adelaida del Castillo challenges
directly Paz's idealization of a passive victimhood, arguing that La Malinche was agent of her own actions. "Doña Marina," del Castillo writes,
"is significant in that she embodies effective, decisive action in the feminine form" (125). Her originary essay, "Malintzín Tenépal: A Preliminary
Look into a New Perspective," read at the 1973 National Association for
Chicano Studies Conference in Austin, forcefully responded to gender relations within movement communities. In this essay, she makes an astute
connection between the Conquest-era La Malinche and contemporary
mestizas, averring that "the denigrations made against her indirectly de-
fame the mexicana/chicana female" (141). Malinche, she argues, is representative of women; thus, the negative portrayal of her reinforces beliefs
about the essential characteristics of women, for example, untrustworthi-
ness. Furthermore, the misogynist image also insists upon a degraded
sexuality. Paz's view of female sexuality, del Castillo points out, refuses
to recognize the desire for and experience of pleasure. Even as she critiqued the characterization of Malinche specifically, del Castillo exposed
the masculinist ethos of Chicano nationalism by broadening her analysis
to include Chicanas more generally.

Using predominantly Spanish and Mexican sources, del Castillo relies upon fairly conventional representations of Conquest-era Aztec society. For example, she calls attention to the story that the Aztecs mistook Cortés for the god Quetzalcoatl. The narrative, which circulates in
accounts commissioned by Spanish clergy and colonial administrators,
has become a convention in telling the tale of the Conquest. The arrival
of the Spanish, the story goes, coincided with Aztec expectations of the

return of Quetzalcoatl in the year specified by the exiled god, One Reed, which translates into 1519 in the European calendar. Additional features of the story claim that the invasion occurred after the Aztecs witnessed certain omens or prophetic signs that indicated impending doom.[11] Del Castillo reproduces and solidifies this narrative in a Chicana/o context, arguing that Doña Marina was a devotee of Quetzalcoatl, favoring peace over bloodshed and the offering of flowers and poetry over human blood and flesh. She sees Malinche's eventual conversion to Catholicism forecast in the choice to worship Quetzalcoatl, "giver of life and peace" (128) over Huitzilopochtli, "bloodthirsty warrior" (128). It is a choice that is assumed rather than proven by del Castillo, although it provides a foundation upon which to explain the alliance with the Spanish and their religious traditions: "Perhaps Malintzin was given some sense of deliverance when she recognized that the Spaniards resembled Quetzalcóatl in more ways than was to be expected for a mere coincidence" (130).

Del Castillo reiterates the anthropological conventions associating Quetzalcoatl with humanity and Huitzilopochtli with blood-lust, as do other writers, like Gloria Anzaldúa. Del Castillo, however, treats the subject of blood sacrifice altogether differently from Anzaldúa. Likewise, del Castillo's representation is dramatically opposed to Luis Valdez's earlier treatment in his 1967 play *The Dark Root of a Scream*. Here, the playwright reinvents ritual human sacrifice as a metaphor for the sacrifice a male activist is willing to make to empower his community. When del Castillo writes of sacrifice, on the other hand, we see a startling parallel to accounts such as William H. Prescott's influential *History of the Conquest of Mexico*. Like Prescott and others, she emphasizes the barbarity of Aztec ritual sacrifice, associating it with a corrupt and "maniacal" priesthood of men. Doña Marina represents for del Castillo a more civilized Native subject who chooses a more civilized religion, Christianity. She argues, in effect, that Doña Marina is drawn to the more humane world of Spanish Catholicism because it corresponds with the ethos of the Cult of Quetzalcoatl to which she was already devoted. Anzaldúa and Valdez reconceptualize the Aztec priesthood and the practice of ritual sacrifice, reclaiming both as the cultural patrimony of Chicanas/os, but del Castillo rejects the Aztec sacerdotal order as "morally degenerate" and "bloodthirsty madmen" (129). She privileges instead women's consciousness—Doña Marina's—over the nationalist consciousness advanced by Valdez.

Del Castillo's choice enables her to formulate Doña Marina's actions as women's resistance to Aztec violence and oppression. Because Malintzin had been a slave, she understood "the trials of the common indio" (129).

It was, according to del Castillo, Malinche's own experiences of injustice and observations of inequalities "under the military state of Huitzilopochtli" that informed both her decision to convert and her actions in support of the campaign against the Aztecs. La Malinche becomes savior of "the common indio," a rhetorical move that initiates a reverse idealization effectively absolving her of the crime of betraying her people and a country that did not yet exist. Del Castillo refashions the role of La Malinche at "the beginning of the mestizo nation": not responsible for the destruction of a civilization, La Malinche is instead to be credited with the creation of another. This recodification of Malinche positions her not as violated victim, but as conscious agent in the birth of the mestizo race and "New World" women's history, a reassessment that would also appear in Carmen Tafolla's 1977 poem "La Malinche." Del Castillo's text is ultimately a celebration of *mestizaje,* a challenge to a more narrowly conceived indigenism that recognizes only very limited aspects of ancestry.

The indigenism that does exist in her text is not a reclamation of Aztec mythic figures in the name of contemporary Chicana feminists. Rather, she uses the deities of an Aztec religious system, Quetzalcoatl and Huitzilopochtli, to theorize Doña Marina's reasons for aligning herself with the Spanish. Del Castillo does not recodify the pantheon, but instead participates in the remythification of a historical figure even as she wants to avoid a further rendering of La Malinche as myth, characterizing her text not as "a historical narrative per se [but] intended [as] more of a mystical interpretation of a historical role" (126). Still, she insists upon her historical foundations, distinguishing Doña Marina "not as a goddess in some mythology, but as an actual force in the making of history" (125). The narrative ultimately appears conflicted, traveling between the demands of history and the allure of myth.[12]

Alarcón informs us that the association of La Malinche with betrayal and the scapegoating of her in the popular consciousness began in the nineteenth century during the time of Mexican independence ("Traddutora" 64 n.16). It is at this point that she became a negative mythic figure, a symbol of women's deceitful nature and the unsavory beginnings of la raza. When Alarcón writes of how Chicanas began "filling her" with their "intentions, significances, and desire," she, too, acknowledges La Malinche's function as myth. La Malinche operates merely as a form, a vessel for alternating and sometimes conflicting meanings that, while seemingly anchored to the "real" story of a real woman, at times lose their connection to a historical past in the service of the mythological message.

Even as Alurista, Valdez, and Anzaldúa embrace the pantheon, they critically approach dominant anthropological accounts of Aztec religion and society. Del Castillo rejects that pantheon, uncritically relying on the conventions of anthropology to legitimate a position that relies upon the realm of the mythic. Her position within Chicana/o indigenism is complicated by this departure from accepted practices of the tradition. Most prominently, she uses the Aztec pantheon as a negative example of the violence of the Aztec regime, refusing to reclaim it as a Chicana/o cultural patrimony. In del Castillo's essay, we find a feminist indigenism that opposes the glorification of male heroes such as Cuahtemoc as she is able both to glorify a Native ancestor and to critique Indigenous cultural practices of domination and violence.[13]

Pre-Columbian Myth and Postmodern Politics

But it is Gloria Anzaldúa's *Borderlands/La Frontera: The New Mestiza,* published in 1987, that is perhaps the most famous example of feminist indigenism. Here, I address Anzaldúa's specific form of Chicana feminist literary indigenism, a response to movement masculinism but also a challenge to Chicana/o homophobia, classism, and linguistic elitism. As a later iteration of both indigenism and feminism, Anzaldúa's work contains within it the echoes of battles waged in movement communities a decade or more before. It is therefore important to situate her work within the trajectory of feminist challenges to Chicano patriarchy, particularly as those challenges were conceptualized through announcements of Indigenous origins.

The history of discursive constructions of the Native is unavoidably present in Chicana and Chicano indigenist writing. As Chicanas/os have struggled to establish historical primacy in the U.S. Southwest, articulations of Indigenous identity have often legitimated those claims. In the case of Anzaldúa, the Indian goddess operates as an object through which to liberate the abused psyche of Chicanas/lesbianas/mestizas/women of color. Anzaldúa's Coatlicue/Shadow-Beast is the author's attempt to construct and to claim the Indigenous in the Chicana. If we accept, however, that the indigeneity of Chicanas/os can be represented metaphorically through Aztec mythology, we position ourselves as modern anthropologists, which raises questions about Chicana/os' relationship to the past and the present of contemporary Indigenous communities in the United States and in Mexico.

Although the construction of a mythic female Indian identity evolves out of earlier formulations of primitivism, its success lies, to an extent, in Anzaldúa's ability to distance herself from a language created by Europeans and European-Americans. By subtly insisting on her Native/Indian identity — she *is* the primitive — the author is able to represent her prose and the knowledge it produces as Indigenous. On the one hand, Anzaldúa's reconstructed pre-Columbian mythology reproduces rhetorical strategies of self-fashioning more widely associated with Chicano (male) indigenists. Less recognized, perhaps, is the degree to which *Borderlands* and other Chicana/o indigenist texts are deeply indebted to language and images first disseminated by European writers as part of colonialist endeavors and, later, as critical reevaluations of the Western social order. This recognition forces new and uncomfortable observations regarding Chicana/o self-fashioning.

Still, it is crucial to acknowledge the deep transformations in languages of theory and conceptualizations of Chicana identity that Anzaldúa's work have generated. Whatever its unstated, unrecognized, and, indeed, even unconscious ideological and discursive debts, *Borderlands/La Frontera: The New Mestiza* presented its audiences with unfamiliar generic forms as it transgressed, merged, and shifted the borders of academic and popular speech, scholarly and creative production, the conventions of masculinity, femininity, and erotic or sexual orientation. Its publication in 1987 brought refreshing change in the fields of Chicana/o Studies, Women's Studies, and beyond, inaugurating the border as the generative metaphor for a range of "hybrid" identity configurations of the 1980s and 1990s. It remains one of the most popular texts to be read outside of a Chicana/o Studies curriculum. In Chicana feminist studies, critical commentary celebrates Anzaldúa's particular attention to the shifting identities of a Chicana borderlands subject. Indeed, much of the significance of the work lies in her elaborate articulation of the multiple situations of Chicana identity. Tey Diana Rebolledo praises Anzaldúa for "[articulating] the tensions, the conflict, the shiftings," and "[recognizing] the multiplicities . . . and ambivalences." "Most important," Rebolledo continues, "in many ways she validated the shiftings, seeing them as coming from a position of resistance" (*Women Singing* 103). Furthermore, Anzaldúa's work is an important marker in the history of Chicana lesbian writing.[14]

A host of theorists writing from outside of Chicana academic circles have also found in Anzaldúa's theory and poetics of the Borderlands a rich terrain of support for their own analyses of subjectivity. Sidonie Smith, like Rebolledo, celebrates "discursive slippages and tongues" and "pronominal fluidity" (178) that reject the conventional dualisms of the pastoral tradition.[15] *Borderlands,* Smith says, "interrupts the cycle of nostalgia—both the nostalgia of nativist history . . . and the nostalgia of personal homelessness" (178–179).

Judith Butler, on the other hand, looks specifically to Anzaldúa's metaphor of the crossroads presented in Chapter 7 of *Borderlands,* "*La conciencia de la mestiza*/Towards a New Consciousness." Butler finds value in the crossroads image as a site "where . . . categories converge[; it is] a crossroads that is not a subject, but, rather, the unfulfillable demand to rework convergent signifiers in and through each other" (117). She later writes of the crossroads as "the non-space of cultural collision . . . which opens up the possibility of a reworking of the very terms by which subjectivization proceeds—and fails to proceed" (124). Butler's language of "convergent signifiers" and "cultural collision" evoke the movement and meeting of discourses. As these discourses "converge" and "collide," they are rearticulated in alternate, reordered form. Anzaldúa provides for Butler the elaboration of a space in which those who are not recognized within the "legitimate" constructions of subjectivity—culture, nation, race, sexuality—resist immobilization and are instead prompted to redefine the very limits of subjectivity as they negotiate the discursive traffic traveling through the "crossroads" of consciousness.

As a final example, I call attention to Kobena Mercer, who, in his theorization of Black Cultural Studies, appeals to "the Chicana concept of *mestizo,* dialogically accentuated by Gloria Anzaldúa." For Mercer, "*mestizo*" is an illustration of the "profusion of rhizomatic connections of the sort that constitute an evolving black queer diaspora community [that] implies another way of conceiving 'the role of the intellectual,' not as heroic leader or patriarchal master, but as a connector located at the hyphenated intersection of disparate discourses . . ." (30). The idea of the rhizome as horizontally-driven sets of breakage and linkage reconceptualizes the intellectual as one who articulates relationships from a place where discourses meet, merge, clash, branch off, and invoke alternative subjectivities. Although he does not name the crossroads metaphor specifically, Mercer's recasting of Anzaldúa appears to privilege features of mestiza consciousness that resonate with Butler's assessment. Butler and Mercer and other cultural theorists have found Anzaldúa's text useful because it exemplified theoretical ideas—anti-nationalism, post-colonialism, and hybridity—at the very moment of their ascendance. Because of their emphasis, however, these critics overlook Anzaldúa's treatments of indigeneity, which is itself a return to origins and thus does not easily align with theories of hybridity or anti-nationalism.

Anzaldúa's text encourages such borrowings. In her preface, she states that "[t]he psychological borderlands, the sexual borderlands, and the spiritual borderlands are not particular to the Southwest. In fact the Borderlands are physically present wherever two or more cultures edge each other, where people of different races occupy the same territory, where under, lower, middle and upper classes touch, where the space between two individuals shrinks with intimacy." It is precisely this ambition to elaborate a general theory of cultural relations that makes Anzaldúa's borderlands so readily available for use beyond Chicana/o cultural studies. Furthermore, among Chicana/o critics, the migration of Anzaldúa's ideas into other fields of analysis is a testament to the generalizable form of the new mestiza and the theory of the borderlands. For instance, Alfred Arteaga has commented that "Anzaldúa embraces nearly everyone as potential subject of the new consciousness, for nearly everyone is marginalized in some way in the borderlands" (35).

Indeed, *Borderlands/La Frontera* is distinct in its commitment to sustaining contradictions and residing in the various and liminal ontological, epistemological, and geographical zones that Anzaldúa has named "the borderlands." The text takes a clear stand against disciplinary and linguistic boundaries as it weaves its answer to paternalism, patriarchy, and homophobia. Yet Anzaldúa also sustains the specificities of her challenge as she consistently takes on narratives of colonization, including those issued by anthropologists, and stakes her claims about the practices and effects of racist ideology in the southwestern United States. So whether Anzaldúa's borderlands function as a general term of service to poststructural, feminist, and race theorists, or evokes the complexities of a specifically Chicana lived experience, the terms of the debates that Anzaldúa initiates remain the same: race, class, gender, nationalism, and sexuality. Despite the assertion of the quasi-universality of *Borderlands,* the immediate context of the book is without question the U.S. Southwest as it addresses directly and particularly the complexities of Chicana/o cultural identities.

One of the strategies by which *Borderlands* does universalize la frontera and the new mestiza, however, is through its reinvestment in pre-Columbian myth, which plays a signifying role throughout the essays. In fact, it is with reference to images from Aztec mythology—recast, refashioned, and revalued—that Anzaldúa represents the characteristics of a repressed, but nonetheless resistant, mestiza consciousness in *Borderlands.* Aztec mythology provides a specifically ethnographic basis for asserting the indigenous side of mestiza consciousness, which is depicted as the site of cultural contact and confrontation. Consequently, indigeneity exists most forcefully in Anzaldúa's text as myth and signifies the denied or unconscious side of mestiza consciousness. And although Anzaldúa strives to give expression to the indigenous elements of Chicana identity in the present, her persistent appeal to an Aztec pantheon represented by Coatlicue/Serpent Skirt, Tlazolteotl, the snake, and smoking mirror effectively dehistoricizes the relations between Chicanas/os and Natives.

Within Chicana/o literary criticism, however, Anzaldúa's revival of the goddesses of Aztec myth motivates an oppositional discourse and has received much acclaim. Alvina Quintana and others have acknowledged Anzaldúa's replacement of the homogeneity and masculinism of conventional nationalisms with a woman-centered political project that "creatively shifts the reader's attention" (128). Similarly, Sonia Saldívar-Hull, in a broad reading of *Borderlands,* isolates the feminist critique that Anzaldúa expresses in images of the Shadow-Beast, pre-Columbian goddesses, and the *indigena.* Through these reclamations and reinventions, Saldívar-Hull argues in her introduction to *Borderlands,* the writer "unearth[s] her multiple subjectivities" (7). And Rafael Pérez-Torres asks us to "recognize the contributions Anzaldúa has made in viewing Chicano culture as racialized, relational, and hybrid" (*Mestizaje* 22).[16]

Anzaldúa's emphasis on these female figures rejects the phallicism of serpent imagery and the conventional treatments of the Aztec pantheon. She combines a number of goddess figures— Coatlicue, Cihuacoatl, and Tlazolteotl, for example—with characteristics drawn from male gods, such as Quetzalcoatl/Feathered Serpent and Tezcatlipoca/Smoking Mirror. Her portrayal of the goddess Coatlicue in *Borderlands* nevertheless draws from the conventions of European, Euro-American, and Mexican representations of pre-Columbian Mexico. Anzaldúa saw "the statue of this life-in-death and death-in-life, headless 'monster' goddess (as the *Village Voice* dubbed her) in the Museum of Natural History in New York City" (47). It is a breathtaking work of sculpture, a monument that occupied the Aztec Templo Mayor until the arrival of the Spanish, and the fact that it had such a profound effect on Anzaldúa is not surprising. The artifact was excavated in 1790, along with what is now known as the Aztec calendar stone, by Antonio León y Gama when it was discovered during a public works project in the Mexico City Zócalo. The Tizoc Stone was excavated a few years later. As mentioned earlier, the statue was reburied when Indigenous people began paying homage, and Hill-Boone notes that it was considered at the time not suitable to exhibit next to Greek and Roman casts (320). It was excavated once more for Alexander von

Humboldt, buried again, and then disinterred permanently in 1824 for another European, William Bullock. Eventually, the statue was exhibited in the Hall of Monoliths in the National Museum of Natural History on Moneda Street and then moved to its current location in the Museum of Anthropology in Chapultepec Park.

Museum culture continues to provide popular access to pre-Columbian artifacts that viewers would never otherwise be able to see, and anthropologists and art historians continue to produce influential interpretations of these objects. Considered an earth goddess, or "Earth Mother" figure, the Coatlicue statue seems to violate conventional aesthetic associations. Burland and Forman call it a "horrifying and monstrous sculpture" (39) and Burr Cartwright Brundage, in *The Fifth Sun: Aztec Gods, Aztec World*, describes it as follows:

> This massive block of stone, looming and powerful, is truly repulsive; it is surely one of the most direct and most unequivocal pieces in art history—nothing can mitigate its horror. The skirt of writhing snakes and the necklace of hands and hearts from which dangles the skull pendant— these form the goddess' accoutrements and strike the viewer first. But even more uncompromising is her form, the bared and flaccid breasts, the clutched hands that are really serpent heads, and the great taloned feet whose thumping tread we can almost hear. Above it all, she is decapitated: what appears to be her leering and idiotic face is a fantasy formed by two symmetrical spurts of blood that have been transfigured as they gush forth into the protruding heads of rattlesnakes. (167)

The misogyny of the passage is disturbing and painful. It is not evident whether Anzaldúa saw the statue before coming into contact with modern descriptions of it such as the above, but what is evident is that she created a version of the goddess to contest directly its representation in "mainstream Mesoamerican studies," to use Broyles-González's phrase. Anzaldúa's feminist recreation of Coatlicue makes the monstrous beautiful, and where many emphasize the goddess' role as devourer, she pointedly draws readers' attention to her creative force. Still, Anzaldúa insists on recognizing the embodiment of contradictions in the statue, capturing features of the goddess deemed central to her mythic persona. Coatlicue is both mother and devourer; her status as mother indicated by breasts that appear to have provided nourishment and her identity as devourer indicated, perhaps more dominantly, by her necklace of skulls, hearts, and hands.

Autobiography provides an entry into the mythic as Anzaldúa represents her personal history, especially her knowledge of Coatlicue, partly through myth, and autobiographical details become sources of both folklore and historical narrative. The reconfiguration of the goddess, Norma Alarcón writes, "resituates Coatlicue through the process of the dreamwork, conjures her from the non-conscious memory, through the serpentine folklore of her youth"("Anzaldúa's *Frontera*" 122). The critic reads Coatlicue as a product of Anzaldúa's unconscious that emerges from dreams and repressed memory. Yet, Alarcón also notes the importance of folklore in her interpretation of Coatlicue's presence in *Borderlands,* gesturing to narrative sources that exist outside of Anzaldúa, but have somehow come to inhabit her unconscious. These remarks suggest only a local context for Anzaldúa's sources inasmuch as "folklore" is a decidedly ethnographic concept that implies the oral transmission of traditions within particular communities. Aztec myth may now possess the status of something like postmodern folklore, in part because of Anzaldúa's recovery of female icons. The pre-Columbian gods and goddesses that people her text, however, have been made available not by the local folklore of Chicanas/os in South Texas, but rather by a modern archaeological discourse that has long concerned itself with documenting and interpreting the Aztec pantheon.

Anzaldúa's treatment of indigenous themes reiterates the indigenism of the Chicano movement and its attempt to position mestizas/os historically. Indigenism in *el movimiento* narrated a Chicana/o history that could establish the legitimacy of mestiza/o presences in the United States. By naming Chicanas/os as indigenous to the Americas, movement indigenism challenged the status of Mexicans as "immigrants" and "foreigners." Furthermore, the claim of indigeneity asserted a historical relationship to land that was no longer occupied by mestizas/os, even if cultivated by mestiza/o hands. "El Plan de Aztlán" and Corky González's "Yo soy Joaquín," both foundational documents of the movement, each assert Chicana/o origins in pre-Conquest Mesoamerica.[17] In a review of Alvina Quintana's *Homegirls: Chicana Literary Voices* and Ana Castillo's *Massacre of the Dreamers: Essays on Xicanisma* in which she examines the "culturalist tendencies" of those texts, Rosaura Sánchez advances a general critique of Chicana/o "appropriation of Aztec myths" as "a prime example of what is for the most part a decontextualized and dehistoricized manipulation of indigenous narratives" ("Reconstructing" 357). Anzaldúa's version of indigeneity continues this trend at the same time that it challenges the masculinism of movement rhetoric, as Sánchez also notes (355).[18] The

Aztec ancestor visualized by such male authors was always the warrior-emperor—for example, Cuahtemoc, the Aztec ruler at the time of the Conquest—who resisted the Spanish conquerors.

Borderlands, in fact, depends upon the evocation of the indigenous through the mythic: *"La India en mí es la sombra: La Chingada, Tlazolteotl, Coatlicue"* (22). "The Indian in me is the Shadow," she writes, conflating female Indianness (*"la india"*), a sign of a gendered racial identity, and mythic personae, symbols of a transcendent indigeneity. This conflation is made clear through the examples she lists: whereas *La Chingada* refers to the historical figure of Doña Marina/La Malinche, interpreter to Cortés, Tlazolteotl and Coatlicue are pre-Columbian goddesses. But the three terms are not equivalent, as the quotation above suggests; rather, the mythic overpowers the historical in this particular formulation of Indigenous identity and more generally throughout *Borderlands.*

The slippage in *Borderlands* between the idea of gendered and racialized subjectivity named *la india* and the numerous goddesses in the Aztec pantheon—among which can be counted Coatlicue, Coatlalopeuh, Tonantsi, Cihuacoatl, and Tlazolteotl—suggests that they operate on the same discursive level. It is a slippage reproduced by Anzaldúa's critics, like Alarcón: "The native woman has many names also—Coatlicue, Cihuacoátl, Ixtacihuátl, etc. In fact, one has only to consult the dictionary of *Mitología Nahuátl,* for example, to discover many more that have not been invoked" ("Chicana Feminism" 251). Alarcón's "native woman" has generally been accepted as a feminist signifier for Chicana subjectivity formed through the experiences of conquest. The recourse to a text of Nahuatl mythology, however, is telling. Alarcón and Anzaldúa each seem to ground their most potent expressions of Indigenous female identity in the chronicles of mythology, folklore, and personal anecdote, rather than in material history or in the immediate moment.

The creative use of autobiography in *Borderlands* further deflects attention from anthropological sources as personal, and family histories function as placeholders for the larger history of the U.S.-Mexico borderlands: "I am a border woman. I grew up between two cultures, the Mexican (with a heavy Indian influence) and the Anglo (as a member of a colonized people in our own territory)" (preface). The frequently referenced first chapter, "The Homeland, Aztlán: *El Otro Mexico,*" locates mestiza identity in the history of South Texas and in the cultural, psychological, and geographical interstices of which Anzaldúa first speaks. It is here that she develops her well-known construction of the U.S.-Mexican border as *"una herida abierta* [an open wound]," powerfully visualizing the material violence of the region. She gradually begins to elaborate her idea of indigeneity in Chapter Two, "*Movimientos de rebeldía y las culturas que traicionan* [movements of rebellion and cultures that betray]" when she invokes the "Shadow-Beast."

Anzaldúa writes that "[t]here is a rebel in me—the Shadow-Beast" (16) and, later in the chapter, that "[m]y Chicana identity is grounded in the Indian woman's history of resistance" (21). These two assertions are connected by their invocations of rebellion, which Anzaldúa appears to claim as the legacy of her Indian blood. The Shadow-Beast, therefore, circulates as a sign of indigeneity. Alarcón makes the connection explicit when she considers the Beast and the Indian woman one and the same: "[T]he 'Shadow Beast' functions as the 'native' women of the Américas, as a sign of savagery—the feminine as a sign of chaos" ("Anzaldúa's *Frontera*" 121). But where Anzaldúa wants to privilege the resistance represented by indigeneity, Alarcón chooses instead to locate the value of the Beast in the "mark" of denigration and mistreatment. The immediate value of indigeneity, for Alarcón, lies in its function as signifier: "The most relevant point in the present is to understand how a pivotal indigenous portion of the *mestiza* may represent a collective female experience as well as 'the mark of the Beast' within us—the maligned and abused indigenous woman" ("Chicana Feminism" 251). Indigeneity serves both as general signifier of "collective female experience" and as a specific representation of a racialized and demeaned identity that is "the maligned and abused indigenous woman."[19] Furthermore, when Alarcón names the Beast as the "sign of savagery" and "chaos," she acknowledges Anzaldúa's challenges to "civilization," even as it is instantiated through the force of brown masculinity. "Woman is carnal, animal, and closer to the undivine," writes Anzaldúa. "She is man's recognized nightmarish pieces, his Shadow-Beast" (17).

Anzaldúa thus manipulates primitivist discourse to create a new subject and deploys the serpent to symbolize female power in its indigenous and mythic forms. Her use of the serpent as a dominant trope of a new mythology carries with it the histories of fascination with ancient Mesoamerica that I charted in the Introduction. Citing C. R. Burland and Werner Forman liberally, Anzaldúa builds her idea of mestiza consciousness around the symbol of the Serpent Skirt goddess, Coatlicue. The prominence of this Aztec goddess is demonstrated in the titles of Chapter 3 of *Borderlands*, "Entering Into the Serpent," and Chapter 4, "*La herencia de Coatlicue*/The Coatlicue State." Coatlicue, the Shadow-Beast of *Borderlands*, opposes the repressive forces of Chicano patriarchy, Anglo hegemonic rationality, imposed heterosexuality, and repressed desire. She is configured to prompt mestizas to recover lost traditions and initiate alternate forms of consciousness.

Yet, even as she recovers and revises Aztec goddess figures, Anzaldúa also invokes a discursive tradition that stemmed from the practices of conquest and colonization and was later reformulated to express critique of Western society. She claims this critical power by recasting the negative terms of primitivism, while continuing to rely on conventional associations with the body, sensuality, femininity, and sexuality. Her schemata finds its effectiveness in a reversal of the binary in which all of the attendant assumptions about female subjectivity, such as diminished rationality and heightened sensuality, are refigured as the positive and unique aspects of women's knowledge. Quintana makes a similar point as she compares *Borderlands* with Susan Griffin's *Woman and Nature:* "each author attempts to rewrite Western thought by representing matriarchal influences that begin with the female's relationship to the earth . . . aimed at building women's self-esteem by providing them with a positive female interpretation of life" (158, n.15). These inversions of accepted conventions, however, ultimately do not challenge radically the grammar of patriarchy.

Anzaldúa launches her transvaluative project when she writes of the Shadow-Beast as her unconscious, ultimately conjoining the Shadow-Beast with the image of the serpent. She tells us that "Coatlicue is one of the powerful images, or archetypes, that inhabits my psyche . . . the symbol of the underground aspects of the psyche" (46). In a footnote to this passage, she cites Carl Jung, as well as James Hillman's *Re-visioning of Psychology,* which she identifies as "instrumental in the development of my thought" (95, n.6). Her invocation of a term so deeply associated with psychoanalysis, as well as her references to psychoanalytic theorists, strengthens her association with modernist practices of using the "savage" to illustrate hidden realms of human consciousness.

Demonstrating her personal knowledge of Coatlicue with an autobiographical account of a childhood fear of the outhouse and the snakes that her mother warned lurked there, Anzaldúa repeats the admonition she heard when told not to go to the *escusado* in the dark: "A snake will crawl into your *nalgas,* make you pregnant" (25). When she does encounter the snake in the field, it is immediately killed by her mother. Anzaldúa tells of a ritual she then performs on herself, cutting an X into each snake bite to make it bleed. She sucks the venom and blood from her own wound, gathers the pieces of the body, and, "plac[ing] them end on end," reconstructs the snake (26). The rebuilt fragments become a complete serpent.

The story, offered as a childhood precursor to Anzaldúa's literary rebuilding of the serpent goddess, suggests that the mythic archetype has an analogue in her own experiences as a Tejana in the borderlands of South Texas. Such personal accounts effectively obscure archaeological and anthropological influences.

In the quotation above, the snake is at once the instrument of impregnation as well as a symbol of the potential for self-creation. As an auto-generative act, the figurative rebuilding of the serpent rejects a dependence on male participation in the process of creation. In her narration of the memory, Anzaldúa explicitly associates the serpent with Coatlicue, the female body, and sexuality. Yet, throughout these autobiographical vignettes, Coatlicue also signifies the shame associated with other, less celebrated, biological facts of women's physiology. In her guise as the serpent in the outhouse and cotton field, Coatlicue signals the onset of menstruation, the secret sin understood as *"la sena,* the mark of the Beast" (42–43). The bleeding that distances the young girl from her peers is the sign of a body that betrays, the instinctual impulses of "her core self, her dark Indian self" (43). Thus, *Borderlands* reproduces the modernist association of the primitive with "uncorrupted" expressions of the body.

When the Indian as pre-Columbian goddess is made to represent "deviant" sexualities and the primitive body, Anzaldúa's text shows how even a radically divergent Chicana discourse can depend upon a symbolic landscape predetermined by the dominant narratives of archaeological investigation and literary primitivism. The writer both queers and feminizes the serpent/Shadow-Beast, redefining a dualistic model as she attempts to create a "third space" that can accommodate those who are "two in one body, both male and female" (19). The choice to make her primitive an icon of demonized sexualities, bisexuality and homosexuality, is perhaps less than original when considered in the context of the many non-primitives who have turned primitive sexuality into a critique of Western hegemonic norms. Art historian Sally Price and anthropologist Daniel Rosenblatt have separately argued that alternative expressions of sexuality (even if that simply means "unrepressed" or unburdened by Judeo-Christian ideas of shame and/or sin) have always been viewed as essential qualities of primitive existence.[20]

The primitive metaphor has also been used to represent the civilized subject's meeting with the unconscious. Anzaldúa confronts repressed desires and fears in a space she names "the Coatlicue state," in which she encounters the smoking mirror, another image borrowed from interpretations of Aztec myth. The invocation of the Aztec god Tezcatlipoca, also known as Smoking Mirror, is another example of the author's manipulation of the characteristics of a powerful male deity. Features of the Tez-catlipoca god are transferred into a Chicana context, where they symbol-ize female power. The smoking mirror becomes the site where Anzaldúa meets the goddess, even as she realizes her own fierce resistance: "I don't want to see what's behind *Coatlicue's* eyes, her hollow sockets. I can't con-front her face to face" (48). Slowly gathering the courage to face the god-dess, however, the writer recognizes that the Beast she fears is herself: "Behind the ice mask I see my own eyes" (48). The particular association of Coatlicue with the idea of the "shadow" crystallizes when we turn to Jungian theory, which interprets the trope of the shadow as the dark side of the psyche, precisely the association that Anzaldúa draws out.[21] She transforms the gaze into a self-emancipatory gesture, a recuperative move that is meant to claim and to valorize that which has been demeaned and hated by racist patriarchies (both Anglo and Chicano), a counter-move to correct and reverse the internalization of homophobia, misogyny, and race hatred. Anzaldúa's most effective innovation of primitivism lies in this feminization of male symbols of power plucked from Aztec my-thology and the academic and artistic discourses that have interpreted and defined them.

The Coatlicue state is the site where writing and self-reflection merge, and to communicate the intensity of this experience, Anzaldúa invokes the Mesoamerican cultural practice most vilified in hegemonic narratives of the Conquest and most often effaced from Chicano indigenist narra-tives: ritual human sacrifice. More importantly, however, Anzaldúa con-flates the participants in the ritual, priestess and victim, in a rewriting of conventional archaeological accounts and masculinist-nationalist Chicano narratives. The woman in the short free verse paragraph that introduces Chapter 4 toys with the idea of surrendering herself to Coatlicue: "the obsidian knife in the air/the building/so high/should she jump/would she feel the breeze/fanning her face/tumbling down the steps/of the temple/ heart offered up to the sun . . ." (41). Her emotional perspective is, how-ever, obscured. Either the thoughts of jumping are an attempt at escape or, perhaps, the preliminary considerations of one who willingly presents herself as an offering, as does D. H. Lawrence's character of the Woman in "The Woman Who Rode Away." The Coatlicue state is conditioned by contradictions, the desire to write and to fear writing, the will to live, and the desire to sacrifice one's self to the creative act:

Writing is my whole life, it is my obsession. This vampire which is my talent does not suffer other suitors. Daily I court it, offer my neck to its teeth. This is the sacrifice that the act of creation requires, a blood sacrifice. For only through the body, through the pulling of flesh, can the human soul be transformed. . . . This work, these images, piercing tongue or ear lobes with cactus needle, are my offerings, are my Aztecan blood sacrifices. (75)

The invocation of self-sacrifice combines received ideas about Aztec culture and female nature in a new mythology that privileges women's subjectivity and the vulnerability associated with creative work.[22] In keeping with her vision of mestiza consciousness, Anzaldúa makes clear that the intellectual acts of thinking and writing have deep and profound effects on the body. Writing is personified as a dangerous yet sexually alluring suitor, the vampire, whose demands exact a physical toll. The beloved victim is forever transformed, physically and emotionally. The submission operates as a contemporary version of devotions that attempt to purchase survival and prosperity with human blood. Anzaldúa restructures the ancient relationship between a god/dess and a community of believers, casting herself as the un/willing supplicant who must offer the sacrificial gift in order to receive the reward, in this case, fluid, evocative prose.

The sacrifice, like the gaze into the smoking mirror, leads to an encounter with Coatlicue. As she begins to understand the nature of the serpent, Anzaldúa realizes and accepts that she is also a serpent. In the face of the goddess, she sees her own image. For example, in narrating her childhood bout with the snake in the cotton field, Anzaldúa recalls a dream of herself as snake: "dreamed rattler fangs filled my mouth, scales covered my body. In the morning I saw through snake eyes, felt snake blood course through my body . . ." (26). She is what she fears, the menstruating female, the snake with the "thousand lidless serpent eyes," the woman with Indian blood (51). She overcomes the fear, becomes the goddess, and accepts the "dark Indian self."

In its organization and syntax, and in the appeal to a cultural/political ethos strategically deployed through the use of autobiographical narrative, Anzaldúa's new mythology suggests that it emerges from the depths of the writer's unconscious, a place to which she has built a bridge or passageway metaphorized in the smoking mirror. Her literary imagination may indeed be overdetermined by earlier and later encounters with the serpent in the field and in the archaeological and other texts she consults. Yet, characterizations of the Shadow-Beast and Coatlicue as figures that have persisted in her imagination since childhood mask the debt to contemporary anthropological and archeological discourse: "I was two or three years old the first time Coatlicue visited my psyche, the first time she 'devoured' me (and I 'fell' into the underworld)" (42). Throughout these chapters of *Borderlands,* Anzaldúa writes herself as psychic, as *curandera,* and roots her "gift" in the experience of marginalization, threat, and violence: "Pain makes us acutely anxious to avoid more of it, so we hone that radar . . ." (39). In doing so, she again directs us to the tradition of the modernist artist who taps into the reservoir of primitive knowledge and becomes the shaman, the seer, the other (Foster, "The 'Primitive' Unconscious" 57).

It is necessary, however, to think about the book's citations in their context as works consulted and cited, considering all the information the author provides, not only the personal stories and mythic imaginings. For these techniques of native self-fashioning belie the extent to which *Borderlands'* images have emerged from sources that Anzaldúa does not fail to note, but nevertheless subsumes in her own prose and in the endnotes following the first section of the book.[23] Along with the celebration of the intriguing modes of invention Anzaldúa has initiated, we must also pursue other, equally fascinating lines of inquiry. To acknowledge Anzaldúa's recodification of modernist primitivism is to reveal new paths in her complex and compelling "serpentine" web of meanings.

Certain strands in this web connect *Borderlands* to various sources. An examination of the book's footnotes points to Spanish chroniclers of the Conquest, like Bernardino de Sahagún, and archeological literature on Aztec culture, including the writings of Jacques Soustelle and Karl W. Luckert.[24] Anzaldúa's most compelling use of source material is her dependence upon *Feathered Serpent and Smoking Mirror,* the coffeetable introduction to Mesoamerican mythology by C. A. Burland and Werner Forman. The startling degree of intertextuality that exists between *Borderlands* and *Feathered Serpent and Smoking Mirror* situates the latter as more than mere influence in the conceptualization of new mestiza consciousness.

One example of Anzaldúa's use of the text can be found in Chapter 4 of *Borderlands,* "*La herencia de Coatlicue*/The Coatlicue State." Although conventional archeological interpretations associate the obsidian mirror with an Aztec god called Tezcatlipoca/Smoking Mirror, as noted earlier, Anzaldúa imports the characteristics of the god and the image of the smoking mirror into her Coatlicue state, where Coatlicue, Cihuacoatl, and Tlazolteotl "cluster" (Anzaldúa 42).[25] Writing in the preface to *Feathered Serpent and Smoking Mirror,* Burland and Forman tell readers that "Tezcatlipoca represent[s] the unconscious 'shadow' in the mind" (7). Later, in keeping with their title, they identify Tezcatlipoca as one side of the "basic dualism in Mexican religion" who represents "the equivalent of what might be called the 'shadow'—the side of our human personality that we do not wish to face openly, and which we consequently hide from ourselves" (56). Anzaldúa uses this idea of the shadow as the repressed unconscious, transforming it into the "Beast" of the mestiza psyche. Her creative strategy of foregrounding serpent imagery and smoking mirrors reproduces, even as it reworks, popular archeological accounts of Aztec mythology.

Anzaldúa takes two images from Burland and Forman, the feathered serpent and the smoking mirror, merges, feminizes, and redeploys them to represent the unconscious. A close analysis of her smoking mirror narrative points to its genesis in her reading of Burland and Forman, who describe Tezcatlipoca and the importance of the obsidian mirror as follows:

> The most powerful of earthly spirits was Tezcatlipoca, whose name means Smoking Mirror. This referred to a mirror, made of the volcanic glass known as obsidian, which seers would gaze at until they fell into a trance. Then within the black, glossy surface, they saw pictures which revealed the future of the tribe and the will of the gods. The Aztecs believed scrying was a powerful kind of magic granted to them by this shadowy god. (55)

Anzaldúa calls the mirror a "door of perception" into the Coatlicue state, and in a combination of summary and direct quotation from Burland and Forman, she rehearses its pre-Conquest Indigenous origins:

> In ancient times the Mexican Indians made mirrors of volcanic glass known as obsidian. Seers would gaze into a mirror until they fell into a trance. Within the black, glossy surface, they saw clouds of smoke which would part to reveal a vision concerning the future of the tribe and the will of the gods. (42)

Recognizing Anzaldúa's dependence on Burland and Forman in this instance does not detract necessarily from the original work of *Borderlands*. It does, however, alert us to the fact that there are sources for Anzaldúa's indigenous imagery outside of a Chicana/o archive of personal experience and textual expression. The example of *Feathered Serpent and Smoking Mirror* and its status within *Borderlands*, moreover, provides additional evidence for situating Anzaldúa within a discursive history of primitivism and its reliance on the excavations of archeology.

In her own commentary on primitivism, Anzaldúa has written that "Modern Western painters have 'borrowed,' copied, or otherwise extrapolated the art of tribal cultures and called it cubism, surrealism, symbolism," indicating her familiarity with the practices of modern primitivism (69). The passage that follows highlights her conflicted impulses as both critic and practitioner:

> Whites, along with a good number of our own people, have cut themselves off from their spiritual roots, and they take our spiritual art objects in an unconscious attempt to get them back. If they're going to do it, I'd like them to be aware of what they are doing and to go about doing it the right way. Let's all stop importing Greek myths and the Western Cartesian split point of view and root ourselves in the mythological soil and soul of this continent. Instead of surreptitiously ripping off the vital energy of people of color and putting it to commercial use, whites could allow themselves to share and exchange and learn from us in a respectful way. By taking up *curanderismo,* Santeria, shamanism, Taoism, Zen and otherwise delving into the spiritual life and ceremonies of multi-colored people, Anglos would perhaps lose the white sterility they have in their kitchens, bathrooms, hospitals, mortuaries and missile bases. . . . Let us hope that the left hand, that of darkness, of femaleness, of "primitiveness," can divert the indifferent, right-handed, "rational" suicidal drive that, unchecked, could blow us into acid rain in a fraction of a millisecond. (69)

Like D. H. Lawrence, Anzaldúa imagines the American continent(s) in fundamental relation to Indigenous mythology. But where Lawrence sees America as a place where the non-Indigenous will be devoured, "the open tomb of my race" (quoted in Ellis 7), Anzaldúa argues for the spiritually nourishing potential of *las Américas*. Pérez-Torres sees Anzaldúa's "resurrection of indigenous religious iconography . . . [as] an attempt to reclaim spirituality in the face of ceaseless Western technological advancement" (*Mestizaje* 23). Certainly, it is that. But the passage is characterized by an indecisiveness, an uncertainty, a sustained contradiction, if you will. And it is that conflicted impulse that I noted above, not the familiar injunction, which compels me as a reader.

Initially, Anzaldúa advances a critique of the cultural appropriation associated with Western primitivism when she writes that Western artists have "taken over" the art forms of non-Western people, indicating an act of aggression, an illegitimate expropriation. This practice is the result of a deep impoverishment, in which Westerners have "cut themselves off from their spiritual roots," yet fail to acknowledge the emptiness that propels their pillaging. When later in the quotation she bemoans the "commercial use" to which such borrowings are directed, she intimates that spiritual "art objects" and practices are cheapened by their treatment as material commodities and romanticizes Indigenous cultures as the source of spirituality needed to counterbalance the materiality of the West. "White" culture is finally not only "cut off" from its "spiritual roots," but might very well have none left to reclaim as Anzaldúa locates the sites of rejuvenation forever outside a Western cultural context.

At the very moment that she presents this critique of primitivism, she chooses to redirect the argument and find fault not in the propensity for "borrowing," but, rather, in misplaced interest and unacknowledged motivations. The "right" way to borrow culture, apparently, is to acknowledge the desire to escape or remedy the diminished spiritual state. White people, she says, must look to America and its mythologies to redress the state of psychic unrest brought on by this void. In her use of the term "importing," Anzaldúa suggests that the mythologies revered by the West, those issuing from Classical Greece, are ill-equipped to address an American context. Whites in America would be better served by the Indigenous mythologies of the continent, which have the capacity to interrupt the cycle of destruction launched by Europe and Euro-America. More than sixty years earlier, D. H. Lawrence expressed a similar sentiment when he wrote "Americans must take up life where the Red Indian, the Aztec, the Maya, the Incas left it off" ("America, Listen to Your Own" 90).

Anzaldúa thus recuperates those acts of cultural appropriation consciously committed to reconnecting with the sacred and rejecting the overvalued "origins" of Western culture. In the second major ideological shift in the quotation, however, Anzaldúa abandons altogether the specific promotion of Indigenous American mythology, claiming that whites must look for renewal in the spiritualities of people of color more generally. She offers her suggestions for religious systems from which whites may legitimately borrow, copy, and extrapolate. "[C]*uranderismo*, Santeria, shamanism, Taoism, Zen and . . . the spiritual life and ceremonies of multi-colored people" are posited as the most viable sites in which to pursue the spiritual quest.

Gloria Anzaldúa was obviously aware of the primitivist tradition, reading it, as I did earlier, as an attempt to recuperate and enrich Western culture. Whether primitivist borrowings are viewed in terms of artistic invention, spiritual reconstitution, or social transformation, they always promote quite consciously a critique of Western norms, as does Anzaldúa. Her identification of "kitchens, bathrooms, hospitals, mortuaries and missile bases" as specific sites of sterility is instructive in its negative assessment of modern industrial Western culture, a critique embedded within the brief litany. The list progresses from the domestic private to the institutional public to the classified and restricted military. Conceptually, it invokes automation, post-industrial compulsory models of hygiene, cold institutional spaces, and the detached, yet precise, weapons of postmodern warfare.

Borderlands tries to provide an alternative to the dehumanizing industrial commercial forces of Western thought, against which Anzaldúa positions "darkness . . . femaleness . . . and 'primitiveness.'" Although she gestures toward a rejection of the "Western Cartesian split point of view," her own substitute for primitivism relies upon a fundamental binary model. The basic structure of primitivist thought is in fact based upon the transvaluation of binaries: civilized and primitive, rational and instinctual, industrial and tribal, individual and collective, right-handed and left-handed. Anzaldúa's answer to Western primitivism reiterates those goals in the elaboration of her own. Thus, her challenge to the dualistic thinking reinforces primitivist ideals even as she resituates and renames them.

The appropriation of the indigenous has always been aimed at understanding the mental landscape of the Western subject, at discovering ways to "release" the Shadow-Beasts that plague us by taking cues from those who are perceived to live more truly. In Anzaldúa's *Borderlands,* we can glimpse the elemental connections between modernist primitivism and postmodern cultural appropriations of Indigenous cultural forms, even as the book enjoys a special legitimacy as a validation of retrieved ancestral knowledge. Yet, even as *Borderlands* creates a new myth to represent an emergent historical perspective, it allows the dehistoricizing function of myth to remain untroubled. Most critical treatments of *Borderlands* have done little to engage the text's processes of mythic construction; Coatlicue is left as if she had sprung fully formed from Anzaldúa's mind rather than, at least in part, from the pages of archeology and art history, and the halls of the British and other museums.

Referring to unspecified debates about the historical accuracy of *Borderlands* upon its publication, Emma Peréz writes that "many historians simply missed the metaphor and read too literally" (25). My point is, however, *precisely* to call attention to the metaphor, to recognize the details of its creation, the multiple sites of its origin. It is then possible to understand that Anzaldúa's "new political stance" (Saldívar-Hull 5) is allegorized by a familiar emblem. Consequently, Anzaldúa's notion of the primitive, represented in terms of the Aztec pantheon, and our own fascination with it reveal that our literary understandings of Chicana/o identity and history continue to rely, not only upon narratives more readily associated with the mytho-nationalist projects of the late 1960s and early 1970s, but also, astonishingly, upon dominant European and Euro-American narratives of the Indian in the Americas.

The attempt to give force to mestiza consciousness depends upon the realm of myth as Anzaldúa invigorates Aztec goddesses and gods to populate her critical statements on material reality, historical convention, alternative spirituality, and renegade consciousness. Ultimately, we find that certain features of the primitive have changed surprisingly little in the migration from Anglo and European textual projects to a Chicana indigenist manifesto. Even as the resistant force of *Borderlands* persists, we might ask if the mythologization of Indigenous ancestry does not overlook or even deny challenges to primitivism that Chicana/o critical discourse is poised to announce.

The manipulations of pre-Columbian mythology by del Castillo and Anzaldúa restructure indigenism and nationalism as representations of Aztec religion, and Indian figures are taken from the control of Chicano indigenists and European anthropologists alike. The representational strategies of these authors are linked by their reliance on a colonial and anthropological archive for information, although they operate differently around this question of myth, one motivated by the use of a historical figure and the other characterized by the centralization of Mesoamerican mythic figures. In contrast with Anzaldúa, who revises and embraces the pre-Columbian pantheon, del Castillo rejects it, uncritically relying on the conventions of anthropology to legitimate a position that exists most convincingly in the realm of myth. More importantly, she uses the Aztec pantheon as a negative example of the violence of the Aztec regime, refusing to reclaim it as a Chicana/o cultural patrimony. In del Castillo's essay, we find a feminist indigenism that reifies Native female ancestry and condemns Indigenous ritual human sacrifice.

Yet, even as these feminist answers to masculinist nationalism might reproduce the conventions of anthropology and modern primitivism, they simultaneously reconstruct dominant tropes of Chicana/o criticism. Although we have, on one hand, the transformation of myth into history and, on the other, history into myth, the approaches are unified, finally, by a common result: the refocusing of Chicana/o critical discourse upon the figure of the Indigenous woman. As these writers work to establish an authority that relies on the forged connection between contemporary mestizas/os and pre-Conquest Mesoamerica, Chicana lived experience becomes the culmination of Indigenous history.

CHAPTER 4

The Contra-mythic in Chicana Literature: Refashioning Indigeneity in Acosta, Cervantes, Gaspar de Alba, and Villanueva

C learly, Chicana/o indigenist use of the Mesoamerican mythic has been inventive and productive. As a tool to challenge dominant narratives that positioned U.S. Mexicans as foreign immigrants, as an indictment of state and religious institutions of imperialism, and as a powerful critique of masculinist nationalism and Anglo-American racist patriarchy, the language of indigenism and its reliance on the mythic has yielded within Chicana/o letters a rich terrain of cultural expression. In all cases, however much writers might deploy mythic signifiers to establish Chicana/o indigeneity, there also exists a fundamental attempt to historicize Chicana/o presence in the Southwest United States.

Poetry has given us some of the most passionate and poignant meditations on and assertions of Chicana/o history and identity, beginning with the movement poetry of the early 1970s. And the work of Lorna Dee Cervantes has long been recognized as integral to a resistant Chicana feminist discourse from within the movement. "Para Un Revolucionario" is a pointed poetic critique of the gender politics within movement communities that confined women to domestic work, without recognizing the centrality of that labor to the success of the movement. And her "Poem for the Young White Man Who Asked Me How I, An Intelligent, Well-Read Person, Could Believe in a War Between the Races" (*Emplumada* 35) continues to serve as a rallying call for those who recognize the increasing difficulty of articulating the instances, not to mention effects, of racism in a world where its machinations have become so highly sophisticated, so subtle, that it is often impossible to concretize experiences in a recognizable semantics. Cervantes' poetry reflects her participation in the movement and, to an extent, she seems to embrace its ideology. Her embrace, however, is made unique by a distinctly critical poetic voice that consciously resists the ease of a return to origins of any kind.

Another of our literature's most finely tuned examples of thoughtful and self-conscious poetic critique is the work of Teresa Palomo Acosta. She has published three poetry collections, *Passing Time* (1984), *Nile and Other Poems* (1999), and *In the Season of Change* (2003). In Acosta's poetry, we meet with speakers who move beyond the mythologized, pre-historicized Indian identity that circulates within many indigenist narratives. I pair the two poets because of this critical strain in their poetic work, the inestimable gestures that challenge the established parameters of Chicana/o identity construction. I have chosen two poems, Cervantes' "Visions of Mexico While at a Writing Symposium in Port Townsend, Washington," which appeared in *Emplumada,* and Acosta's "Preguntas y frases para una bisabuela española," from her second collection, *Nile and Other Poems: A 1985–1994 Notebook.* Both poems transgress now-accepted conventions of writing an oppositional Chicana/o identity. They do so through highly distinct strategies that reshuffle Chicana/o inherited narratives of descent and challenge indigenist Chicana/o sensibilities.

In addition, the short fiction of Alicia Gaspar de Alba and Alma Luz Villanueva also provide unusual and provocative meditations on indigeneity in Chicana/o literature. "La Mariscal" and "Free Women" each create a touristic experience in Mexico, approaching the theme with striking similarity *and* difference. Gaspar de Alba's "La Mariscal" focuses on a white male sociologist, Jack, purchasing pleasure in a border bar; Villanueva shows us four Chicana doctors indulging poolside at a resort in "the interior." Like Cervantes and Acosta, the stories call our attention to ruptures that dislodge easy assumptions about particular identity configurations, the tourist, and the Chicana. Gaspar de Alba launches a critique of gringo border tourism as Villanueva casts an eye toward Chicana touristic consumption. The two stories together highlight the fact that the myth-inspired primitivism authored by European and Mexican academics and writers continues to proliferate with remarkable influence.

Teresa Palomo Acosta's Questions to a Spanish Great-Grandmother

Acosta's "Preguntas y frases para una bisabuela española" (*Nile and Other Poems* 25) is written from the perspective of a poetic speaker who reflects on her *Spanish* ancestry, by no means a new thematic in Chicana literature. The privileging of Spanish ancestry is most often associated with a Nuevo Mexicano/New Mexican Hispano tradition, in which recovered autobiographical texts display specific class and racial distinctions, clearly marking the differences among Indian, mestiza/o, and Hispano identities. Recovery work, however, has also located such texts emerging from the experiences of a once-elite Californio ranching class.[1] *Caballero,* a novel written by folklorist Jovita González, who was a native Texan and a student of J. Frank Dobie, and Eve Raleigh, provides further evidence that proving Spanish ancestry was equally important for Tejanos, who might trace their roots to the criollos and Canary Islanders who established San Antonio de Bexár in 1718 or to the Spaniards who settled along the South Texas border in 1749.[2]

Chicana and Chicano literary critics have long since begun the process of reading early Spanish colonial narratives as predecessors to contemporary Chicana/o literary expression. In 1971, Philip D. Ortego (aka Felipe de Ortego y Gasca) located the beginning of the "Hispanic period of American literature" at the settlement of St. Augustine, Florida, in 1565 (296), as he argues for a recognition of the "sleeping Mexican-American [literary] giant [who] has begun to flex *his* dormant muscles" (295, emphasis added).[3] Genaro Padilla has insisted that "[w]e must recover this literature not to celebrate a vanished imperial discourse but to reestablish the lines of a socioideologic complexity that will illuminate the continuity in discontinuity that characterizes the formation of our literature before and after 1846" ("Discontinuous" 32). On the other hand, Chicana critics such as María Herrera-Sobek and Tey Diana Rebolledo have suggested looking to early Spanish *crónicas* and *diarios* to recover a women's history through the "Spanish-Mexicana" presence in New Spain. Herrera-Sobek and Rebolledo view this recovery work as significant to contemporary projects that reinvigorate and valorize Chicana identity.[4]

In understanding that "traditional history is the history of power narratives, defined as primarily political, economic, and military," Rebolledo looks to "evidence of a different kind: folklore, ritual, religious ceremonies, and even food preparation," a strategy that continues the Chicana/o literary critical tradition of "viewing Chicano literature [as proceeding] out of a folk base."[5] She also asks that we read "histories and official accounts in new ways" to recover the experiences of the Hispana gendered subaltern.[6] With no access to texts written by women during the colonial period, Rebolledo argues that nevertheless we can "see glimpses and hints of their lives in songs and plays, *dichos, cuentos,* and *memorate*" (sayings, stories, and memorabilia) ("Y dónde" 141). She also recognizes, as does Ranajit Guha when he speaks of the uses of "elitist historiography,"[7] that "we must understand that the images of women were always presented within male discourses and from male perspectives" ("Y dónde" 140). At the same time, she believes in the possibility, unlike Gayatri Chakravorty

Spivak, that we can "begin to hear the voices of the women themselves, albeit within mediated discourses" ("Y dónde" 141) when oral traditions are transcribed.[8]

My own interests differ from those of Padilla and Rebolledo, who are very much engaged in projects of writing literary histories. Instead, I explore the way in which subjectivity and identity are expressed by reaching backward into narratives of mythology and ancestry. The dominant trend has been, and continues to be, the use of the placemarker of indigenous ancestry to propel contemporary accounts of Chicana/o legitimacy in the United States. There also exist, however, narrative traditions that emphasize Spanish ancestry in the mestiza/o line of descent, although these are often considered narratives of a dispossessed elite, for example, the hacendados of the nineteenth-century Southwest.[9] One finds this emphasis in María Amparo Ruíz de Burton's *The Squatter and the Don,* an autobiography recovered from the mid-1800s and published in 1992 by the Arte Público Press for the Recovering the U.S. Hispanic Literary Heritage Project. The historical novel, *Caballero,* written by Jovita González and Eve Raleigh in the 1930s and 1940s but unpublished until 1996, also fictionalizes a mestiza/o elite emphasis upon European ancestry and culture, but from a twentieth-century perspective. And Pat Mora's autobiography, *House of Houses,* published in 1997, offers a more recent example that places the narrator within a familial and cultural history of Spanish-identified *tías* in the Mora family.

Claiming Spanish lineage might be considered retrograde in the context of Chicano movement activity of the early 1970s and the rise of the symbol of Aztlán. Within and between these realms of Chicana/o discourse, and in the context of their competition for legitimacy, however, Acosta's text emerges as distinct. In contrast with both "Hispanophile" and indigenist narratives, "Preguntas y frases para una bisabuela española" offers an imbricated history of mestizas in the U.S. Southwest, a self-conscious and historically persistent kind of mythopoetics that treats myth not as recovered legacy, but as the imaginings of an insistent and troubled speaker trying to understand the historical complexities of ancestry. Her questions and imaginings deftly move from a playful, yet provocative, invitation to a mythic great-grandmother to tell of her life, to meditations on colonial power relations between Spaniards and Natives, to the phenotypic diversity of mestizas/os and the cultural denigration of contemporary Chicana/o colloquial Spanish. The poem ends on a note of concern, as the speaker wonders just how she and her Spanish great-grandmother will be able to "account" for their shared history.

Reflecting on the novelty of a Spanish great-grandmother—an idea that first hovers at the edge of consciousness, and then attains full recognition and active consideration—a mestiza speaker muses: "Sabe, bisabuela, I just barely thought about you tonight./For the first time considered that I might be related to you." Struck by the anomaly of such a thought, she answers in the next two lines the question of *why* she might not dare to conjure such an ancestor: "Because we mestizas cafecitas con los high cheekbones believe/We're almost ninety-nine percent Indian." Alluding to the "Indian" features in mestiza physical appearance, brown skin and high cheekbones, the speaker confirms her understanding of the commonly held assumption that "the Indian" dominates the mestiza gene pool: "And we may be ninety-nine percent right."

But certain physical and cultural traits cannot be explained through Indian ancestry, such as wavy instead of straight hair, or the centrality of the Spanish language to Chicana/o subjectivity: "Still, como me llamo Teresa Palomo Acosta." In fantasizing about belonging to a great-grandmother "[w]ho spoke totally proper Spanish," the speaker testifies to the effects of institutional denigration of the Spanish language in Texas borderlands. Gloria Anzaldúa discusses this educational practice in "How to Tame a Wild Tongue," a chapter from *Borderlands:*

> I remember being caught speaking Spanish at recess—that was good for three licks on the knuckles with a sharp ruler. I remember being sent to the corner of the classroom for "talking back" to the Anglo teacher when all I was trying to do was tell her how to pronounce my name. (53)

Later in the chapter, she coins a term, "linguistic terrorism," which she uses to refer to the unfortunate practice of "us[ing] our language differences against each other" (58). Anzaldúa points to the challenges to authenticity of which I earlier spoke, that is, the delegitimation of Mexican identity *within* Chicano or Latino communities. In other words, those who more "properly" speak the language challenge the identity claims of others based on a perceived lack of language acquisition and cultural knowledge.

The term can also speak to the literal terrorizing of Spanish-dominant mestiza/o schoolchildren in Texas, a reality to which Anzaldúa refers in the previous quotation. The institutionalized practices of linguistic terrorism, which included public embarrassment and humiliation, corporal punishment delivered at the hands of school administrators, and expulsion for speaking Spanish even in the putative "free zone" of recess, were common well into the 1960s and even 1970s in some areas.[10] Anzaldúa chronicles the violence in her metaphor of the dentist's office and the taming of the wild tongue: "We're going to have to control your tongue," says the dentist as he attempts to perform a root canal. "*Deslenguadas.* [Detongued.] *Somos los del español deficiente . . . somos huerfanos.* [We are those of the deficient Spanish. We are orphans]. We speak an orphan tongue," Anzaldúa writes (58). Acosta's treatment of this internalized understanding of one's "illegitimacy"—the drama of the "bastard tongue"—may not evoke the violent history that Anzaldúa makes explicit for us, but charts an other, equally compelling, path.

Rather than naming a female ancestor to explain a racialized identity, Acosta's speaker looks for one who will allow her to claim fully her linguistic and cultural identity. The speaker indulges a fantasy in which she exhibits her fluency to an ancestor who, she expects, judges her based on the dictates of *el Castellano.* This imagining might well be read as a symbolic reversal of the linguistic positioning of many Tejanas educated in the Texas public school system. Many have refrained from teaching their children their own "bad Spanish." Some might even take courses at local educational institutions in order to learn to speak "totally proper Spanish," an important and valuable skill in the current economic moment. Although later in the poem, the speaker confidently asserts her right to and knowledge of her language, "we pochas know the difference between/ Pues y pos," she nevertheless begins by betraying herself as *huerfana.*

But the desire for ownership of the language and membership in a community of those who speak it "properly" is subverted quickly:

> And so, bisabuela, I need to know—just between us two—
> Did you wear mantillas de encaje,
> A chongo, a trenza, or a shawl?
> Were you a gitana, a castanet-flaying flamenco bailante,
> A pre-fandango mujer, Precursor to us
> Who've grown fond of el tacuachito
> In our mezcla de tambora de rancho y acordeón,
> Un bajo sexto: los beginnings de otra onda. (25)

In deploying "*estereotipos*" of Spanish women, the speaker launches an alternative visual narrative of exotic ancestry. Positioning the pious, shawl-covered Spanish great-grandmother alongside the "gypsy" flamenco dancer, the speaker implicates that proper Spanish speaker, whoever she was, in the evolution of contemporary mestiza culture.

Acosta directly engages both "Hispanophile" and Anglo constructions of the Mexican in America. There is more than a touch of irony as the figure of the chaste, upstanding, and church-going Spanish woman gives way to the flamenco dancer, an image that reminds us of the all-too-common eroticization of "Latin" women. Probably originating in Spain, the fandango, on the other hand, is considered a "native Mexican" dance, and provided no small shock to arriving Anglo settlers in the nineteenth century. Arnoldo De León, in his study of Anglo attitudes toward Mexicans in Texas, writes: "In addition to all their other discoveries about Mexicans, whites in the period between 1821 and 1836 thought Tejanos lax in virtue. A number of aspects of Mexican morality bothered them, including the native *fandango,* a dance of a sinuous sort with sexually suggestive moves" (*Greasers* 9). Noting the important symbolic value of the fandango as a *female* erotic act, De León suggests that "[t]he love of the *fandango* was thought to be universal with the Mexican women, and one of the last pleasures they would willingly renounce" (*Greasers* 37). As with most forms of cultural performance characterized as "uninhibited," "sensual," and therefore "primitive," fandango was further associated with "the poor, the uneducated, the mixed-bloods" (*Greasers* 37). The "fandango mujer," with her excessive sexuality and insufficient capital, finds her precursor in the Spanish great-grandmother, perhaps a flamenco dancer, perhaps a modest and upstanding matriarch. She is, in any case, the direct ancestor of the mestiza speaker.

It is not insignificant that Acosta makes "the Spaniard" female. In doing so, she engages another convention of Chicana/o critical discourse: the metaphor of the Conquest as a rape and the Spaniard as *always* the male rapist.[11] From the outset of the poem, we can see that Acosta's text is no simple recovery of "female voice," but, rather, a complex and self-critical commentary on Chicana/o self-fashioning. Yet, in privileging women's storytelling, recovering and valorizing women's history and experiences, Acosta participates in the larger project of reconstructing a distinctly Chicana history in the Americas.

But she continues to trouble our notions of "the Spaniard" by placing the Spanish great-grandmother and, we could say, Spanish culture more generally, as precursor to Chicano working-class cultural expression and the history of scholarship, principally among Chicano folklorists, that reads such expression as resistance.[12] Furthermore, Acosta's allusion to *"el tacuachito,"* quite the working-class Chicano folk dance, claims a new cultural form that nevertheless evolved from Spanish influences in the speaker's chronology. A "low-dipping," "swaying shuffle" danced to a different tempo than the flamenco or fandango, *el tacuachito* emerged in the late 1940s in South Texas and distinguished the Texas-Mexican polka style, according to Manuel Peña.[13] The conjunto that provided the music included at one time the "tambora," a drum that accompanied the bajo sexto. Of the tambora, Peña writes that it was

> apparently of purely folk origins; that is, it was never commercially pro-
> duced, though the body may have been fashioned from old, second-hand
> parade drums. . . . According to don Pedro Ayala, on a still night the
> sound of the *tambora* could be heard for miles, serving as a primitive sort
> of advertisement that somewhere in the vicinity a dance celebration was
> under way. (38)

Associated with working-class and pachuco culture, these gatherings were to be avoided, Peña writes, "by young men and women *de buenas familias* (i.e., of middle-class orientation)" (140). In fact, conjunto music is still considered to be "low-class" by some. "You'd have to go to a dive to hear that," I was told once, although it is now not unusual for organizations such as the Guadalupe Cultural Arts Center in San Antonio to pay homage to the form with crowd-drawing conjunto festivals.

This reconstructed history that the speaker outlines brings together the racial arrogance of a Spanish colonial woman and the romantic indigenism of a current-day Chicana; it weds the chaste image of religious devotion with the exhibitionism of the fandango and the populism of the *pachanga* (party). It is a history that could be considered scandalous on a number of levels. As the pious great-grandmother's reputation is marred by this Chicana history lesson, so too is the Chicana/o claim to indigenous ancestry being ever-so-slightly readjusted. But this is not the history lesson of an evolving Hispanophile. The challenge is leveled against not only Chicana/o narrative strategies that simply mark "the Spaniard" as male elite, but also the imagined elitism of a Spanish ancestor:

> There's more, bis, bisabuela.
> Were you haughty and arrogant?
> Ready to do in la india clutched by el soldado español
> As he crossed your path?
> Or did you also hide from him
> In a corner of your hacienda? (25)

As we read the Spanish great-grandmother's haughtiness and arrogance as markers of her socio-racial status, we also recognize the attempt to account for the history of conquest and violence that undergirds Chicana/o oppositional narratives. The poem acknowledges Spanish dominance over Native peoples in the Americas and also works to revise a gendered stereotype of the Spaniard. For example, the speaker identifies the Spanish *woman* as an ancestor who committed violence against Native women: "Ready to *do in* la india." She immediately complicates the española's hatred of the Native woman by pointing to their shared fear of the Spanish soldier. The threat of rape, concretized in the image of "la india clutched by el soldado español," and a reality for Indigenous women well documented by historian Antonia Castañeda, is also a threat to the Spanish señora.

Not only does Castañeda illuminate a historical record of violence against Native women in Alta California, she also places that violence within the context of the devaluation of women in relation to men and Indigenous people in relation to Europeans. Castañeda reminds us that the norms of morality and conduct were established for women of the ruling classes, but used to judge all others: "These norms were rooted in questions of the acquisition of economic and political power and of women's relationship to that power" (27). Because Native people were excluded from property and inheritance structures, they were also excluded from the "corresponding concepts and structures of social legitimacy" (27). A Native woman could never be fully authorized as a subject because of her racial, as well as gender identification; therefore, her children would never be considered viable heirs. Because they do not fulfill the primary social responsibility of women, to produce heirs, the Native woman becomes the "bad woman," Castañeda argues, "corrupted, inferior, unusable, immoral, without virtue . . ." (27). The poetic imagining of the Spanish great-grandmother and *una indígena* demonstrates colonial-era relations of power between women of different racial and economic classes. We can imagine the Spanish ancestor deploying the misogynist tools of patriarchy to establish her own legitimacy through the ideological devaluation and physical oppression of the Native woman.

A strategic "or," however, reveals another version of the Spanish great-grandmother: "Or did you also hide from him/In a corner of your hacienda?" (25). Rather than the figure of the angry woman on the offensive, ready to "do in" the brown woman (the object of the Spanish soldier's desire, as well as hatred), the second image depicts one who *also* seeks a retreat from his aggressions. The relationship between *la señora* and *la india,* however, is clearly not one of easy alliance or solidarity. For, as Acosta's speaker makes apparent, any interaction between the two is marked necessarily by power differences.

This power dynamic is made apparent through the class and race signifiers Acosta includes. As I said earlier, the "haughty and arrogant" de-
meanor of the Spanish female ancestor, the great pride in herself and the
disdain for others, reflect a class and race consciousness that distinguishes
her from *la india*. She is pictured in an "hacienda," which indicates the
privilege, in relation to a husband, father, or brother, of course, of land
ownership. One imagines the Native woman hiding, not in her own hacienda, but in a dwelling of significantly less proportion and comfort.
Although the great-grandmother may hide *like* the Indian woman, but in
her own house, the "also" might *also* indicate that they hide in the same
house. I am not suggesting a parallel between the Spanish colonialist and
the dispossessed Native. I mean, rather, to return to Acosta's intertwined
vision of the two. If the Native woman were indeed *also* hiding in the hacienda, she is certainly not there as *la señora*. The two hide in the hacienda
as master and servant.

Feminist literary criticism has addressed the importance of the colonialist female subject in the civilizing mission abroad. Critics such as Rosemary Marangoly George and Cynthia Enloe have made interventions that
insist upon the significance of female authority in the colonies.[14] This
authority was effectively deployed in the realm of the domestic, where
settler women were responsible for "managing" domestic workers. The
duty of the colonialist mother was to rear good citizens, a responsibility
that played no small part in perpetuating the "civilizing" mission right
inside the home. In other words, Native domestic workers, as infantil-
ized colonial subjects, fall within the purview of the colonialist female's
"opportunity to function as contributing national subject" (George 101).
George challenges Nancy Armstrong's claim in *Desire and Domestic Fiction*
that "the modern individual was first and foremost a female"(66, quoted
in George 97), instead arguing that "the modern [eighteenth-century]
individual woman was first and foremost an imperialist" (George 97). As
George claims further, "This authoritative self was defined against a racial
Other in encounters that were located in space that was paradoxically domestic as well as public: the English home in the colonies" (George 97).
Servants to colonialist women were therefore marked as non-authoritative
Others not only by economic positioning, but also by racialized identity:
these servants were not white. The recognition of the domestic sphere as
a site of imperial power and authority, however mediated by a larger patriarchal colonial context, is useful in teasing out the nuances of Acosta's
poetic language.

Acosta's detail effectively alerts us to the power dynamic set in motion between a Spanish female colonialist and a Native woman. Her speaker tries to confront the contradictions that her musings uncover, the most profound being her historical relationship to both the conquering Spaniard and the dispossessed Native. She considers this confrontation a challenge that nevertheless will help to make sense of the dissonances in Chicana/o history:

> Oye, mi bisabuela
> These days I have to face the música,
> Figure out how our lives intertwine
> Even though we got colored in so many tints:
> This high café
> This café con crema,
> This crema con strong black tea
> And this crema solita. (25)

The task she assigns to herself is to "face the music." The use of this common expression, inflected by Acosta's movements between Spanish and English, suggests an obligation to *admit* to something, to own up to a situation that one has perhaps been avoiding. The responsibility subtly expressed by this mestiza is that of *facing* a truly mestiza history, one in which the "ninety-nine percent" Indian narrative is joined to the history of a Spanish great-grandmother. Again, Acosta's poetic language refracts multiply, a richly complex expression of mestiza identity. The speaker of the poem points out the wide variations in skin tone among Chicanas that might not be immediately considered European: the high coffee color, the cream-colored coffee, the cream darkened by the "strong black tea," and the cream alone. Indigenist discourse assumes the predominance of the Indian in mestiza/o phenotypes, and Acosta's poem supports this assumption to a degree. The "presence of the Indian," many would argue, dominates mestiza phenotypes. Chicano critic Alfred Arteaga has made this point: "For while the miscegenation had to begin in a one to one ratio, Spaniard male to Indian female, the subsequent course of the mestizaje was overwhelmingly Indian" (11). But Arteaga, and Chicano literary criticism more generally, have been unable to account for the nuances of more troubling "historical facts," such as the Mexican history of Indian-hating and exploitation of Native labor. Acosta's poem can edge us toward unhinging these unexamined placemarkers of Chicana/o identity.

In the final verse paragraph, the speaker's gesture of good will and friendship toward the Spanish great-grandmother symbolically enacts the possibilities for a community understanding of this polyvalent mestiza history: "Te mandan saludos y abrazos/Y yo también."[15] Yet, in her final words to *la bisabuela,* we again note the speaker's ambivalence, the persisting sense of unease, and the recognition of the high stakes she has waged:

> But I'm still worried about all that responsibilidad
> We both carry:
> To set some crooked things en nuestra historia
> At least at a slant,
> If not straight,
> Between us (25)

Speaking of "nuestra historia," our history, as "crooked," suggests that much has been bypassed; historical narratives have taken routes perhaps not altogether appropriate to or functional in representing the complexity of mestiza history. The final line is richly ambiguous: "Between us." Perhaps the line refers to the history of "we" mestizas, or perhaps the interwoven histories of the *española* and the mestiza. In either case, the concluding lines suggest an attempt to figure out how lives and histories intertwine and an attempt to straighten the crooked to at least a slant. Invoking the opening assurance to the fantasy great-grandmother—"just between us two"—the final line suggests that the idea is maybe just to get the story straight between two women. But there is also the matter of history, and how it is written, and how it is produced. The now slanted trajectory articulates a new historical narrative, one that extends from the Spanish great-grandmother to the "ninety-nine percent Indian" mestiza.

"Preguntas y frases para una bisabuela española" transgresses accepted conventions of writing a progressive or oppositional Chicana/o identity. Such conventions have demanded a rejection of "the Spaniard" even as Chicanas/os claim intimacy with the Spanish language and a group identity that stems from it. The poet alludes to the conflict between Spaniards and Indians, a contentious history that certainly involved women on both sides, but she also troubles easy oppositions that anchor indigenist self-fashioning. *La española* and *la india* represent the symbolic paternal and maternal grandmothers of mestizas/os. In between is *el soldado español,* the son of *la bisabuela* and the rapist of *la indígena.*

Furthermore, Acosta subverts Chicano indigenist nationalism by asserting the possibility of affiliation through gender, even as she problematizes that affiliation by subtly interweaving the history of colonialism. Hinting at the potential for solidarity between women threatened by patriarchy and militarization, she simultaneously acknowledges particularities that made and continue to make such alliances impossible. Foregrounding the Spanish language as the *link* to repressed Chicana/o narratives of conquest, Acosta reveals the tensions that exist between claiming, at once, marginality based on a collective linguistic identity—that is, "Spanish-speakers"—and marginality based on the ancestral identity of "Indian." In doing so, Acosta seems to bring her speaker closer to conveying a linguistic and cultural identity that may seem to oppose the indigenist narrative—Spanish *is* a colonial language, after all—while at the same time insisting on the historicization of mestiza racial identity. Indigenism has enabled the celebration of a uniquely denigrated aspect of Chicana/o identity, dark skin, a reality of existence for which we must account. But I suggest here, and I believe Acosta suggests as well, that such an accounting must *be* an accounting. In other words, the accounting is not simply a report of or offering of the reasons for, but a *reckoning with* painful, and even shameful, facts of mestiza/o history.

I would like to return to an early section of the poem, the narrative of origin that explains mestiza physical appearance through its "Indian" features: "And we may be ninety-nine percent right." It is within the realm of that remaining one percent that Acosta is able to launch an other narrative of mestiza identity and history, one that we may recognize as, rather than crooked, maybe a bit more *honest* in its accounting of and for the past, one that reflects a fuller range of *mestizaje*—its nuances, its valences, and even its repressed secrets.

Resisting the Return:
Chicana Subjectivity in Cervantes' *Emplumada*

Like Acosta, Lorna Dee Cervantes takes up "pocha," or Anglicized, identity, while more directly engaging the idea of Mexico. Her highly acclaimed collection of poetry, *Emplumada,* appeared in 1981, placing her on the cusp of a decline in popular support of a Chicano cultural nationalist agenda. The second third of the collection is signaled by the following epigraph, a quote taken from the Italian poet, Antonio Porchia: "This world understands nothing but words and you have come into it with almost none." Indeed, this collection is self-consciously about language, about claiming it, crafting it, and yet remaining alienated from it. This tension is played out in texts that exhibit a sense of inadequacy with Spanish: "The words are foreign, stumbling/On my tongue" ("Refugee Ship," *Emplumada* 41). The speakers in Cervantes' poems are unable to make authoritative claims, such as "know[ing] the difference between pues y pos" (Acosta 25). Both poetic personas are alienated from the Spanish language and unable to assume fully Mexican identities. But while Acosta's pocha speaker asserts legitimate knowledge of Spanish, the woman in Cervantes' "Oaxaca, 1974" struggles with the recognition of her ignorance: "I didn't ask to be brought up tonta!" (*Emplumada* 44).

The paradox of linguistic identity and its centrality to Chicana cultural identity intersect with Cervantes' sophisticated commentaries on racialization. Cervantes also creates speakers who appear to understand profoundly and painfully the contradictions that Chicana/o indigenism and nationalism have left untroubled. In other words, "brown bodies" and "bronzed skin and black hair" do not necessarily grant a prerogative to a "Mexican" identity, particularly one that relies on familiarity with the Spanish language and/or assumptions about Indian ancestry. Finally, however, the unsettling recognition is that it is the *English* language that empowers a female speaker to represent "her people's" history and struggles: "And as pain sends seabirds south from the cold/I go north to gather my feathers for quills" ("Visions," *Emplumada* 47).

But images of birds and the sea also characterize the entire collection, and texture Section II with a predominant theme: migration. This was noticed by Marta Sánchez, who wrote the following of "Visions of Mexico While at a Writing Symposium in Port Townsend, Washington":

> The major structural device of this poem is the theme of migration, and the central image is the migrating bird that is always in transit between one home and another. The theme of migration has strong implications for a Mexican-Chicano community whose history has been shaped by patterns of migration, both internal (within Mexico and within the United States) and external (between Mexico and the United States). Like the migrating bird, the speaker hovers between two homelands, Mexico and the state of Washington, identifying with each place but also alienated from each. (97)

The speaker most strongly associates herself with the seabird, a migrating bird that Cervantes evokes in other poems as well. As Sánchez suggests, Mexican patterns of migration are present in the metaphor of the migrating bird and the speaker's own pattern of migration. Her status in each place finds expression in the image of the seagull. Although seagulls, some of which migrate, encourage ideas of travel and return, they are also well suited to articulating Cervantes' accompanying reflections on language. In "From Where We Sit: Corpus Christi," another poem in the second section of *Emplumada*, the first-person persona speaks in the plural and claims knowledge of the seabird's language:

We who have learned the language
They speak as they beg
understand what they really say
as they lower and bite. (33)

Rather than alluding to the harmonious melodies of songbirds, the learned language is compared to the discontinuous nasal-sounding bursts of Corpus Christi seagulls. Seagulls are often considered a nuisance, particularly along beach areas and especially when unwitting tourists answer the calls for food. The expectation of an enjoyable interaction with the local wildlife is dashed quickly as the seabirds continue to insist, "mispronouncing" the pleasant and lilting sounds birds are supposed to make.

As do other poems in this section of *Emplumada*, "Visions of Mexico" wrestles with the turmoil of landlessness, being without a homeland. In Mexico, the speaker of "Visions" imagines herself liberated, a desire expressed through the metaphor of molting feathers. Feathers figure as "the old words," the constraints of which are lifted as she sheds them. But the title, "Visions of Mexico While at a Writing Symposium in Port Townsend, Washington," highlights the fact that what follows is a constructed and romanticized *vision*, or mental image, of Mexico, which is initially figured as homeland in the poem. The second verse paragraph of this first section of the poem, titled "México," also works against the impulse to ground identity in the recovery of an Indigenous past. Unable to make the subsequent claim to geographic territory, the Chicana speaker effectively denaturalizes this poetic rendering of her claim to homeland. The romanticized vision of Mexico exists most powerfully when she is *not there*, as communicated by the grammatical structure of the opening line: "When I'm *that* far south, the old words/molt off my skin, the feathers/ of all my nervousness" ("Visions," *Emplumada* 45). By using a pronoun that designates something farther away or *other*, "that," Cervantes' poetic persona places herself clearly somewhere else. She is in a place where she retains her "old words" and where the "feathers of [her] nervousness" do not molt off. She is at a writing symposium in Port Townsend, Washington, imagining Mexico.

The use of Indigenous place names such as Michoacán, Tenochtitlan, and Oaxaca is not incidental. As she builds her vision of Mexico through references to present-day signifiers of Indigenous cultures, the speaker places herself squarely within a tradition of Chicana/o identity construction that announces Indigenous ancestry and first presence in the Americas. The iteration of a "Chicana/Indian" identity, however, is short-lived:

> I watch and understand.
> My frail body has never packed mud
> or gathered in the full weight of the harvest.
> Alone with the women in the adobe, I watch men,
> their taut faces holding in all their youth.
> This far south we are governed by the law
> of the next whole meal. We work
> and watch seabirds elbow their wings
> in migratory ways, those mispronouncing gulls
> coming south
> to refuge or gameland. (45)

Her status as observer, rather than participant, betrays the reality of her position. The reckoning with her lack of experience in stereotypically Indigenous activities, such as packing mud for adobe or gathering *maíz* during the harvest, reins in a potentially indulgent indigenism. This maneuver is complicated, however, by a sudden rhetorical shift: "This far south we are governed . . . ." The speaker's identification shifts temporarily from her place in the north, envisioning the south, to being *in* the south: "*This* far south . . . ." Again, the subtle shifting of the pronoun, from connoting something farther away to referencing something close to the speaker, has significant effect. The speaker now places herself within the south, although it is a different south than the México she initially idealizes. "*This* far south," she is part of a community that lives from hand to mouth, able to earn only enough to provide, or perhaps not, "for the next whole meal."

Cervantes continues to dismantle the "vision" of Mexico throughout the poem. After relying on stereotypical touristic images of Native Mexican culture—images that might likely be linked to the archaeological and ethnographic (Indigenous sites, ancient handball rituals, adobe, harvest, *maíz*)—the speaker jars the ideal by admitting the limits of her knowledge. The indigenous-sounding names, the handball courts of Mitla in Oaxaca that evoke imagined events of ritualized sport, the pastoral hills that overlook acres of *maíz,* these are *all she knows* of her México: "I don't want to pretend I know more/and can speak all the names. I can't" (45). She is, perhaps, just like the "mispronouncing gulls" that migrate and scavenge along the way, indulging in poetic affiliation with the people of Mexico whose lives are governed by the laws of transnational economics and migration of labor. She, too, travels south for "refuge or gamelands," seeking haven, but also seeking pleasure.[16]

Admitting her alienation from a language that is not her own "old words," she confesses that she cannot speak the names that in the previous version of the vision "somersault as naturally as my name." What she knows of this land, Mexico, ripples through her veins, not like blood, but like the "chant of an epic corrido." Within Chicana/o academic discourse, the corrido—a narrative song that both records and disseminates historical events of usually male heroism—is read as a response to cultural conflict. The corrido as a form of Chicano cultural expression is bound intimately to the notion of contextual resistance and political critique, an idea that remains Américo Paredes' foundational contribution to Chicana/o studies and border studies.[17] That it is the image of a corrido coursing through mestiza/o veins, rather than blood, allows Cervantes to privilege the function of culture in the construction of identity. The poetic persona challenges naturalized visions of "blood-consciousness" or familiarity with Mexico based on the retrieval of an ancestral past. The corrido serves as historical record, making known historical events that have heretofore not been narrativized in written form: "I come from a long line of eloquent illiterates/whose history reveals what words don't say" (45). As records of injustice, corridos also communicate the resistant acts of communities that have been wronged: "Our anger is our way of speaking,/the gesture is an utterance more pure than word"("Visions" 45). Teresa McKenna writes:

> Despite changes in its form and content, the corrido has survived because of its power to recall paradigmatic resistance to political and cultural domination. For example, whereas the classic corrido tells the tale of an individual hero, others exalt the image of a collective persona as hero of a community. . . . The corrido gives form to the Mexican's struggle for survival in oppressive times and in an environment once positive but now sapping and hostile. (14)

The injustices faced by Tejano and other rural communities from *this* side of the U.S./Mexico border in the nineteenth and early twentieth centuries persist in the urban locales to which Mexicans have migrated.

In the concrete jungle, reliance on perception and reflex reemerge as the guarantors of survival. Precise gestures emphasize and clarify meanings that remain unspoken, yet entirely understood: "We are not animals/but our senses are keen and our reflexes,/accurate punctuation." As violence against and within communities persists in the "knifings . . . low-voiced scufflings, sirens, gunnings" of urban space, the recorder of history, the poet, howls, both in sorrow and against oblivion: "We hear them/and the poet within us bays" ("Visions" 46).

The second section of the poem, "Washington," places the speaker in the north. The place in which Cervantes locates her speaker mirrors the geographic location of the poet—perhaps Cervantes, perhaps not—who sits in a writing symposium, sharing work, receiving feedback, and imagining Mexico. "Washington" alludes to a U.S. "Founding Father," George Washington, first president and leader of military campaigns against Native peoples in the Northeast, but it also refers to a state in the Pacific Northwest that is now home to large numbers of Mexican-descent migrant workers who followed the crops north and then settled there. Nevertheless, the situation presents us with a slight irony as the poet finds herself in Port Townsend, trendy and coastal, rather than in the Yakima Valley agricultural basin. In the north, the poet/speaker confronts stereotypes of another Mexico as a "stumbling comedy/A loose-legged Cantinflas woman/acting with Pancho Villa drunkenness" (46).

This second section carries out the parallel structure of the poem, which illustrates Mexico from southern and then northern perspectives. In each section, the second verse-paragraphs provide the poet's commentary on extant imagery (Mexico as agrarian, Indian, and economically disenfranchised, and also as ridiculous, yet eroticized). In these final verse paragraphs, the poet communicates both her desire to represent more accurately the experiences of her community and the painful understanding that it is in the north, in Washington, that she is able, ironically, to equip herself with the words through which she can articulate that history.[18] Yet, she is at home in neither place, as Sánchez rightly observes, and in *either* place still very far removed from the corrido composer. It is through the process of migration that she is (un)able to unify her identity. Her alienation from both places is finally a valuable creative space in which she can dismantle stereotypes and create new imagery. She does not "belong this far north," but neither does she belong that far south, where she must remain honest about what she does not understand and is unable to speak.

But it is the songs in her head, perhaps corridos, that would displace these commodified versions of Mexican culture—mariachis, caricatured machismo (Speedy Gonzalez, Pancho Villa)—that circulate in the north. In order to translate those songs, however, the speaker needs "words." She compares her accumulation of them to an act of illicit lovemaking in which the words are "nymphs between white sheets of paper." The words she desires are figured as feminine, obedient, and obligatory, perfectly accommodating to her use.[19] Marta Sánchez interprets the final stanza and its interlacing of the images of feathers and writing as "[t]he unifying of two extremes in the mythic bird [Quetzalcoatl, union of bird 'quetzal' and snake 'coatl']," a resolution of the "tensions between poetry and community, oral and written, high and low, north and south" (103). But I would suggest that the effect of Cervantes' poetry, particularly the texts I have chosen, is not to attempt, but to *preclude* resolution. The tensions that reside in Cervantes' work are neither solved nor resolved. Their heuristic potential in relation to Chicana/o identity construction lies precisely in the lack of resolution, the failure of the attempt to explain. In this sense, she is one of the poets whose writing perhaps most accurately reflects the realities of Chicana/o experiences and the limitations of nationalist, indigenist, and even some feminist narratives. Chicana/o identity is contradictory, unsettled, unresolved, racially ambiguous, geographically unmoored, and linguistically compromised:

> as pain sends seabirds south from the cold
> I come north
> to gather my feathers
> for quills ("Visions" 47)

These final words redeploy the image of the Chicana self as migrating seabird. Her pain, however, does not emerge solely from her experiences in the north. In the south, alienated from the Mexico that she imagines and encounters, ill-equipped to communicate in her "own words," she must return north to gather again the "old words" of the English language in which she is fluent: "obedient words obligatory words words I steal/ in the dark when no one can hear me" (47). Ironically, "the old words" are those with which she is most familiar, the words that she accumulates surreptitiously for subversive use. They are words that she perhaps has no "right" to claim, but nevertheless, they obey her and are bound to follow her purpose: to write and speak the experiences of people excluded from written histories.

We can look toward another poem in that second section of *Emplu-*

mada, one mentioned earlier, "Oaxaca, 1974," to understand more fully the complexity of Cervantes' engagement with "Indian Mexico." Again, signifiers of Indigenous culture are noticeable, especially as the city and state of Oaxaca are heavily associated with Indigenous communities in the discourses of tourism and anthropology. In *Zapotec Women,* anthropologist Lynn Stephen provides the following information about Oaxaca in the 1980s, soon after the publication of *Emplumada:*

> The state of Oaxaca holds several distinctions in relation to the other thirty-one states of Mexico. Located in the south, next to Chiapas, Oaxaca is one of the most heavily populated indigenous areas of Mexico. Approximately 35 percent of the population of Oaxaca is defined as indigenous according to languages (Instituto Nacional de Estadística, Geografía e Informática, 1984:I:1275). Currently there are fourteen different indigenous languages in Oaxaca, including Amuzgo, Chatino, Chinanteco, Chocho, Chontal, Cuicateco, Huave, Mazateco, Mixe, Mixteco, Nahuatl, Triqui, Zapoteco, and Zoque. In 1980, there were 347,006 Zapotec speakers (Instituto Nacional de Estadística, Geografía e Informática 1984: II:633). (64)

"Oaxaca, 1974" is again a poem about alienation from language and the fact that cultural socialization has a greater purchase on identity than do ancestral bloodlines. The awkward name of the literal poet, "Lorna Dee," tags along as reminder when the speaker compares her name to a "loose tooth" (*"Oaxaca"* 44). The Anglo-sounding name resists her easy assimilation to Native ways of thinking and being. Reminding everyone of her national and cultural identity, it is an obstacle to attempts to forge a new identity grounded in Mexico and, in particular, the streets of Oaxaca.

The city and state attract significant tourism because of the communities of Native peoples and their festivals. The speaker, therefore, looks for her vision of México in the streets of one of the most "indigenous" cities in the country. The "words of another language" may be Spanish, but might also be the words of a non-European language. The children who sell their wares in the Zócalo and plazas of the city are often Indigenous and, while conversing with buyers may speak Spanish, but often use Indigenous languages when communicating with each other or with other members of their communities. The speaker in "Oaxaca, 1974" is confused, unable to see or think in the midst of laughing children in the city. Anzaldúa's image of the mestiza who finds herself "norteada"—a far more popularized version of the confused mestiza—is imbued with an alternative significance when one reads back into the Chicana poetic archive.

Cervantes deeply challenges the idea of an inherited "consciousness" or identity grounded in biology. The speaker of "Oaxaca, 1974" thinks "white," indicating her socialization in Euro-American North America. She looks for a way to become more native, but does not understand the language or the mores: "My brown body searches the streets/for the dye that will color my thoughts" (44). In describing herself as a "bland po-chaseed," she illustrates her lack of development, feeling both indistinct and immature, lacking language and culture. This is an idea stated more explicitly in "Refugee Ship": "Mama raised me without language./I'm orphaned from my Spanish name" (41).

Compounding the sense of alienation, however, is the fact that the poet/speaker *looks* Mexican, or perhaps even Indian: "My brown body" she writes in "Oaxaca, 1974," and "I see in the mirror/my reflection: bronzed skin, black hair" in "Refugee Ship." Here Cervantes addresses an issue that Acosta also takes up, that is, the need to account for a racialized identity. The more legitimate subjects might be Mexican nationals, Chicanas/os who speak Spanish well or "properly," or Native people in Oaxaca whom she might expect to respond to her with recognition. In all cases, however, the speaker must confront the fact that she does not belong and is not claimed: "But México gags,/Esputa!/on this bland pochaseed" ("Oaxaca, 1974" 44).

Through her meditations on language, race, and geography, Cervantes unmoors the assumptions of Chicana/o oppositional identity construction. Denying her speakers access to homeland, even as she identifies migration as a Chicana/o experience, Cervantes' poems preclude and resist the mythologization of history and culture. Cervantes places Indian Mexico in contemporary moment, 1974, thereby granting it a coevalness that is denied in indigenist nationalism and certain forms of indigenist feminism.[20]

Borderlands Azteca: Alicia Gaspar de Alba's "La Mariscal"

The setting of Alicia Gaspar de Alba's short story, "La Mariscal" casts a familiar stereotype: a white American male sits in a border bar drinking tequila and beer. He has money in excess, enough to tip his server twice as much as his drinks cost, enough to elicit the bartender's help in pursing the object of his erotic interest, enough to secure the sexual attentions of that woman for a time. The place is the "combat zone," as Jack Dublin calls it, or "la mariscal," as it is called in Spanish, a pleasure strip that sits just inside *that* side of the U.S./Mexico border, across from a nameless town and a nameless university at which Jack is employed as a professor of sociology. Perhaps the only real surprise in Gaspar de Alba's border tale is Jack's identity. He is a white academic who crosses the border to engage in activities more often associated with white college students transgressing the drinking age laws of the United States and the rules of social decorum that govern their everyday behavior. "La Mariscal" makes apparent, however, that the excesses of border tourism are enjoyed by a much wider population (not to target academics certainly) than we might typically assume.

The narrative casts another familiar image, one that is typical enough in the Chicana/o cultural arts and in critical discourse: the Aztec. Gaspar de Alba feminizes the conventional version of the Aztec warrior, choosing instead to create the fantasy of the Aztec princess in the middle of a Mexican border bar. And it is in the interactions between the East Coast academic and the borderlands princess—the admiring and assenting looks, the extending of and accepting of the gift of a drink, the unsolicited touching and the resistant response, the aversion to and insistence on smoking, and, finally, the exchange of currency—that "La Mariscal" reveals to us, on one hand, the seductive power of an image and, on the other, the asymmetrical power dynamics of transborder relations.

Jack encounters Susana in a bar called the Red Canary. He has chosen to separate from "[h]is colleagues from the Sociology Department [who] were watching the strip show across the street at the Mona Lisa Club, the most popular brothel on the Mariscal" (41) in favor of "drink[ing] quietly for a few hours, maybe even buy[ing] himself some company for the rest of the evening" (41). He spots Susana sitting at the bar with a drunk GI and is immediately captivated by the incongruence of her regal beauty and what he perceives to be the reason she is in the Red Canary:

> He looked towards the bar again, where the GI had fallen off his stool, and realized that the girl beside the GI was a working girl, though she didn't look it from the way she was dressed. It was really the drunken soldier who gave her away. With her smooth, olive complexion, the bloom of peacock feathers in her blue-black hair, her embroidered Mexican dress, she looked more like an Aztec princess. Maybe she wasn't a working girl, after all. The GI got back on his stool and looped his arm around her neck. Wrong, Jack, he said to himself, taking a long draw on his beer. (42)

Jack is seduced by the figure of the Aztec princess, although the degree to which Susana cultivates the image is not clear. As fetish object, however, Susana's intentions are irrelevant. Jack's desire and the meanings that he attaches to this particular Mexican woman's body fuel the encounter, with Jack advancing on the hope or belief that the Aztec he sees before him represents something genuine, authentic, more than an empty carica- ture, even as he simultaneously reminds himself of Susana's actual role in the bar. He conceives of his sexual attraction as a desire to "serve Susana, kneel before her and taste her native blood, swallow the Aztec seed of her, save her from the cage of the Red Canary" (45). The irony of this fantasy is that she really has to serve him, yet he is able, theoretically at least, to pur- chase the illusion that his servitude is desirable. The strictly consumptive nature of his lust is revealed in the wish to "taste her native blood," which actually places Jack in role of dominator rather than servant. Figuratively speaking, he becomes the agent of a ritual human sacrifice in which, ac- cording to conventional accounts, the victim's heart is carved from her chest and eaten by the Aztec priest.

Susana recognizes Jack's fantasy and insists to him that she is not "a working girl." She tells him that she is from Chihuahua, that she is not a bar employee, and that she is waiting for her sister, a nurse in the back. The bartender, however, confirms for Jack what the gringo suspects. Her name is Berta, the bartender says, but she uses Susana with the gringos. In the final scene of the story, Jack enters a smoke-filled room in the back, after having been inspected and passed through by the nurse with the red cross tin into which he deposits a dollar. He sees Susana sitting on a bed underneath a velvet painting of an "Aztec princess offering her bronze breasts to the conquistador" (46). The velvet scene inscribes Jack's illu- sion, that he is the conquistador and Susana the Aztec princess, despite her working girl identity, despite the fact that she has filled the room with smoke after he has told her that the image of a woman smoking "molests" him, redeploying Susana's mistranslation of the Spanish.

Although Jack finds a different Susana when he enters the room, we are given the impression that he is not deterred. With the molesting ciga- rette in her hand, false eyelashes, and red lipstick applied, she is no longer the untouched ingénue, the Aztec princess. She has instead contaminated the illusion, subverted it, choosing to announce its inauthenticity and to make its constructed nature all the more obvious. Our last glimpse of the two is when Jack reaches out to kiss her and she turns her head away. "I don't kiss for money" she says (46). Susana effectively shatters Jack's fan- tasy of the Aztec princess whom he can conquer, exposing the contractual relationship between them and setting the limits for their encounter.

In her analysis of "La Mariscal," Catrióna Rueda Esquibel reads Susana as fully aware of the particular contours of Jack's desire for an Aztec princess. Certainly, the feathers in her hair unequivocally signify "Indian," and her application of make-up and insistence on cigarette smoking suggest a conscious tarnishing of the public image she has presented in the bar. Esquibel argues that Gaspar de Alba's "postmodern princess prostitute" (61) shifts the terrain and alters the conventions of the Aztec princess narrative that "romanticizes and effaces the sexual violence perpetrated against native women of the Americas" (63). Rather, Gaspar de Alba's version exposes "the colonial sexual fantasy, ironizes the Anglo male academic and the wish fulfillment in play in his construction of 'the' Mexican woman" (63). Esquibel interprets the final scene as the disruption of Jack's fantasy and the illusion of sexual control he imagined exercising over Susana, who retains power and has the last laugh at the joke that is the gringo john.

True, Susana/Berta appears to establish the boundaries of the transaction even as Jack has paid her to do his bidding. We are left, perhaps too optimistically, with the impression that she remains inaccessible to the presumptuous Jack. The seemingly obvious exertions of will—playing hard-to-get, choosing to smoke when she knows that Jack does not like it, making up her face to destroy the "purity" of the Aztec princess—suggest concrete exercises of agency in which she maintains a form of power over Jack. Her observable disdain for him, her aloofness, and her disobedience all convey dislike, disrespect, and disingenuousness, characteristics that readers applaud in her treatment of Jack. Susana may end up allowing him access to her body, but according to rules that she has decided upon. The game, however, is not of her own design.

The conclusion of the story might suggest Susana's/Berta's ultimate power and control in her relationship with Jack. Our reading of this abrupt conclusion of Gaspar de Alba's short story perhaps offers us a slight sense of satisfaction that Susana has gotten the best of Jack. In actuality, what likely occurs is that Susana is left to engage in sex with a man that she does not know and seems not to like; she is to allow him access to her body and then prepare herself to do it all over again. In the end, Jack still has money and a gendered and racialized national identity that signifies and deploys power. Even if he does experience some sort of public humiliation—public in that it is witnessed by bartender, nurse, and, most immediately, the princess—Jack will still have the power to reenter the Red Canary at a later date, cleansed of his humiliation, his newly regained authority procured with the symbolic currency granted to "gringos" in recognition of their dominance in the world order.

"La Mariscal" also turns our attention to the debate regarding sex work within feminist studies. That debate is crystallized in the character of Susana, a Third World female sex worker. One of the questions to address regards the highly circumscribed reality of Susana's agency. While that agency should not be denied (she *does* say she will not kiss on the mouth and we probably assume that Jack conforms), another theoretical problem involves the pressure on sex workers to partition themselves in some way, to abstract emotions from the experiences of the physical body. Given the likelihood that Susana's sexual interactions with Jack might well be distasteful, undesirable, physically uncomfortable, and perhaps even painful, a woman in her position conceivably must engage in some sort of abstraction in which the activities being performed by and upon her body are recategorized as occurring to another body, not her own. The question becomes whether prostitution represents an exercise of Susana's, or any other woman's, rights or a violation of them. To claim the latter is to afford her no agency and to claim the former is to ignore the very real relations of power that structure the relationship between her and Jack; the reality that enables him to secure her attention and her body from another man, a transfer of goods facilitated by the bartender who helps Jack carry out the drunk GI. Additionally, the story highlights the material context of border sex work, as Esquibel also notes (63). Berta/Susana's situation is contained within a racialized economic order in which Jack is an agent of the state, a civilian functionary who can strengthen the structures of domination both by creating knowledge about natives of the border zone as well as by playing his part to perpetuate an economic system that constantly redistributes power from brown to white, from women to men.

"La Mariscal," at its most obvious level, works as a critique of male misogyny exercised through gringo fantasies of the exotic. But the story also invites readers to dwell upon the symbol of the Mexican Indian, namely, the Aztec and even more specifically, the Aztec princess or "Native Woman," to recall the term popularized by Norma Alarcón. We very often encounter the Native woman as a victim in Chicana/o critical discourse, yet in this story we question whether Susana is indeed solely a victim. Gaspar de Alba's representation remains reminiscent of narratives of objectified Indian women who enable cultural exchange, or even dominance. We could take La Malinche as a case in point. If we imagine that La Malinche exhibited the confidence of a Susana/Berta in those Conquest-era exchanges with Cortés, we might well be able to augment feminist readings of Doña Marina that cast her as agent of her own destiny. Still, we are left with the final chapter of her life as we know it—rejected by Cortés in favor of his European wife, transferred as property to another man, and divested of her role as parent to the child fathered by the conqueror. None of this seals Susana's/Berta's fate, however, and we can recognize the exercise of power by two women—one a character of fiction, the other an at-times fictionalized historical figure—as they negotiate the narrow limits of their potential and actual influence.

On the other hand, Gaspar de Alba's story also offers to us a critique of the fetishization of the pre-Columbian Native woman, a call to be aware of its artifice. "La Mariscal" demonstrates starkly the seductive power of the Indian as the author deploys a version of the Native woman that has not yet received much attention, one who manipulates Indianness for its alluring power. Gaspar de Alba creates an illusion of the Aztec princess to satisfy the fetish of a gringo john. The critique is directed most clearly toward Anglo romanticizing tendencies as the story seems to suggest that all the Mexicanos are somehow in on the joke being played on Jack. Chicanas/os presumably share the insider knowledge of the barroom employees, disdaining Anglo desires for the ethnically esoteric and exotic and the quest for access that drives the white "culture vulture." So where does a Chicana/o history of Indian fetishism fit in here? In the end, "La Mariscal" leaves that history untroubled.[21]

Chicana Tourism and the Ethnic Fetish:
Alma Luz Villanueva's "Free Women"

Alma Luz Villanueva's "Free Women," from her collection *Weeping Woman: La Llorona and Other Stories,* targets quite explicitly the Chicana First World touristic subject in Mexico. The scene is a resort hotel pool, where four Chicana doctors lounge during time off from a professional symposium. María, Marta, Yolanda, and Consuelo amuse themselves, at Marta's urging, by sharing their fantasies of the perfect orgasm. A white shell is passed among them and as each tells her story, she holds the shell to her forehead. They giggle and cast glances at the Mexican men by the pool, all the while unaware that they are being mercilessly ridiculed as pocha tourists by the people who serve them.

Mexican contempt for the Chicanas is made most apparent through the interactions of Consuelo, a child psychologist, with the twelve- or thirteen-year-old server, known only as "the busboy" or "the boy," a Central American refugee. Recognizing Consuelo's secretive glances at him and surmising correctly that the women find him attractive, if young, the boy begins to imagine compensation beyond the generous tips were he to make himself available sexually to "La Doctora Puta," Consuelo. As he casts his eyes upon and appreciates her breasts, he fantasizes about the black motorcycle that he wants and muses over the fact that "[m]y father's dead and I have nothing" (72).

The boy's ruminations are preceded by a brief history of his and his mother's flight from their homeland after the disappearance of the father and oldest brother. They arrive in the Mexican resort where she "[takes] in laundry, sewing, catering to the tourists" (72) while he works as a busboy at the hotel. He thinks of his mother's warning "to stay away from the tourist women. 'They're all gringas, no matter what color they are. Mujeres sin vergüenza. They pay you for what's between your legs, just like a man pays a woman. ¡Qué putas!'" (71)

The story makes much of the women's status as tourists in Mexico, a status that might seem to be complicated by their racial and cultural identity as Chicanas. But the mother's words highlight the narrative assumptions about Mexican views of Mexican-Americans. Despite their phenotypic similarity to the workers, the cultural identity assigned to them is "gringa." Racial identity becomes not a matter of skin color, but of national positioning. Additionally, the Chicanas' gringa status is assigned based on their behavior. The men around the pool, while smiling and playing the role of welcoming hosts, see in the women's dress (the choice to wear bikinis) and drinking habits (successive margaritas) evidence of their corrupt moral status, as well as their cultural difference.

We find similar perspectives in the conversation between Lupe and Juanita, two hotel workers, as they discuss the women on their way home. While Lupe thinks wistfully about how different her life would be if she had the freedom of the Chicana tourists, Juanita condemns them as "whores." The last portion of their conversation reveals, as Gaspar de Alba's "La Mariscal" implies, a Mexican manipulation of tourist gullibility. The women speak briefly about the bag of shells that Lupe takes home for her children to paint and sell to the tourists. The two mimic the expected delight gringas will take in the charm of objects that are probably not recognized as having been created for the sole purpose of fulfilling touristic desire. This practice of collection is linked to the history of exportation—through coercion, manipulation, theft—of Indigenous artifacts from their sites of origin. At this point in time, however, foreign travelers are no longer able to secure authentic pre-Columbian artifacts to take home and display in their curiosity cabinets. Such items are rare and their removal from the country illegal. Neither do these objects made by the children classify as "authentic" native art. As tourist art, their production is motivated by the presence of foreign travelers, their designs conceived to fulfill the longing for access to and possession of something beautiful, magical, and primitive.[22]

Again, the joke is on the gringa tourist who does not see that ethnic authenticity is here manufactured for her consumption. Lupe feels some guilt for manipulating the tourists in this way, telling Juanita that "it's like stealing" (77). Ultimately, however, both Lupe and Juanita, like the men at the pool, recognize the women as sources of income, but not for a minute as *familia*. And the shell that operates as empowering aid to the Chicanas' rejection of the repressive limitations on sexual expression and experience becomes here a symbol of their naiveté and predatory consumption.

As his mother's counsel reverberates in his mind, the boy is able to see himself as provider of sexual services to Consuelo, the one who seems most interested in him in spite of herself. Ironically, his mother has planted an idea for action, rather than succeeding in turning him away from the tourists. The boy imagines himself as commodity and Consuelo as consumer and, at the end of the story, passes a note to her that says "I like you, Señora" (72). Consuelo later responds with a whispered "Tonight" (79).

The final paragraph reveals Consuelo's thoughts as she lies tanning in the sun, after she has issued her answer to the busboy:

Consuelo smiled, spreading her legs to the hot Mexican sun. She wanted her innermost thighs to darken, to burn. She wondered, suddenly, what it felt like to have your heart cut out of your body. Would you be able to see it, for a moment, in the priest's bloody hands? She shivered with fear and excitement and continued to lie to her friends, so leisurely, in English. (80)

Although Consuelo has been positioned as the devourer, the mother who consumes the child in violation of the standards of acceptable female behavior, in this last scene she imagines herself relinquishing authority, giving herself over to the "hot Mexican sun" and the Aztec priest, a fantasy not altogether different from the Woman's in D. H. Lawrence's "The Woman Who Rode Away." The association of Mexico with the death-wish is a touristic image that recalls most particularly for us here Lawrence's writing, but is also evident in Malcolm Lowry's *Under the Volcano* and in Graham Greene's *The Power and the Glory*, to name only a couple of examples. Most interesting in the case of "Free Women," however, is that the narrative appears quite consciously to place the Chicana tourists within the tradition of gringo tourism and travel in Mexico and makes its critical point most convincingly in the introduction of Aztec imagery.

Consuelo's fixation on ritual human sacrifice and her daydream of herself as sacrificial victim again challenge the usual, although not complete, Chicana/o indigenist omission. Consuelo's role as the offering evokes Anzaldúa's treatment of the theme in *Borderlands,* in which she uses sacrifice as a metaphor for the toll exacted upon one by the writing process. In "Free Women," however, Consuelo's indulgent fantasy prompts us to recognize, not the Native status that Anzaldúa's text attempts, but, rather, the character's distance from the host culture and the structured limits of her understanding of *el otro lado.* Her fascination with death wishes and blood thirst once again direct us toward an archaeological record that has been made available in public culture through the museum, the travelogue, the novel. This archaeological record has been transformed into a primitivist narrative that emphasizes Aztec religious hierarchy and a barbarity that is assumed to lie just beneath the surface of contemporary Mexican civilization. Consequently, Villanueva's final portrait of Consuelo exposes her positioning as a First World Chicana subject inoculated by the history of primitivist renderings of Mexico.

Reclamation and Transformation: Chicana/o Literary Indigenism

I have called these works by Lorna Dee Cervantes, Teresa Palomo Acosta, Alicia Gaspar de Alba, and Alma Luz Villanueva "contra-mythic" because they direct attention to Chicana/o indigenism: its naturalization of a socially constructed racial category, "Indian," and its links to the anthropological archive mentioned earlier. Although I make no argument here regarding intent—I do not assume that any of these authors wrote specifically to critique indigenism—their texts nevertheless lead to insights that can urge us toward a reassessment of some of the accepted strategies of indigenist writing.

I have brought the analyses in *Blood Lines* to bear upon a wide-ranging selection of literary texts. While trying to expose subtle features of both European and Chicana/o indigenism, I have also tried to acknowledge the empowering and transformative potential of Chicana/o indigenist thought. The inventive approaches to pre-Columbian myth that we find in Anzaldúa, Alurista, del Castillo, and Valdez are in no way diminished by their shortcomings, or by the contra-mythic approaches of the writers in this last chapter.

Stuart Hall has argued for a recognition of the "constant transformation" that so characterizes the production of identity:

> Far from being grounded in a mere "recovery" of the past, which is waiting to be found, and which, when found, will secure our sense of ourselves into eternity, identities are the names we give to the different ways we are positioned by, and position ourselves within, the narratives of the past. ("Diaspora" 225)

Hall speaks of the ways in which we place ourselves within historical narratives. In the case of Chicanas/os, it is within narratives of the Conquest of the Americas and Anglo-American settlement of the U.S. Southwest, most particularly, that we have struggled to be heard.

Since the movement activities of the late 1960s and 1970s, Chicanas and Chicanos have marked their place as the colonized in this history, a gesture effected through the reclamation of an indigenous past, or indigenous ancestry. Naming ourselves as "colonized" or "subaltern" has both granted access to the image—facilitating interventions in classrooms, history books, and self-representation—as well as closed off avenues of production deemed inappropriate to re-presenting a Chicana/o oppositional identity. Taken together, the readings in *Blood Lines* urge us to dwell upon the relationship between Chicana/o indigenist identity construction and the histories of collection and interpretation that have structured European and Euro-American knowledge of pre-Columbian Mesoamerica. We are then in a better position to address the implications of using Aztec and other forms of Mesoamerican myth to place Chicanas/os in history.

Coda

C hicana/o indigenism emerges in relation to the complex histories of "discovery," theft, and exhibition that made popular knowledge of pre-Columbian Mesoamerica possible. State and private economic sponsorship of excavation, removal, and preservation of artifacts, and the global circuits through which these objects moved, enabled European and Euro-American pursuit of the pre-history of Mexico, whether from the floor of the museum space or the trenches of the archaeological site. Before the institutionalization of archaeology and anthropology, the production of this knowledge was first the province of Spaniards present at the time of the Conquest, or those who arrived in post-Conquest "New Spain" to govern, missionize, and militarize. Mexican prehistory also became the domain of usually very wealthy men who cast themselves in the role of the "lone explorer," setting off into the jungle, the desert, the lowlands, and the highlands of the Other.[1]

When Mexico achieved independence in 1821, this field of inquiry that had been dominated by Europeans was reorganized in the pursuit of a national identity that would unify and distinguish creole and mestizo populations struggling to define themselves against the colonial power. This state ideology, the beginnings of which Florescano and Bernal locate in "Creole anxiety" of the seventeenth century, would eventually become known as *indigenismo,* and in the Mexican post-Revolutionary period, it achieved some of its most famous expressions in the work of artists and intellectuals such as Diego Rivera and Manuel Gamio. Leading up to this period, European artists had been taking note of pre-Columbian artifacts, visually impressed by monumental sculptural forms and oddly seduced by the exoticism of human sacrifice, with Georges Bataille as the most prominent example of the latter.[2] In the era of Modernism, writers and visual

artists launched a version of primitivist thinking that began to include ancient Mesoamerica. The pantheons and plastic arts of the Aztecs reached
new audiences through the work of figures such as D. H. Lawrence and
Henry Moore, at the same time that the Mexican state was solidifying the
centrality of Tenochtitlan in Mexican nationalist self-fashioning.

The Mesoamerican imaginings of Chicana/o writers both disrupt and
continue a history of narrative absorption with pre-Conquest civilizations
of the Americas that has accounted for particular strains of primitivist
cultural expression. The sources of the pre-Columbian material accessed
by Chicana/o indigenist writers have not been confined to the elite spaces
of the academy. Indeed, since the Conquest, chronicles and interpretations of Mesoamerican cultures have been made available for popular
consumption, creating and nourishing the desire to capture the mystique
of civilizations believed to be at once fundamentally barbaric and emi-
nently advanced. The indigenism of writers like Alurista, Rendon, Valdez,
Anzaldúa, and del Castillo were at times developed in academic contexts.
During the period of movement indigenism, Alurista was studying at
San Diego State College, where he received his Bachelor of Arts degree
in 1970 and helped to found Chicano Studies in 1968–1969. Similarly,
Anzaldúa worked on *Borderlands* while in graduate school at the University of California Santa Cruz. Clearly, the work of Adelaida del Castillo
conforms to particular conventions of academic scholarship, and her essay
was presented at an academic conference. Yet, the academy is not the only
environment in which to pursue a curiosity in pre-Columbian religion
and culture. Anzaldúa saw the Coatlicue statue in a Museum of Natural
History. Teatro Campesino pursued their Theater of the Sphere outside of
the academy, consulting sources that challenged traditional Mesoamerican scholarship, although other material, such as the *Popul Vuh,* was made
available precisely because of academic interest.

The pre-Columbian anthropological and archaeological archive is not
the sole influence on Chicana/o literary indigenism, yet it is time to acknowledge its presence. Doing so will certainly alter the cultural constel-
lation of indigenism. It will also resituate Chicana/o literary discourse,
illuminating intertextualities and creative borrowings that complicate the
practices, old and new, of identity construction. Hal Foster has called for
a counterdiscourse to primitivism that would anchor what conventional
primitivism "sets adrift" (52). Chicana/o indigenism has tried to anchor
itself in the history of conquest, a project that has at times been thwarted
by the constraints of primitivist discourse.

Chicanas/os occupy a peculiar place as a mestiza/o population in the

Americas, which alerts us to the multiple forms that indigeneity takes. With little access to institutional and other structures of indigeneity in the United States, Chicana and Chicano writers have explored other ways to assert the relationship to land. These strategies have not always been effective, or displayed an awareness of their fuller ideological context, yet they convey attempts to make sense of Chicanas'/os' status in the Americas and to situate ourselves in history. The mythification of Indigenous history that characterizes Chicana/o indigenism has set itself against the primitivizing impulses of early anthropologists and modernist novelists. But the reliance on and manipulation of Mesoamerican myth, and the use of "Indians" as emblems of resistance or vessels of critique, are not new projects. Although Chicana/o indigenism may mobilize Indigenous figures as versions of the cherished Self rather than the barbaric Other, the practice of elevating the Indian past does not break radically with existing and dominant traditions.

Chicanas/os have added layers of invention to traditions that have already been reinvented by Mesoamerican studies scholars trying to piece together pre-Conquest culture and history from the fragments that escaped Spanish zealotry. The idea that "original" meaning could ever be arrived at, even with access to original pre-Conquest artifacts, is dubious. Original contexts are forever inaccessible and the specificities of those cultural signs rendered perpetually elusive.

Chicana/o indigenism is at times aware of its own paradox, that is, the longing for a pre-colonial past that can never be known. The allure of Indigenous myth is strong as it may seem to provide a new grammar with which to challenge European and Euro-American domination of Native America. Thus, the critical discussion of indigenism is so very important because it remains one of the grounds upon which resistance to empires, old and new, finds expression.

Notes

Prelude

1. Miguel León-Portilla writes that "by the mid-sixteenth century, children of Spaniards and indigenous women were numerous" (*Endangered Cultures* 109). León Portilla takes this information from Francisco A. de Icaza's *Diccionario autobiográfico de conquistadores y pobladores de Nueva España,* published in 1923. León-Portilla also tells us that "toward the middle of the seventeenth century there were more than three hundred thousand mestizos" (110) and "[c]alculations of New Spain's population toward the end of the eighteenth century demonstrate that of approximately six million inhabitants, nearly a third were mestizo" (112). Martha Menchaca troubles this simpler version of Spanish-Indigenous *mestizaje,* as does Gloria Anzaldúa. See *Recovering History, Constructing Race: The Indian, Black, and White Roots of Mexican Americans* (2001) and *Borderlands/La Frontera: The New Mestiza* (1987).

2. This social education can perhaps be summarized in terms of my own childhood experiences as a viewer of a popular eco-conscious advertisement featuring a Native man sitting on a pinto and sorrowfully regarding a choked, polluted stream. The indictment of U.S. society and its avaricious consumerism and consumption is crystallized in the single tear slowly trickling down his face. Obviously, what we encounter here is the Indian as Noble Savage passing quiet, gentle, somber judgment on Euro-America. The poster version of the advertisement, "Pollution: It's a Crying Shame," was designed for the Keep America Beautiful campaign and distributed by the Advertising Council, Inc., in 1972 (Berkhofer 138). The actor, identified as Iron Eyes Cody, effectively embodies "two standard images of the Indian: the image of the stoic Indian (who never weeps) and the image of the Indian who respects nature and possesses an ingrained sense of ecology . . . an effective countercultural use of a reverse image to make a point about ecological concerns" (138).

3. At the time of León-Portilla's translation of the manuscript known as *Séptima relación,* held in the Bibliothèque Nationale de France (BNP), the significance of Chimalpahin's work had not yet been realized. Since that time, the number

of additional materials attributed to him has more than doubled in size. Susan Schroeder, an editor and translator of Chimalpahin's work, has argued that a text previously attributed to Bernardino de Sahagún, *Exercicio quotidiano,* for example, is written in Chimalpahin's hand ("Annals" 6), as well as the single known contemporary copy of *Crónica Mexicayotl,* authorship of which is usually assigned to Hernando de Alvarado Tezozómoc (2). Chimalpahin manuscripts have been located in Mexico (1971) and Cambridge, England (1983). Also, Chimalpahin's own copy of Francisco López de Gómara's *Conquista de México* (1522), complete with corrective marginalia, was found in Yuma, Arizona (6). The spelling of a portion of the chronicler's name varies, at times appearing as "Quauhtlehuanitzin," at others as "Cuauhtlehuanitzin." I have chosen to use "Quauhtlehuanitzin" in keeping with Lockhart, Schroeder, and Namala in their 2006 editing and translation of a manuscript titled the *Fonds Mexicain 220,* housed in the BNP and published as *Annals of his Time* (2006). Now-published works by Chimalpahin also include *Compendio de la historia mexicana. Extracts from a lost manuscript* (1975); *Historia Mexicana: A Short History of Ancient Mexico* (1978); and *Codex Chimalpahin: Society and Politics in Mexico, Tenochtitlan, Tlatelolco, Texcoco, Culhuacan, and Other Nahua Altepetl in Central Mexico. The Nahuatl and Spanish Annals and Accounts Collected and Recorded by don Domingo de San Antón Muñón Chimalpahin Quauhtlehuanitzin* (1997).

4. Carrasco calls it the Museum of Anthropology, but Bernal identifies it as the National Museum of Natural History (322).

5. "Aztec" as a term was popularized in the nineteenth century by European and Anglo-American anthropologists and archaeologists; "Mexica" probably more closely resembles the name by which the "Aztecs" referred to themselves. "Nahua" refers to historic and contemporary Nahuatl-speaking people of Mesoamerica. The Aztecs were but one group of Nahuatl speakers among many. For example, the Tlaxcaltecas, who aligned with the Spanish against the Aztecs, were and are Nahua as well.

6. The hall contained, according to Florescano, "the Stone of the Sun, the Coatlicue, the Tizoc Stone or Cuauhxicalli, a Chac-Mol brought from Yucatan, the colossal head of Coyolxauhqui, some feathered serpents, and other pieces of enormous proportions" ("Creation" 93).

Introduction

1. The theorization of colonial administrative discourse was, of course, launched in the work of the Subaltern Studies Group, although colonial discourse analysis covers quite a broad range of textual genres.

2. See "'Primitive' Thinking and the 'Civilized' Mind" in *Myth and Meaning,* 16.

3. Andrew Von Hendy provides a cogent overview of critiques of Lévi-Strauss' theories of myth. See *The Modern Construction of Myth,* 231–251.

4. In drawing out the relationship between myth and the Left, Barthes argues that there can be no myth on the Left because myth is anti-revolutionary. The Left, in Von Hendy's parsing of Barthes, "has no ideology of everyday life of

its own but can only borrow from its bourgeois antagonist; it has no 'fabulizing' power to invent myth for itself because 'the Left always defines itself in relation to the oppressed (Barthes 148)'" (293). Finally, however, Von Hendy contends that "myth as ideology is limited by its purely antithetical status; it is locked in endless dialectical struggle with its mortal enemy" (338).

5. Rubin footnotes his use of "tribal," explaining that it is not used in the anthropological sense, but, rather, according to the definition in *Webster's New International Dictionary, 2nd ed.*: "Any aggregation of peoples, especially in a primitive or nomadic state, believed to be of common stock and acting under a more or less central authority, like that of a headman or chief" (74 n.1). The use of the term in his essay, Rubin argues, highlights features of the Western "primitivist perspective" and does not attempt to describe actual so-called primitive peoples.

6. In MOMA's description of the 1907 painting, "five prostitutes seductively invite the viewer into a splintered and faceted space that confounds our understanding of the image." According to MOMA, the painting is "often celebrated as a cornerstone of modernism" and represents "a pivotal work in the development of modern art and in The Museum of Modern Art's permanent collection" (*"Les Demoiselles de Avignon"*).

7. Foster quotes from Rubin's "Modernist Primitivism: An Introduction": "We owe to the voyagers, colonials, and ethnologists the arrival of these objects in the West. But we owe primarily to the convictions of the pioneer modern artists their promotion from the rank of curiosities and artifacts to that of major art, indeed to the status of art at all" (Foster n.10, 47). Sally Price details this history of expropriation of material artifacts from Indigenous communities in *Primitive Art in Civilized Places*.

8. In Foster's reading, Rubin's terminological argument makes the primitive neither "dead" like the archaic nor historical, thus banishing it "into a nebulous past and/or into an idealist realm of 'primitive' essences" (52).

9. She continues: "However, they did have a significant impact on several individuals in Picasso's circle in the prewar period" and lists André Derain, Diego Rivera, David Alfaro Siqueiros, Henri Rousseau, and Guillaume Apollinaire (38).

10. See Brassaï's *Picasso and Company*, 242.

11. For an extensive history of Mexico's presence at World's Fairs, refer to Tenorio-Trillo, especially the analysis of the Mexican Pavilion at the 1889 Paris Exposition, Chapters 4–8.

12. See Read 47–64. In an 1888 letter to Emile Bernard, Gauguin writes that Van Gogh had advised that "the future is to be the painters of the tropics, which have not yet been painted" (102).

13. The Mexican state declined to participate in the display not only on the advice of a prominent Mexican historian, Francisco del Paso y Troncoso, but also, argues Mauricio Tenorio-Trillo, because "[t]he truth was that, in terms of exoticism, for Mexico one Aztec Palace was enough, and the government was reluctant to disperse its theatrical effect in various palaces" (85).

14. Read quotes from *Complete Letters of Vincent Van Gogh*. Benjamin Keen mistakenly attributes this quotation to Paul Gauguin, having misread Read. See Keen 510.

15. Catherwood also authored his own volumes, such as *Views of Ancient Monuments in Central America, Chiapas, and Yucatan.*

16. In the 1930s and 1940s, Holly Barnet-Sánchez argues, pre-Columbian art achieved a wider reception in the United States, promoted through museum culture as part of government efforts to strengthen relations between North, Central, and South America (180). Franklin Roosevelt's administration approached hemispheric unity as a necessary protection against the rise of fascism, and it was during this time that the Office of the Coordinator of Inter-American Affairs was created and Nelson Rockefeller named its first leader (177–180).

17. Barbara Braun documents this trend in relation to the personal history of Henry Moore (95–98).

18. Braun's article on Moore beautifully displays photographs of the artist's work juxtaposed with the pre-Columbian sculptural models from which he drew inspiration. These reproductions represent the fundamental influence of pre-Columbian art on Moore's work with stunning clarity.

19. Recent examples include Josefina Saldaña-Portillo, "Who's the Indian in Aztlán? Re-Writing Mestizaje, Indianism, and Chicanismo from the Lacandón" and Guisela Latorre, "Gender, Muralism and the Politics of Identity: Chicana Muralism and Indigenist Aesthetics." Martha Menchaca's "Chicano Indianism: A Historical Account of Racial Repression in the United States" is unconventional in this regard.

20. Domingo Francisco de San Antón Muñón Chimalpahin Quauhtlehuanitzin, Fernando de Alvarado Tezozómoc, Diego Muñoz Camargo, Juan Bautista Pomar, and Fernando de Alva Ixtlilxóchitl all either produced or safeguarded manuscripts narrating the history of pre- and post-Conquest Mexico.

21. Alan Knight clarifies the two terms through the lens of integrationism, with indigenism as an integrationist movement and Indianism as anti-integrationist. Knight continues on to establish several different forms of Indianism, one of which is a "vicarious romanticization of Indian history and culture, usually on the part of urban middle-class mestizos: parlour Aztecófilos, 'erudite contemporary idolaters,' as Octavio Paz has called them, people straight from the pages of Lawrence's *Plumed Serpent*" (81).

22. According to the Yale-Edinburgh Group on the History of the Missionary Movement and Non-Western Christianity, Bonfil-Batalla was responsible for convincing the World Council of Churches to become involved in the controversial discussions being held in the field of anthropology regarding the collusion among religious missionaries, anthropologists, and colonial regimes. See Andrew F. Walls and Lamin Sanneh, "Missions and Human Rights: A Conference Prospectus" www.library.yale.edu/div/theme2.htm.

23. Forbes writes that he circulated the "mimeographed manuscript," entitled "The Mexican Heritage of Aztlán (the Southwest) to 1821" through "the Movimiento Nativo-Americano in 1962 and 1963 to Chicanos in California and the Southwest. As far as is known, this was the first use of the term Aztlán to refer to the Chicano homeland" (17).

24. See, for example, Alfredo López Austin and Leonardo López Luján, *El Pasado Indígena.*

25. Martha Menchaca offers an excellent and detailed analysis of racialization

and land claims immediately following the Treaty of Guadalupe Hidalgo. See *Recovering History, Constructing Race: The Indian, Black, and White Roots of Mexican Americans,* Chapter 7, "The Treaty of Guadalupe Hidalgo and the Racialization of the Mexican Population," 215–276.

26. Gloria Anzaldúa acknowledges this feature of Chicana/o history repeatedly in *Borderlands/La Frontera: The New Mestiza.* More recently, Martha Menchaca has conducted an auto-ethnographic examination of the presence, and absence, of African ancestry in her own family. See *Recovering History, Constructing Race: The Indian, Black, and White Roots of Mexican Americans.* Additionally, Evelyn Hu DeHart's work on the Chinese in Latin America is invaluable. See, for example, "Coolies, Shopkeepers, Pioneers: The Chinese of Mexico and Peru (1849–1930)"; "Racism and Anti-Chinese Persecution in Mexico"; and "Immigrants to a Developing Society: The Chinese in Northern Mexico, 1875–1932."

27. Jack Forbes advanced this premise (151) and this is indeed a grounding principle of sorts in Bonfil-Batalla's *Mexico Profundo,* although, of course, the context is Mexico.

28. Martha Menchaca's recent work offers the most sustained treatment of this issue to date. See *Recovering History, Constructing Race: The Indian, Black, and White Roots of Mexican Americans.*

29. Critics have argued in Mexico and in the United States that the Zapatista rebellion is not an Indigenous rebellion, but one that mobilizes categories of national identity and citizenship. See Saldaña-Portillo 404. Nevertheless, it remains important to recognize the persistent goal of the Zapatista movement to improve, first and foremost, the lives of Indigenous peoples.

30. *La Voz de Aztlan* advances positions that are at the fringes of Chicana/o political discourse. Although few might challenge allegiances to the Zapatista movement expressed in the pages of *La Voz,* many would distance themselves from the conspiracy theories promulgated in articles on the World Trade Center bombing and U.S. support of Israeli military campaigns.

31. Martha Menchaca, focusing on citizenship and racial legislation from 1848–1947, argues that many Mexican-descent people, particularly those of "predominantly Indian descent," experienced legislative pressure to claim "Mexican/mestizo" rather than "Indian" identity following the Treaty of Guadalupe Hidalgo in 1848. See Martha Menchaca, "Chicano Indianism: A Historical Account of Racial Repression in the United States." For a different perspective, see Tomás Almaguer's *Racial Fault Lines: The Historical Origins of White Supremacy in California,* in which he carefully delineates the historical differences between Mexicans and Indians in California, particularly as manifested in citizenship, indenture, and vagrancy legislation.

Chapter One

1. For example, Burr Cartwright Brundage, *The Fifth Sun: Aztec Gods, Aztec World,* 102–128; C. A. Burland and Werner Forman, *Feathered Serpent and Smoking Mirror,* 43–53; and Enrique Florescano, *The Myth of Quetzalcóatl.* In Florescano, see Chapter 3, especially the table of interpretations, and Chapter 4.

2. Michael D. Coe dates the middle pre-Classic period from 1200–400 BCE and the late post-Classic, the period of Aztec civilization, from 1200–1521 AD.

3. L. D. Clark provides a detailed list of Lawrence's sources in his introduction to the 1987 Cambridge edition of the novel (xxv n.49 and xxxii n.89).

4. Ross Parmenter, in *Lawrence in Oaxaca: A Quest for the Novelist in Mexico,* names Zelia Nuttall as a significant source because of Lawrence's visits with her in 1923 and 1924. Parmenter argues that the influences of the archaeologist's *Principles of Old and New World Civilizations* (1902) are "striking and unmistakable" in *The Plumed Serpent* (292). Parmenter commits at least one factual error, however, when he writes that when Lawrence met Nuttall, she had published only two books, when, in fact, she had published many more by that time. Parmenter also contends that Lewis Spence's 1923 *Gods of Mexico* was Lawrence's source for Aztec cosmology, based on the novelist's description of the five suns in "Corasmin and the Parrots," a sketch from his *Mornings in Mexico* (1927), as well as on artist Dorothy Brett's own memoir of her time with the writer, *Lawrence and Brett: A Friendship.* See Parmenter, 91.

5. Although the influence of psychoanalysis on Lawrence has been debated, he had at least passing familiarity with the field. In spite of the fact that he is known by biographers to have read only Jung's *Psychology and the Unconscious,* his own critiques of Freudian psychology, i.e., *Psychoanalysis and the Unconscious* and *Fantasia of the Unconscious,* were trenchant. Biographer David Ellis in his 1998 book, *D. H. Lawrence: Dying Game, 1922–1930,* comments that although Lawrence "disparaged" Jung's work, "he did in fact adopt several of its positions against Freud in his own psychology books" (646, n.13). More importantly, Ellis comments, "Like DHL . . . Jung was led to feel strongly that the Indians could help whites to find a better way of life" (647, n.13). I was directed to the above Jung quotation by Dirk Laureyssens, whose website brings together string theory, big tube theory, and, in the midst of all that, a discussion of the uroborus. See www .mu6.com/uroboros.html.

6. Richard F. Townsend, *The Aztecs,* 77.

7. This appropriation of the eagle and serpent myth may be seen as part of the practice of dispossession whereby Indigenous subjects in Mexico are denied access to their own ancestral sites as well as to the production of knowledge about their history. This is, of course, in addition to the profound and devastating acts of state and private expropriations of land that continue to displace Native peoples in Mexico.

8. John Worthen discusses Lawrence's penchant for frugality and timely payment of bills (160). Mabel Dodge Luhan, one of Lawrence's repeated hosts, writes that "Lawrence really had very little sense of leisure" (68), and later details his attempts to teach her to mop floors, an endeavor at which she admits her lack of success (74–75). Similarly, in a passage often referred to by Lawrence biographers (for example, Ellis 61), Witter Bynner tells of Lawrence's first stay at the poet's house en route to Taos in 1922: "In the morning I was up ahead of the alarm clock for once, to make sure that the guests should have a decent breakfast. . . . Every dish had been washed. The table was laid with an ample breakfast. The bed had been neatly made in the room beyond. . . . Just then my maid appeared from across the street where she lived; but the Lawrences had finished a complete job. The maid looked ashamed; but the guests were beaming as well as hungry" (7).

9. Williams states that Lawrence "takes over the major criticism of industrialism from the 19th century tradition," which he inherits from Thomas Carlyle in particular (*Culture and Society* 200).

10. See E. P. Thompson, "Revolution Again! Or Shut Your Ears and Run," *New Left Review,* 6 and Hall, 32–35 of same issue.

11. *Mornings in Mexico* (1927) is an especially striking case in point.

12. *Letters IV* indicates that Lawrence's correspondence with Luhan did not begin until November 5, 1921.

13. Kinkead-Weekes writes that "the same issue carried a rejoinder by Walter Lippman, and the issue of 5 January a protest against Lippman by Mary Austin" (858, n.8).

14. Rudnick says that "Lawrence stressed the importance of America's lack of a past and traditions. He expressed his belief in the possibilities of a new aesthetic arising from a continent that had the opportunity to regenerate its art and society. . . . Although Lawrence was never of one mind about the Indians, he shared Mabel's belief that the Indians cherished some esoteric life secret. While he was aware of the materialism of the East, he was optimistic about the Indian West" (194). Kinkead-Weekes summarizes that "he had come to see America as the future, which can only come about by freeing itself from the past" (600). Both writers also note Lawrence's references to the Aztec and Maya.

15. This quotation resonates more strongly with "The Woman Who Rode Away" than *The Plumed Serpent.*

16. In June 1922, Lawrence writes in a letter to Luhan before his September arrival that "I build quite a lot on Taos—and the pueblo [in *Aaron's Rod, Fantasia of the Unconscious,* and *Psychoanalysis and the Unconscious*]. I shall be so glad if I can write an American novel from that centre" (*Letters IV* 260). And in July he writes to Robert Mountsier, "I should like, if I could, to write a New Mexico novel with Indians in it. Wonder if that would be possible" (*Letters IV* 274).

17. "Hopi Snake Dance" appears in *Mornings in Mexico* and the other two essays appeared in the *Dial* after Christmas, 1922. "New Mexico" was written after Lawrence had left the continent and was commissioned by Mabel Dodge Luhan. Ellis reports that it was first published in the *Survey Graphic,* May 1, 1931 (701 n.12), but written in December 1928 (621 n.36).

18. I take the term "Mexican-American novel" from Worthen, who uses it to refer to *The Plumed Serpent.* Wayne Templeton, in particular, acknowledges the context of Native political activism characterizing the New Mexico Lawrence encountered (24). Templeton also astutely observes the "liberal contingent['s] investment in Native 'self-government' as opposed to the more radical concept of self-determination" (30). Lawrence did, however, write an article on the Bursum Bill, legislation sponsored by New Mexico Senator Holm Bursum that would have profoundly diminished Native land tenure rights. The article was published in the *New York Times Magazine* in December 1922 under the title "Certain Americans and an Englishman." See Nicholas Joost and Alvin Sullivan, *D. H. Lawrence and the Dial,* 79. The essay is reprinted in *Phoenix II,* ed. Warren Roberts and Harry T. Moore, London: Heinemann, 1968: 238–243.

19. See *The Aztec Palimpsest: Mexico in the Modern Imagination.*

20. Dr. Atl, also known as Gerardo Murillo, was an early proponent of Mexican folk art and a fixture at the National Preparatory School's National Academy

of the Arts. José Clemente Orozco describes him as an "agitator" who instilled in the young artists of the Academy the knowledge that "[w]e too had a character, which was quite the equal of any other" (20).

21. See Mary Kay Vaughan's *Cultural Politics in Revolution: Teachers, Peasants, and Schools in Mexico, 1930–1940,* for an analysis of a later post-Revolutionary period.

22. See *José Clemente Orozco: An Autobiography,* 94–96, 104–108, and Charlot 12.

23. John B. Humma called *The Plumed Serpent* "Lawrence's most ambitious failure" in *Metaphor and Meaning in D. H. Lawrence's Later Novels,* 62. Gunn, citing William York Tindall, writes, "Worse, such a belief in the self-contained destiny of each people brought Lawrence to a position essentially one with fascism" and that the tone of the novel is "shrill, and many of its ideas unworthy of Lawrence's talent" (135). See Mary Freeman 191 and Parmenter 301–308 for defenses of Lawrence against charges of fascism. See Walker's chapter on *The Plumed Serpent* for an overview of criticism of the novel to 1978 and Humma's chapter for an overview of negative criticism in particular (62–76). Nixon documents Lawrence's political and philosophical "turns," claiming that "[b]y 1917, Lawrence believed that personal salvation was to be found in submission to a male leader, a natural hero possessed of wisdom and power. Women in particular would have to learn that submission was for their own good; in Lawrence's new utopia, even the most inferior man would have one follower, namely, his wife. That man would in turn be pledged to a greater, and so on up the hierarchy of dominance. This great army of manhood would march away from their women to build a new world" (4). See her "Introduction." Judith Ruderman writes that "The movement into violence during Lawrence's leadership period is steady, culminating in the bloodbaths of *The Plumed Serpent* (135).

24. See Parmenter, Chapter 11, "How *The Plumed Serpent* Was Changed in Oaxaca," for a discussion of the content of the revisions. Kimberley Van Hoosier-Carey has also written an analysis of the changes in the manuscript, focusing on the character of Kate. See "Struggling With the Master: The Position of Kate and the Reader in Lawrence's *Quetzalcoatl* and *The Plumed Serpent.*"

25. The editors of the Cambridge edition of the novel write in an explanatory note that "DHL borrowed the fictional name from a lake and a village 25 miles s.w. of Lake Chapala" (454).

26. Parmenter claims that the character of Ramón is based on Manuel Gamio, but most other critics take him to be a combination of José Vasconcelos, and perhaps Gamio.

27. See Luhan 173. John Burt Foster Jr. attributes the symbol to Nietzsche's influence on Lawrence: "It is no exaggeration to say that Zarathustra's animals permeate the novel, taking on various forms to comment on its tendencies. A normative example would be the emblem for Ramón's Quetzalcoatl movement. . . . Eagle and snake have joined to suggest bipolar unity" (237). Robert E. Montgomery writes, "There is an important *relation* between Nietzsche and Lawrence, but, as in the case of Schopenhauer, the question of influence is a vexed one. . . . Yet, strangely, it is impossible to tell which of Nietzsche's works Lawrence actually read, or if indeed he read any" (73).

28. Lawrence's presumptions about the need for Mexican Indians to return to their old sacrificial ways, thoughts he expressed in fiction and letters, as well as in conversations with fellow travelers such as Bynner, seem to have borrowed heavily from William H. Prescott's accounts of Aztec zeal in *A History of the Conquest of Mexico,* published in 1843: "The amount of victims immolated on its accursed altars would stagger the faith of the least scrupulous believer. Scarcely any author pretends to estimate the yearly sacrifices throughout the empire at less than twenty thousand, and some carry the number as high as fifty!" (31). Prescott, however, insists that these acts of sacrifice and cannibalism were always in service to the dictates of Aztec religion rather than for the sheer joy of drinking blood because the Aztec Empire also operated for him as a "golden age" of civilization. Prescott's description of the actual ritual suggests itself as a precursor to Lawrence's depiction of the Chilchui ritual in "The Woman Who Rode Away" (Prescott 29–31). Mabel Dodge Luhan, who claimed that the story was Lawrence's attempt to kill her off, describes a visit she made with Lawrence to a cave in New Mexico. Luhan's account bears a striking resemblance to the cave in which Lawrence sets the suspended sacrifice of the Woman (Luhan 209–210).

29. The character of Mrs. Norris generally is agreed to have been based on the real-life Zelia Nuttall, an archeologist who published a number of texts on Mexican ancient history and mythology at the turn of the century and into the 1920s. Harry T. Moore writes that Nuttall offered the Lawrences a house in Coyoacán and that Frieda told William York Tindall that she recalled Lawrence reading *The Fundamental Principles of Old and New World Civilizations,* published in 1901. Tindall, in *D. H. Lawrence and Susan His Cow,* Moore says, was the first to make this connection and establish Nuttall's influence on *The Plumed Serpent,* but "Tindall was wrong in saying that Lawrence had stayed at Mrs. Nuttall's; she says he went there for lunch three times. Tindall was correct, however, in identifying Mrs. Nuttall as the original of Mrs. Norris, the suburban hostess. . . ." See Tindall (114–115) for his discussion of the discovery of this previously unknown source for Lawrence, information that was suggested to him by George Valliant, then curator of Mexican Archaeology at the American Museum of Natural History. Parmenter also points to discrepancies regarding whether Lawrence had access to Nuttall's library, as some biographers suggest, but nevertheless holds that *The Plumed Serpent* was greatly influenced by Nuttall's work (292). Ellis' biography of Lawrence, published as part of the extensively documented Cambridge editions, does not make much of her influence or the possibility that Lawrence read her work and neither does L. D. Clark in his introduction to the Cambridge edition of *The Plumed Serpent.*

30. Antonia Castañeda's groundbreaking work on the role of sexual violence in the advancement of colonization and conquest chronicles that historical reality and, in doing so, alters the paradigm through which conquest-era social relations must be viewed. See "Sexual Violence in the Politics and Policies of Conquest: Amerindian Women and the Spanish Conquest of Alta California."

31. This sentence occurs in the midst of a shocking commentary about the superiority of the Spanish form of conquest. Vasconcelos writes that when "the dominating race stands apart and takes no interest in the life of the inferior," the consequence is unchecked reproduction in order "to compensate through

numbers what the dominating race achieves through quality" ("The Race Problem" 100). In the full version of this quotation, Vasconcelos includes "the Negro" and "the Asiatic," which makes the racism of his argument more relevant to American and British colonial contexts and contemporary audiences.

32. Parmenter argues that Ramón's education and profession parallel that of Manuel Gamio, who was, incidentally, a good friend of Nuttall (279).

33. Infantilization of Native peoples is a recognizable feature, not only of primitivist, but also of early ethnographic and art historical discourses. Consider the following written by American museum curator René d'Harnoncourt, published in *Mexican Folkways* in 1928: "The toymaker's customers are the Indians who never outgrow their desire for something to play with. . . . Neither the toymaker or his clients take his efforts toward efficiency very seriously. . . . Pancho considers himself free to fashion a quaint world after his own will and fancy. . . . Pancho and his art are not really children of the twentieth century. He is often unconscious of the merit of his own work. . . . We most fervently hope that we shall never lose him and his playthings—the most charming souvenirs of a time of delightful inefficiency" (quoted in Florence H. Pettit and Robert M. Pettit, *Mexican Folk Toys: Festival Decorations and Ritual Objects* 15).

34. The story of Quetzalcoatl is complicated precisely because there is not simply one story. The figure has been the subject of much academic interest by anthropologists, religious historians, and others. Enrique Florescano's *The Myth of Quetzalcoatl* attempts to chart and interpret the vast system of textual referencing of Quetzalcoatl throughout Mesoamerica, and Davíd Carrasco, in *Quetzalcoatl and the Irony of Empire,* theorizes Quetzalcoatl's significance within a specifically Aztec pantheon.

35. C. A. Burland, among others, relates the myth of Huitzilopochtli in which he killed his sister Coyolxauhqui at the moment of his birth; she later became the moon (*The Gods of Mexico* 176). Laurette Séjourné writes that he is "the only deity of Aztec origin . . . but, as with all the others, it is impossible to define his characteristics without recourse to the teaching of Quetzalcoatl" (*Burning Water: Thought and Religion in Ancient Mexico* 29). Huitzilopochtli also sometimes appears as Tezcatlipoca (León-Portilla, *Aztec Thought* 35). Miguel León-Portilla explains the transformation of Huitzilopochtli from "patron deity of a poor and intimidated tribe" to his final appearance as "the most powerful god, the one to whom the ancient prayers of Nahuatl religion were directed" (*The Broken Spears* 161). George Vaillant reports that the "Tenochcas, the Mexico City Aztecs," found "an idol of Huitzilopochtli (Hummingbird Wizard), which had the useful ability to speak and give them good advice" (75–76).

Although Prescott's text, first published in 1843, continues to be recognized as one of the premiere accounts of the Conquest, the initial praise has been tempered as more Mexican scholars contribute to the conversation. Additionally, more sophisticated knowledge and interpretation of pre-Conquest Indigenous societies has revised Prescott's status. Prescott made use of vast amounts of primary materials, but his account favors Hernán Cortés as the great hero and demonizes the Aztecs with embellished accounts of sacrifice and cannibalism. Benjamin Keen summarizes critical responses to Prescott in *The Aztec Image in Western Thought* (354–364). See also chapters on Prescott in Eric Wertheimer, *Imagined Empires:*

Incas, Aztecs, and the New World of American Literature, 1771–1876, and Scott Michaelsen, *The Limits of Multiculturalism: Interrogating the Origins of American Anthropology.*

36. Lawrence modeled these dances on the Apache dances he observed in New Mexico with Tony Luhan.

37. Lawrence ends "The Woman Who Rode Away" by suspending the moment at which the Chilchui priest plunges his obsidian knife into the beating chest of the Woman.

38. Cooper Alarcón (45–48) cogently summarizes this emergence, and critical representations of it. He critiques Walker for "demonstrat[ing] a disturbing propensity to see Mexico as 'collaborating' with writers in developing the Infernal Paradise myth" (41).

Chapter Two

1. The role of the farmworker movement as a motivating source of Chicana/o political activity is widely recognized. Gómez-Quiñones identifies the Farmworkers Union as one of several "seminal initiating forces" (*Mexican Students* 12), and Limón holds that "it may well be said that the Mexican-American student movement started in the mid-sixties initially as a series of farmworker support committees on campuses in the Southwest and across the country" (*Mexican Ballads* 83). Carlos Muñoz, while acknowledging the farmworker movement as a source of inspiration, challenges Rodolfo Acuña's claim that César Chávez was a national leader for the Chicano movement (quoted in Muñoz 7) and contends that Chávez was actually "never . . . integral" (7).

2. Yolanda Broyles-González argues, however, that the troupe was transformed into a "Chicano icon for the academy" by the 1970s (xii).

3. Two instances are Bruce-Novoa's *Chicano Poetry: A Response to Chaos* 14–25 (see especially his rich footnote on pachucos 218–219, n.2); and José E. Limón, *Mexican Ballads, Chicano Poems: History and Influence in Mexican-American Social Poetry* 106–108.

4. The prominence of the figure of the Indian seer in Rudolfo A. Anaya's *Heart of Aztlán* (1976) is an interesting example. Guisela Latorre provides a history of indigenism and gender in mural production in "Gender, Muralism and the Politics of Identity: Chicana Muralism and Indigenist Aesthetics."

5. Jack Forbes has written that he first used the term Aztlán in a mimeographed manuscript, "The Mexican Heritage of Aztlán (the Southwest) to 1821," circulated in 1962. See his *Aztecas del Norte* 17.

6. See "Episode One: Quest for a Homeland," *Chicano! History of the Mexican American Civil Rights Movement* (1996).

7. Mary Pat Brady has uncovered an 1878 reference to Aztlán in an address given by Ignacio Bonillas, celebrating Mexico's sixty-eight-year-old independence. See *Extinct Lands, Temporal Geographies* 33–36.

8. Pérez-Torres provides a thorough overview of how the debate over the cultural versus the political implications of Aztlán has marked the concept itself.

9. Jorge Klor de Alva has developed perhaps the most sustained critiques of

indigenism. See "California Chicano Literature and Pre-Columbian Motifs: Foil and Fetish" and "The Invention of Ethnic Origins and the Negotiation of Latino Identity, 1969–1981."

10. Klor de Alva writes of "brown power" as a "non-metaphoric effort at reconstituting their corporate identity as a racially founded nationalism," as "a strategy for unification . . . and as a way to explain the source of their oppressed condition" ("Invention" 58).

11. Klor de Alva refers to this process as a "redemptive bifurcation of cultural traits." See his table and explanation ("Invention" 58).

12. See Arnoldo de León's *They Called Them Greasers: Anglo Attitudes toward Mexicans, 1821–1900* (8–9).

13. Marked by wide lapels, padded shoulders, and pegged trousers, the zoot suit was sometimes adorned with a chain dangling from the side pocket. Generally considered to have first appeared in African-American communities, most particularly Harlem in New York, the zoot suit was popular in urban Chicano communities. Luis Valdez's 1979 play *Zoot Suit* is based upon the Sleepy Lagoon trial and ensuing "Zoot Suit" riots. For additional reading on the trial and riots, see Rodolfo Acuña, *Occupied America: A History of Chicanos* (268–273); Eduardo Obregón Pagán, *Murder at the Sleepy Lagoon: Zoot Suits, Race, and Riot in Wartime L.A.;* and Frank P. Barajas, "The Defense Committees of Sleepy Lagoon: A Convergent Struggle against Fascism, 1942–1944." In 2002, the Public Broadcasting Service (PBS) produced an American Experience documentary, "Zoot Suit Riots."

14. Sánchez also tries to establish the "legally white" status of Mexican-Americans, which, he argues, grants to them avenues of legal recourse against segregation (125–126).

15. See "Sexual Violence in the Politics and Policies of Conquest: Amerindian Women and the Spanish Conquest of Alta California" (24).

16. Although not as prominent as female goddesses like Coatlicue and Coyolxauhqui, Quetzalcoatl still retains a presence in Chicana feminist texts like Gloria Anzaldúa's *Borderlands/La Frontera: The New Mestiza.* Consider also the title of Lorna Dee Cervantes' 1981 poetry collection, *Emplumada.* I discuss both of these works in following chapters.

17. Keen uses an accent in the name, i.e., "Quetzalcóatl." This practice has been largely abandoned by scholars of Mesoamerica.

18. Coe outlines for us the challenges to the narrative of omens and mistaken identity. Nigel Davies argues that the prophecy of Quetzalcoatl's return was a detail added to the original legend after the Conquest. Coe is convinced by Susan Gillespie's argument that Aztec informants invented the story of Cortés being mistaken for Quetzalcoatl, again, after the Conquest (Coe 18). Stuart B. Schwartz suggests that Indigenous accounts may have been influenced by informants' desire to satisfy Spanish interests (10). Furthermore, he calls attention to the reinterpretation of pre-Conquest accounts that holds that they may not have been entirely Native in origin (29–30).

19. See, for example, Enrique Florescano, *The Myth of Quetzalcóatl* and *Memory, Myth and Time in Mexico* (1–29).

20. See Muñoz 6. Angie Chabram-Dernersesian has written cogently about the

use of the "brown woman" in Rendon. See "I Throw Punches for My Race, but I Don't Want to Be a Man: Writing Us—Chica-nos (Girl, Us)/Chican*as*—into the Movement Script" and "On the Social Construction of Whiteness within Selected Chicana/o Discourses." I will take up Rendon's discussion of "malinchismo" in the next chapter.

21. See Enrique Florescano, *Memory, Myth and Time in Mexico: From the Aztecs to Independence,* and Richard F. Townsend, *The Aztecs* (116–122).

22. See Jorge Huerta's *Chicano Drama* for an example of theater scholarship that centralizes Valdez's role. Huerta also provides a brief and helpful biography of Valdez. See especially 26–44.

23. Yolanda Broyles-González provides a thorough history of the productions of the play and its eventual transference to film. See *El Teatro Campesino* (177–214).

24. Broyles-González has written the authoritative account of Theater of the Sphere. See *El Teatro Campesino* (79–127). Mark Pizzaro has addressed the Aztec signifiers in *Zoot Suit,* particularly in the connection to violence. See his "Brechtian and Aztec Violence in Valdez's 'Zoot Suit.'"

25. Although Broyles-González has challenged the single-authored status of some of the *Actos,* particularly *Soldado Razo,* she attributes *Pensamiento Serpentino* to Valdez and does not discuss *The Dark Root of a Scream.* See her Chapter 3, "Towards a Re-vision of Chicano Theater History: The Roles of Women in El Teatro Campesino."

26. See Broyles-González's summary and refutation of critiques of Theater of the Sphere (119–127) and also Yolanda Yarbro-Bejarano's treatment of the subject in "From Acto to Mito: A Critical Appraisal of the Teatro Campesino."

27. See Broyles-González's discussion of his work and influence (90–95 and 119–127). She devotes significant attention to the *danzas* performed in the context of the Theater of the Sphere. Certainly, *danza* remains a significant expression of indigenism, in Mexico as well as among Chicanas/os in the United States. It does not fall into the purview of this study, however, and I look forward to the future work of scholars on this topic.

28. The original hieroglyphic version of the Mayan sacred text *Popul Vuh* is assumed to have been destroyed (although scholars admit they fantasize otherwise), as only four known books survived the religiously-sanctioned destruction of Mayan texts by missionaries. An alphabetic version written in Quiché was composed in the mid-sixteenth century, and at the very beginning of the eighteenth century, it received the attention of Francisco Ximénez, a parish priest who made a copy of it and translated it into Spanish. The original Quiché text is lost, as was Ximénez's text until about 1830. Thus, the text comes to most modern readers through at least two translations, from pictograph to alphabet, from Quiché to Spanish and, at times, to English. According to Dennis Tedlock, who published an English translation in 1985, the text suggests that pictures were included, but these were not reproduced by Ximénez. Tedlock notes that the text narrates a creation myth, but he takes care to point out its other functions. He translates the characterization of the manuscript by its Indigenous authors, who were probably reproducing it from memory, as an instrument to guide them into the future, a "seeing instrument" or "place to see," from the Quiché *ilb'al* (21–28).

29. See Enrique Florescano, *The Myth of Quetzalcóatl.*

30. Valdez and El Teatro Campesino began to develop the Theater of the Sphere in the 1970s, a form of dramaturgy that relied heavily on Mayan myth, especially the *Popul Vuh.* For an extended analysis of the Theater of the Sphere, see Yolanda Broyles-González's Chapter 2, "Theater of the Sphere: Toward the Formulation of a Native Performance Theory and Practice" in *El Teatro Campesino.*

31. Valdez follows the older practice of placing accents, a European convention, in Nahuatl names—e.g., Quetzalcóatl, Mixcóatl—and so I have preserved them.

32. Cuahtemoc was the last Aztec ruler, executed by Córtes in 1525; Nezahualcoyotl was the Texcocoan poet-king who lived prior to the Conquest. Some surviving texts attributed to Nezahualcoyotl have been collected in León-Portilla and Shorris, *In the Language of Kings: An Anthology of Mesoamerican Literature—Pre-Columbian to the Present,* 146–152.

33. There are others, of course. I discuss Gloria Anzaldúa's treatment of this theme in Chapter 4.

34. This also reproduces the confusion of Topiltzin-Quetzalcoatl the king and Quetzalcoatl the god found in Mesoamerican myth and history. See Coe 114.

35. Many thanks to the graduate students in the Border Literatures class I taught in fall 2006, Rain Cranford, Nicole Shannanaquat Shepherd, Rikk Mulligan, and Joseph Darowski, who were unconvinced of Lizard's status as priest.

36. See Florescano, *Memory, Myth and Time in Mexico,* Chapter 1.

37. Specifically, León-Portilla's *The Broken Spears: The Aztec Account of the Conquest of Mexico* (1962); *Los Antiguos Mexicanos a Través de sus Crónicas y Cantares* (1961); and *Aztec Thought and Culture: A Study of the Ancient Nahuatl Mind* (1963). Also, Edmund Bordeaux's *The Soul of Ancient Mexico* (1968); Laurette Séjourné's *El Universo del Quetzalcoatl* (1962); Edward H. Thompson's *People of the Serpent: Life and Adventure among the Mayas* (1932); and Agustí Bartra's poetry collection entitled *Quetzalcoatl* (1960). Interestingly, Bartra was a Catalan exile in Mexico who played very purposefully with the depiction of Quetzalcoatl in his creative work.

38. One version of the Quetzalcoatl myth says that Cihuacoatl ground up the bones in the underworld Mictlan or Mictlanteuchtli from which Quetzalcoatl and the other gods created humanity. See Enrique Florescano, *Memory, Myth and Time in Mexico* 9. Alurista uses accents in the Nahuatl character names, and I have preserved these when referring specifically to characters in the play.

39. The editors of *Aztlán: Essays on the Chicano Homeland* note that their published version of "El Plan" is taken from *Documents of the Chicano Struggle.* See "El Plan" 5.

40. Vine Deloria Jr.'s *God is Red* was published in 1973, yet it is surely not the first example of an oppositional political use of the term. The reading list documents Alurista's familiarity with American Indian literature and politics, listing *Black Elk Speaks: Being the Life Story of a Holy Man of the Oglala Sioux, as Told through John G. Neihardt* (1961) and *The Sacred Pipe: Black Elk's Account of the Seven Rites of the Oglala Sioux* (1971); Frank Waters' *Book of the Hopi: Drawings and Source Material recorded by Oswald White Bear Fredericks* (1963); and, much less authoritative in the realm of American Indian critical discourse, as well as in contemporary

academic anthropology, Carlos Castaneda's *The Teachings of Don Juan: A Yaqui Way of Knowledge* (1968) and *A Separate Reality: Further Conversations with Don Juan* (1971).

41. Jack Forbes is the most prominent exception. See *Aztecas del Norte*.

Chapter Three

1. For example, contemporary readings of the Virgin of Guadalupe focus on her origin at the site of a temple devoted to the goddess Tonantzin. There the Virgin appeared to Juan Diego in 1531, speaking to him in Nahuatl. Her brown-skinned features, her appearance to an Indigenous man and her use of an Indigenous language instantiate her as a "Goddess of the Americas," setting her apart from the European Virgin Mary. The representation of the Virgin of Guadalupe as goddess, as she is named in *Goddess of the Americas,* a collection of writings edited by Ana Castillo, asserts her association with Indigenous mythology and the argument that the Virgin of Guadalupe is, at her source, Tonantzin refashioned for a Catholic pantheon. Feminists and others have worked with the image of the Virgin, making her into a figure more accessible to everyday women who can never embody the ideal of chaste motherhood that the Virgin represents. See, for example, the work of artists Alma López, particularly her digital image *Our Lady* (http://chicanas.com/alma.html), and Yolanda M. López, especially her *Portrait of the Artist as the Virgin of Guadalupe.*

2. At the 2003 meetings of the Society for the Study of Multi-Ethnic Literatures, Moraga gave a keynote address in which Coyolxauhqui figured prominently. Moraga is not the first writer to invoke Coyolxauhqui; the goddess also appears in Anzaldúa's text. But the appearance of Huitzilopochtli's "re-membered" sister as a central icon in Moraga's work speaks to the continued relevance of such figures to Chicana feminism.

3. Alarcón treats the subject of La Malinche specifically in her article "Traddutora, Traditora: A Paradigmatic Figure of Chicana Feminism." The article cited here, "Chicana Feminism: In the Tracks of 'the' Native Woman," merely alludes to La Malinche as a model: "The strategic invocation and recodification of 'the' native woman in the present has the effect of conjoining the historical repression of the 'non-civilized' dark woman—which continues to operate through the 'regulative psychobiographies' of good and evil women such as that of Guadalupe, Malinche, Llorona and many others . . ." (252).

4. Chicana literary criticism has addressed this history of recodification, with Norma Alarcón's work holding a particular prominence. Her "Traddutora, Traditora: A Paradigmatic Figure of Chicana Feminism" offers an extended contemplation of the relationship between the narrative of La Malinche and the struggle to assert Chicana voice as Alarcón also provides a genealogy of Chicana and Mexican creative and critical revisions. More recently, Rita Cano Alcalá has argued for a recognition of the similarities between the now legendary account of La Malinche and certain Aztec mythic narratives such as the story of Huitzilopochtli's sisters, Coyolxauhqui and Malinalxochitl. See "From Chingada to Chingona: La Malinche Redefined, or a Long Line of Hermanas."

5. Ana Nieto-Gómez, "Chicanas Identify" (1971); Mirta Vidal, *Chicanas Speak Out. Women: New Voice of La Raza* (1971); Martha Cotera, *The Chicana Feminist* (1977); Alfredo Mirandé and Evangelina Enríquez, *La Chicana: The Mexican-American Woman* (1979).

6. Chabram-Dernersesian writes that Rendon elevates "machismo as the symbolic principle of Chicano revolt" ("I Throw" 83), stressing the degree to which men not only managed movement communities, but also viewed community vitality as dependent upon the unquestioned authority of male power.

7. Recovery work on the historical figure, however, has attested to her relatively empowered status in post-Conquest Mexico—for example, her access to the spoils of conquest in the form of land. Rita Cano Alcalá's fascinating research places the narrative of La Malinche in the context of Aztec myth and also provides a thoroughgoing review of the historiography and literary criticism surrounding this figure (33–61).

8. Alarcón writes that "[a]lthough Paz's views are often the contemporary point of departure for current revision of the legend and myth of Malintzin, there are two previous stages in its almost five hundred year trajectory" ("Traddutora" 64). She breaks these down into a first stage comprised of the accounts of chroniclers of the Conquest and a second stage that emerges in the nineteenth century during Mexican independence and involves scapegoating and the branding of La Malinche as traitor (64 and n.16).

9. Alarcón notes that Paz's work takes up the theme of La Malinche as "metaphor par excellence of Mexico" where Alfonso Reyes leaves off in *Visión de Anáhuac* (1519) ("Traddutora" 64).

10. See "Traddutora, Traditora" 69 and n.28.

11. As mentioned earlier, this feature of Indigenous accounts of the Conquest has been questioned by contemporary scholars. See Davies 257–260 and Schwartz 10.

12. Alarcón notes this tension, telling us that because there is no record of Doña Marina's voice, only interpretations of that voice, the attribution of "motives, qualities, and desires" necessarily comes into existence as myth ("Traddutora" 74).

13. Cuahtemoc was the last Aztec emperor. He resisted the Spanish until his assassination.

14. See Catrióna Rueda Esquibel's introduction to *With Her Machete in Her Hand* for an overview of that history (1–21).

15. In *Disrupting Savagism: Intersecting Chicana/o, Mexican Immigrant and Native American Struggles for Self-Representation,* Arturo Aldama contends that Smith "mistakenly argues that Anzaldúa writes within a pastoral tradition" (111). It is true that Smith invokes a literary tradition grounded in the specificity of European industrial development, yet she characterizes *Borderlands* as a challenge to and critique of that tradition, rather than a perpetuation of it: "I do not mean to imply here that Anzaldúa writes in the pastoral tradition, for that would be to define her manifesto through and contain it within the very history she challenges" (169). And although it is tremendously important to continue the work of terminological invention—creating new categories that acknowledge and describe the specificities of Chicana/o history and cultural production—it is

also imperative to understand the dialectical relationships that exist between Chicana/o literature and dominant literary discourses.

16. Since the mid-1990s or so, a critical conversation has developed that questions Anzaldúa's indigenism. Pérez-Torres provides an overview of this criticism as he challenges Saldaña-Portillo's argument that Anzaldúa reproduces the indigenism of the Mexican state and erases contemporary Indigenous realities. He argues that the contextual differences between Mexican state *indigenismo* and Chicana/o indigenism are deep enough to dismiss the charge that Chicana/o Indian fantasies marginalize living Indigenous subjects. Furthermore, he argues, Anzaldúa's indigenism is a response to "discrimination and political exclusion" and has as its goal the creation of new political alliances (16). Ultimately, however, Pérez-Torres provides little evidence of a Chicana/o indigenist concern with, for example, Native land rights in the United States. His example of political alliance between Chicanas/os and Natives dates to the 1970s, contains little detail, and, unfortunately, does not convince (n.8, 224). I agree with Saldaña as I find no engagement with the distinct material and political realities of American Indians in contemporary, as opposed to movement, Chicana/o literary indigenism. This is a point, however, not central to this book. See Josefina Saldaña, "Who's the Indian in Aztlán? Re-Writing Mestizaje, Indianism, and Chicanismo from the Lacandón."

17. Corky González writes, for example: "I am Cuauhtémoc, proud and noble,/ leader of men, king of an empire civilized/beyond the dreams of the *gachupín* Cortés,/who also is the blood, the image of myself./I am the Maya prince. . . . I am Aztec prince and Christian Christ." See "Yo Soy Joaquín."

18. Norma Alarcón acknowledges a "neo-nationalism" in *Borderlands* that enables Anzaldúa to promote a nationalist space that is open to all as "she rejects a masculinist ethnonationalism that would exclude the Queer" ("Anzaldúa's *Frontera*" 120). Alvina Quintana calls attention to Anzaldúa's perpetuation of a symbolic tradition when she writes that "[u]nlike the rhetoric of Chicano nationalism, Anzaldúa's brand of new-age feminist nationalism privileges Coatlicue over her son, the Aztec war-god Huitzilopochtli" (136). She also makes a passing reference to what she views as the similarity between *Borderlands* and Alurista's nationalist poetry of the movement period. Although Rosaura Sánchez comments upon the reworking of Chicano and Mexicano indigenist narratives, she devotes significant attention to Quintana's text ("Reconstructing" 351–356).

19. This abuse is delivered not only by the forces of European and Euro-American domination, but also within mestiza/o communities. Anzaldúa makes clear her critique of Chicano sexism through references to her own everyday forms of rebellion against the demands of Tejano patriarchy. She writes: "*Repelé. Hablé pa' 'tras. Fuí muy hocicona. Era indiferente a muchos valores de mi cultura. No me dejé de los hombres. No fuí buena ni obediente*/I complained. I talked back. I was a real bigmouth. I was indifferent to many of the values of my culture. I didn't let the men take advantage of me. I was neither good nor obedient" (15).

20. Daniel Rosenblatt writes that "modern primitives in the United States today valorize a primitive that, like its predecessors, is more open about sexual desire and less concerned with consumer goods." See "The Antisocial Skin: Structure, Resistance, and 'Modern Primitive' Adornment in the United States" 296.

In *Primitive Art in Civilized Places,* Sally Price characterizes Western conceptions of the primitive in terms of imagery that "employs a standard rhetoric of fear, darkness, pagan spirits, and eroticism" (37).

21. See Jung's "The Shadow" in *Aion. Researches into the Phenomenology of the Self.* For a contemporary interpretation, see Robert A. Johnson, *Owning Your Own Shadow: Understanding the Dark Side of the Psyche.*

22. AnaLouise Keating offers an interesting juxtaposition of Anzaldúa's *"mestizaje écriture"* with Helene Cixous' *"écriture féminine."* The argument relies on Keating's own advancement of Anzaldúa's claim to "Mexican Indian heritage" (Keating 125), a term that mobilizes a "monolithic concept of female identity" (Keating 126). Keating argues, however, that Anzaldúa actively prevents readers from visualizing identity in this way (126).

23. Many would argue that Anzaldúa's peculiar and particular pattern of documentation is a strategy by which she both acquiesces and deconstructs academic symbolic structures. The citations are directed toward those readers who require the "legitimation" of academic authority (See Alarcón, "Anzaldúa's *Frontera*" 121). If I were to further that line of argument, I could claim that the documentary elisions challenge the basis of such authority and that the knowledge Anzaldúa relies upon, Indigenous and pre-Columbian, by virtue of historical precedence, supercedes and renders such arbitrary systems meaningless.

24. For example, Anzaldúa cites Jacques Soustelle's *Daily Life of the Aztecs on the Eve of the Spanish Conquest* and Karl W. Luckert's *Olmec Religion: A Key to Middle America and Beyond,* specifically 68, 69, 87, and 109. See Anzaldúa 94, n.25 and n.29.

25. In *The Aztecs,* Richard F. Townsend writes that Tezcatlipoca is "associated with the notion of destiny or fate" and "is the object of the most lengthy and reverent prayers in the rites of kingship" (109). The rival of Quetzalcoatl, Tezcatlipoca, according to George Valliant, was honored with the sacrifice of "the handsomest and bravest prisoner of war." See *Aztecs of Mexico: Origin, Rise and Fall of the Aztec Nation* 202.

Chapter Four

1. See Rosaura Sánchez, *Telling Identities: The Californio Testimonios* (1995).

2. Historians Arnoldo De León, Gilberto M. Hinojosa, and Gerald E. Poyo have facilitated significant revisions in the writing of Texas history by focusing on "Mexican" settlement of Texas, particularly the settlement of San Antonio de Béxar beginning in 1718 with the establishment of the presidio. See the edited collection of Poyo and Hinojosa, *Tejano Origins in Eighteenth-Century San Antonio;* Poyo's edited collection, *Tejano Journey: 1770–1850,* which focuses on Tejano communities more broadly; and de León's *The Tejano Community, 1836–1900.*

3. Ortego calls for a redefinition of American literature, which "actually begins with the formation of the United States as a political entity. Thus, the literary period from the founding of the first permanent British settlement at Jamestown, Virginia, in 1607, represents only the British period of American literature. More appropriately, the British and Spanish periods should both be listed under

the rubric 'Colonial American Literature.' The Mexican period of the Southwest (1821–1848) should simply be labeled 'The Mexican Period'" (296). See "The Chicano Renaissance."

4. Rebolledo examines archival material collected in the 1930s and 1940s as part of the New Mexico Federal Writers' Project. See "'Y Dónde Estaban las Mujeres?' In Pursuit of an *Hispana* Literary and Historical Heritage in Colonial New Mexico, 1580–1840." In her introduction to *Beyond Stereotypes: The Critical Analysis of Chicana Literature,* Herrera-Sobek writes that "[m]odern-day Chicanas can trace their ancestors to these hardy women [i.e., Spaniards] who accompanied their husbands in their explorations of new worlds" (16).

5. Teresa McKenna does an excellent job of plotting the history of Chicano literary criticism and its debt to the foundational work of folklorist and *corrido*-specialist Américo Paredes. See her Chapter 2 *"Chicano Poetry and the Political Age. The Canales/Córdova Corridos as Social Drama"* in *Migrant Song: Politics and Process in Contemporary Chicano Literature,* especially pages 27–34.

6. Rosaura Sánchez has consistently characterized *Californio* narratives as "subaltern," for example, in her introduction to Maria Amparo Ruíz de Burton's *The Squatter and the Don* and in her book-length study, *Telling Identities.* In both cases, we can see how contemporary scholarship unfortunately contributes to the erasure of American Indian occupation of the U.S. Southwest and West, even as it strategically mines the category of "native" to position ideologically a dispossessed settler population.

7. See Guha, "On Some Aspects of the Historiography of Colonial India."

8. Rebolledo further argues that Native women were more historically present than Spanish women in that "[w]hile they [Spanish explorers] took for granted the women who accompanied them, the men displayed great interest in the Indian peoples they came across. We therefore often know more about the Indian women than we do about the Spanish Mexicanas" ("Y Dónde" 143).

9. See, for example, Genaro Padilla, *My History, Not Yours. The Formation of Mexican American Autobiography.*

10. With the recent resurgence of xenophobic activism throughout the United States, it would not be surprising to see these tactics again become popular.

11. Jenny Sharpe argues for the abandonment of the concept-metaphor of rape in *Allegories of Empire: The Figure of the Woman in the Colonial Text,* a study of the theme of rape in British and Anglo-Indian fiction. She writes: "The story of a doomed love between a white woman and brown-skinned man, a story that Anglo-Indians can read only according to the sexual violence of rape, is one that reinforces a Victorian ideal of manliness. This may explain why, when deployed as a concept-metaphor for imperialism, 'rape' does not designate the penetration and control of a female colonial body; rather, it designates the emasculation of a male one" (155).

12. The most influential text is, of course, Américo Paredes' *"With His Pistol in His Hand," A Border Ballad and Its Hero* (1958). Two contemporary studies, both undertaken by students of Paredes, are Manuel Peña's *The Texas-Mexican Conjunto: History of a Working-Class Music* (1985) and José E. Limón's *Dancing With the Devil: Society and Cultural Poetics in Mexican-American South Texas* (1994).

13. Thank you to José Limón for the first detail. The second I owe to Manuel

Peña's work (80). Both the low dip and the sway probably account for the dance's name, literally "the little possum."

14. Their studies are useful, even if not directly addressing Spanish colonization of the Americas. Enloe's work, *Bananas, Beaches and Bases: Making Feminist Sense of International Politics,* addresses U.S. foreign policy. George's article, "Homes in the Empire, Empires in the Home," advances the claim that "the sojourn of Englishwomen in the empire writes a crucial chapter in the history of the formation that we today know as Western feminism" (96).

15. "They send you greetings and hugs/And so do I" (translation mine).

16. Marta Sánchez reads the image of the "mispronouncing gulls" as "probably a reference to American tourists who descend upon Mexico, mispronouncing Spanish as they move toward their vacation resorts, seeking 'refuge' and 'gameland' from their tax obligations. The speaker is like the migrating bird who leaves the warm southern climate to come north to build its nest" (101).

17. Teresa McKenna has written: "That Chicano literature proceeds out of a folk base has been a common assumption of most Chicano critics. That it evolves out of an oral tradition is a widely held corollary to this belief" (29).

18. "In order to write, she must accept the pain of reality associated with the north rather than the nostalgia of romance associated with the south because the north is a print culture. She comes north to gather her 'feathers' to build her nest—words she needs to write poems. The repetition of 'songs' in lines 21–24 and of 'words' in lines 26–28 stresses the urgency the speaker feels about fulfilling her objectives as a mediator between an oral people and a reading audience" (M. Sánchez 102).

19. Marta Sánchez reads this image as the poet's view of the act of writing as a "birthing."

20. The term "coeval" comes from Johannes Fabian. See *Time and the Other: How Anthropology Makes Its Object.*

21. Esquibel's interpretation of Terri de la Peña's "La Maya" engages a critique of the Chicana/o Pre-Columbian fetish. See 57–60.

22. As children's art, the shells could very easily be placed in the bona fide art historical category of primitive art, although perhaps the more applicable term might be "naïve art." See Errington's valuable discussion in Part I, "The Death of Primitive Art," in *The Death of Primitive Art and Other Tales of Progress* (47–146), in which she documents a history of tourist fascination with "authentic" Native art objects.

Coda

1. See Curtis Hinsley's "In Search of the New World Classical."

2. See, for example, "Sacrifices and Wars of the Aztecs," *The Accursed Share: An Essay on General Economy* 45–62.

Works Cited

Acosta, Teresa Palomo. *In the Season of Change*. Austin: Eakin Press, 2003.

———. *Passing Time*. Austin: n.p., 1984.

———. "Preguntas y frases para una bisabuela española." *Nile and Other Poems: A 1985–1994 Notebook*. Austin: n.p., 1999. 25.

Acuña, Rodolfo. *Occupied America: A History of Chicanos*. New York: Longman, 2000.

Alarcón, Norma. "Anzaldúa's *Frontera*: Inscribing Gynetics." *Decolonial Voices: Chicana and Chicano Cultural Studies in the 21st Century*. Ed. Arturo J. Aldama and Naomi H. Quiñonez. Bloomington: Indiana University Press, 2002. 113–126.

———. "Chicana Feminism: In the Tracks of 'the' Native Woman." *Cultural Studies* 4 (1990): 248–256.

———. "Cognitive Desires: An Allegory of/for Chicana Critics." *Listening to Silences: New Essays in Feminist Criticism*. Ed. Elaine Hedges and Shelley Fisher Fishkin. New York: Oxford University Press, 1994. 260–273.

———. "Traddutora, Traditora: A Paradigmatic Figure of Chicana Feminism." *Cultural Critique* (Fall 1989): 57–87.

Alcalá, Rita Cano. "From Chingada to Chingona: La Malinche Redefined, or a Long Line of Hermanas." *Aztlán* 26:2 (Fall 2001): 33–61.

Aldama, Arturo J. *Disrupting Savagism: Intersecting Chicana/o, Mexican Immigrant, and Native American Struggles for Self-Representation*. Durham: Duke University Press, 2001.

Almaguer, Tomás. *Racial Fault Lines: The Historical Origins of White Supremacy in California*. Berkeley: University of California Press, 1994.

Alurista. "Aztlan: Reality or Myth?" Alurista Papers, 1968–1979, Benson Latin American Collection, The University of Texas at Austin Libraries.

———. "Chicano Studies: A Future." Alurista Papers, 1968–1979, Benson Latin American Collection, The University of Texas at Austin Libraries.

———. "Dawn." In "Chicano Drama," special issue, *El Grito*. 7:4 (1974): 55–84.

———. *Floricanto En Aztlan*, 2nd ed. Los Angeles: UCLA Chicano Studies Center, 1976.

————. *Nationchild Plumaroja: 1969–1972.* San Diego: Toltecas en Aztlan, Centro Cultura de la Raza, 1972.

Anaya, Rudolfo. *Heart of Aztlán.* Berkeley: Justa Publications, 1976.

Anzaldúa, Gloria. *Borderlands/La Frontera: The New Mestiza.* San Francisco: Aunt Lute Books, 1987.

Armstrong, Nancy. *Desire and Domestic Fiction: A Political History of the Novel.* New York: Oxford University Press, 1987.

Arteaga, Alfred. *Chicano Poetics: Heterotexts and Hybridities.* Cambridge: Cambridge University Press, 1997.

Ayres, Edward Duran. "Edward Duran Ayres Report." *Readings on La Raza: The Twentieth Century.* Ed. Matt S. Meier and Feliciano Rivera. New York: Hill and Wang, 1974. 127–133.

Baldwin, Neil. *Legends of the Plumed Serpent: Biography of a Mexican God.* New York: Public Affairs, 1998.

Barajas, Frank P. "The Defense Committees of Sleepy Lagoon: A Convergent Struggle against Fascism, 1942–1944." *Aztlán* 31 (Spring 2006): 33–62.

Barnet-Sánchez, Holly. "The Necessity of Pre-Columbian Art in the United States: Appropriations and Transformations of Heritage, 1933–1945." *Collecting the Pre-Columbian Past.* Ed. Elizabeth Hill-Boone. Washington, D.C.: Dunbarton Oaks, 1993. 177–208.

Barrera, Mario, Carlos Muñoz, and Charles Ornelas. "The Barrio as Internal Colony." *La Causa Politica: A Chicano Politics Reader.* Ed. F. Chris Garcia. Notre Dame: University of Notre Dame Press, 1974. 465–498.

Barthes, Roland. *Mythologies.* Trans. Annette Lavers. New York: Hill and Wang, 1972.

Bartra, Agustí. *Quetzalcoatl.* México, D.F.: Universidad Autónoma Metropolitana, Dirección de Difusión Cultural, Departamento Editorial, 1988.

Bataille, Georges. *The Accursed Share: An Essay on General Economy,* Vol. 1. Trans. Robert Hurley. New York: Zone Books, 1991.

Berkhofer, Robert F. *The White Man's Indian, from Columbus to the Present.* New York: Vintage Books, 1979.

Berman, Marshall. *All That Is Solid Melts into Air: The Experience of Modernity.* New York: Penguin Books, 1988.

Bernal, Ignacio. "The Museum of Anthropology of Mexico." *Current Anthropology* 7 (June 1966): 320–326.

Black Elk. *Black Elk Speaks; Being the Life Story of a Holy Man of the Oglala Sioux, as Told through John G. Neihardt.* Lincoln: University of Nebraska Press, 1961.

————. *The Sacred Pipe; Black Elk's Account of the Seven Rites of the Oglala Sioux.* Recorded and edited by Joseph Epes Brown. Baltimore: Penguin Books, 1971.

Bonfil-Batalla, Guillermo. *México Profundo. Reclaiming a Civilization.* Trans. Philip A. Dennis. Austin: University of Texas Press, 1996.

Bordeaux, Edmond S. *The Soul of Ancient Mexico.* U.S.A.: Mille Meditations, 1968.

Boulton, James T., and Lindeth Vasey, eds. *The Letters of D. H. Lawrence,* Vol. 5 (March 1924–March 1927). Cambridge: Cambridge University Press, 1989.

Brady, Mary Pat. *Extinct Lands, Temporal Geographies.* Durham: Duke University Press, 2002.

Brassaï. *Picasso and Company*. Trans. Francis Price. Garden City, N.Y.: Doubleday, 1966.

Braun, Barbara. *Pre-Columbian Art and the Post-Columbian World: Ancient American Sources of Modern Art*. New York: Harry N. Abrams, 1993.

Britton, John A. *Revolution and Ideology: Images of the Mexican Revolution in the United States*. Lexington: University of Kentucky, 1995.

Brown, Betty Ann. "The Past Idealized: Diego Rivera's Use of Pre-Columbian Imagery." *Diego Rivera: A Retrospective*. New York: Detroit Institute of Art, 1986.

Broyles-González, Yolanda. *El Teatro Campesino: Theater in the Chicano Movement*. Austin: University of Texas Press, 1994.

Bruce-Novoa, Juan. *Chicano Poetry: A Response to Chaos*. Austin: University of Texas Press, 1982.

Brundage, Burr Cartwright. *The Fifth Sun: Aztec Gods, Aztec World*. Austin: University of Texas Press, 1979.

Burland, C. A. *The Gods of Mexico*. New York: G. P. Putnam's Sons, 1967.

Burland, C. A., and Werner Forman. *Feathered Serpent and Smoking Mirror*. New York: G. P. Putnam's Sons, 1975.

Butler, Judith. *Bodies That Matter: On the Discursive Limits of "Sex"*. New York and London: Routledge, 1993.

Bynner, Witter. *Journey with Genius: Recollections and Reflections Concerning the D. H. Lawrences*. New York: John Day Company, 1951.

Candelaria, Cordelia. "La Malinche, Feminist Prototype." *Frontiers* 2 (1980): 1–6.

Carpenter, Rebecca. "'Bottom-Dog Insolence' and 'the Harem Mentality': Race and Gender in *The Plumed Serpent*." *D. H. Lawrence Review* 25: 1–3 (1993 and 1994): 119–129.

Carrasco, Davíd. "Aztec Moments and Chicano Cosmovision: Aztlán Recalled to Life." *Moctezuma's Mexico: Visions of the Aztec World*, rev. ed. Ed. Davíd Carrasco and Eduardo Matos Moctezuma. Boulder: University Press of Colorado, 2003. 175–198.

Carrasco, Davíd. *Quetzalcoatl and the Irony of Empire: Myths and Prophecies in the Aztec Tradition*. Chicago: University of Chicago Press, 1982.

Carreon, Hector. "Aztlan Joins Zapatistas on March into Tenochtitlan." March 8, 2001. *La Voz de Aztlan*. www.aztlan.net/zocalo.htm. Accessed June 15, 2005.

Castañeda, Antonia I. "Sexual Violence in the Politics and Policies of Conquest: Amerindian Women and the Spanish Conquest of Alta California." *Building with Our Hands: New Direction in Chicana Studies*. Ed. Adela de la Torre and Beatríz Pesquera. Berkeley: University of California Press, 1993. 15–33.

Castaneda, Carlos. *A Separate Reality: Further Conversations with Don Juan*. New York: Simon and Schuster, 1971.

———. *The Teachings of Don Juan: A Yaqui Way of Knowledge*. Berkeley: University of California Press, 1968.

Castillo, Ana. *Goddess of the Americas. La diosa de las Américas: Writings on the Virgin of Guadalupe*. New York: Riverhead Books, 1996.

———. *Massacre of the Dreamers: Essays on Xicanisma*. Albuquerque: University of New Mexico Press, 1994.

Catherwood, Frederick. *Views of Ancient Monuments in Central America, Chiapas, and Yucatan*. New York: Barlett and Welford, 1844.

Cervantes, Lorna Dee. *Emplumada*. Pittsburgh: University of Pittsburg, 1981.

———. "Para un Revolucionario." *Infinite Divisions. An Anthology of Chicana Literature*. Ed. Tey Diana Rebolledo and Eliana S. Rivero. Tucson: University of Arizona Press, 1993. 151.

Chabram, Angie, and Rosa Linda Fregoso. "Introduction. Chicana/o Cultural Representations: Reframing Alternative Critical Discourses." *Cultural Studies* 4 (1990): 203–212.

Chabram-Dernersesian, Angie. "I Throw Punches for My Race, but I Don't Want to Be a Man: Writing Us—Chica-Nos (Girl, Us)/Chican*as*—into the Movement Script." *Cultural Studies*. Ed. Lawrence Grossberg, Cary Nelson, and Paula Treichler. New York: Routledge, 1992. 81–95.

———. "On the Social Construction of Whiteness within Selected Chicana/o Discourses." *Displacing Whiteness: Essays in Social and Cultural Criticism*. Ed. Ruth Frankenberg. Durham: Duke University Press, 1997. 107–164.

Charlot, Jean. *Mexican Mural Renaissance. 1920–1925*. New Haven and London: Yale University Press, 1967.

Chimalpahin Quauhtlehuanitzin, Domingo Francisco de San Antón Muñón. *Annals of His Time*. Ed. and trans. James Lockhart, Susan Schroeder, and Doris Namala. Stanford, Calif.: Stanford University Press, 2006.

———. *Codex Chimalpahin. Society and Politics in Mexico Tenochtitlan, Tlatelolco, Texcoco, Culhuacan, and Other Nahua Altepetl in Central Mexico. The Nahuatl and Spanish Annals and Accounts Collected and Recorded by don Domingo de San Anton Munon Chimalpahin Quauhtlehuanitzin*, Vols. 1–2. Ed. Arthur J. O. Anderson and Susan Schroeder. Norman: University of Oklahoma Press, 1997.

———. *Compendio de la Historia Mexicana: Extracts from a Lost Manuscript*. Ed. John B. Glass. Trans. Gordon Whittaker. Lincoln Center, Mass.: Conemex Associates, 1975.

Churchill, Ward. *Struggle for the Land: Indigenous Resistance to Genocide, Ecocide and Expropriation in Contemporary North America*. Monroe, Maine: Common Courage Press, 1993.

Clark, L. D. "Introduction." *The Plumed Serpent by D. H. Lawrence*. Cambridge: Cambridge University Press, 1987.

Coe, Michael D. *Mexico: From the Olmecs to the Aztecs*. New York: Thames and Hudson, 1994.

Consejo Regional Indígena del Cauca. "Plataforma Política Del CRIC." *Utopía y Revolución. El pensamiento político contemporáneo de los Indios en América Latina*. Ed. Guillermo Bonfil-Batalla. México, D.F.: Editorial Nueva Imagen, 1981. 300–314.

Contreras, Sheila M. "'These Were Just Natives to Her': Chilchui Indians and D. H. Lawrence's 'The Woman Who Rode Away'." *D. H. Lawrence Review* 25: 1–3 (1993 and 1994): 91–103.

Cooper Alarcón, Daniel. *The Aztec Palimpsest: Mexico in the Modern Imagination*. Tucson: University of Arizona Press, 1997.

Cotera, Martha. *The Chicana Feminist*. Austin: Information Systems Development, 1977.

———. *Diosa Y Hembra*. Austin: Information Systems Development, 1977.

Cowan, James C. D. H. *Lawrence's American Journey: A Study in Literature and Myth*. Cleveland/London: The Press of Case Western Reserve University, 1970.

Culler, Jonathan. *Structuralist Poetics: Structuralism, Linguistics, and the Study of Literature*. Ithaca: Cornell University Press, 1975.

Davies, Nigel. *The Aztecs. A History*. Norman: University of Oklahoma Press, 1982.

De León, Arnoldo. *The Tejano Community, 1836–1900*. Albuquerque: University of New Mexico Press, 1982.

———. *They Called Them Greasers: Anglo Attitudes toward Mexicans in Texas, 1821–1900*. Austin: University of Texas Press, 1983.

del Castillo, Adelaida. "Malintzín Tenépal: A Preliminary Look Into a New Perspective." *Essays on La Mujer*. Ed. Rosaura Sánchez and Rosa Martinez Cruz. Los Angeles: Chicano Studies Center Publications, University of California, Los Angeles, 1977. 124–149.

d'Harnoncourt, René. "Pancho the Toymaker." *Mexican Folk Toys: Festival Decorations and Ritual Objects*. Ed. Florence H. and Robert M. Pettit. New York: Hastings House Publishers, 1978. 15.

Díaz del Castillo, Bernal. *The Discovery and Conquest of Mexico, 1517–1521*. Trans. A. P. Maudslay. New York: Da Capo Press, 1996.

Dunbar-Ortiz, Roxanne. *Indians of the Americas. Human Rights and Self-Determination*. London: Zed Books, Ltd., 1984.

Durán, Diego. *The History of the Indies of New Spain*. Trans. Doris Heyden and Fernando Horcasitas. New York: Orion Press, 1964.

Eagleton, Terry. *Literary Theory: An Introduction*. Minneapolis: University of Minnesota, 1983.

Ejército Zapatista de Liberación Nacional (EZLN). "Editorial. El Despertador Mexicano." *Zapatistas! Documents of the New Mexican Revolution*. New York: Autonomedia, 1994. 35–36. Latin American Network Information Center (LANIC). http://lanic.utexas.edu/project/Zapatistas/chapter01.html. Accessed June 9, 2007.

Ellis, David. *D. H. Lawrence: Dying Game 1922–1930*. The Cambridge Biography. Cambridge: Cambridge University Press, 1998.

"El Plan Espiritual De Aztlán." *Aztlán: Essays on the Chicano Homeland*. Ed. Rudolfo A. Anaya and Francisco Lomelí. Albuquerque: University of New Mexico Press, 1989. 1–5.

Enloe, Cynthia. *Bananas, Beaches and Bases: Making Feminist Sense of International Politics*. Berkeley: University of California Press, 1989.

Errington, Shelly. *The Death of Primitive Art and Other Tales of Progress*. Berkeley: University of California Press, 1998.

———. "Progressivist Stories and the Pre-Columbian Past: Notes on Mexico and the United States." *Collecting the Pre-Columbian Past*. Ed. Elizabeth Hill-Boone. Washington, D.C.: Dumbarton Oaks, 1993. 209–249.

Esquibel, Catrióna Rueda. *With Her Machete in Her Hand.* Austin: University of Texas Press, 2006.

Fabian, Johannes. *Time and the Other: How Anthropology Makes Its Object.* New York: Columbia University Press, 1983.

Fanon, Frantz. *The Wretched of the Earth.* New York: Grove Press, 1963.

Fiedler, Leslie. *The Return of the Vanishing American.* New York: Stein and Day, 1968.

Florescano, Enrique. "The Creation of the Museo Nacional de Antropología of Mexico and its Scientific, Educational and Political Purposes." *Collecting the Pre-Columbian Past.* Ed. Elizabeth Hill-Boone. Washington, D.C.: Dumbarton Oaks, 1993. 81–103.

———. *Memory, Myth and Time in Mexico.* Trans. Albert G. Bork and Kathryn R. Bork. Austin: University of Texas Press, 1994.

———. *The Myth of Quetzalcoatl.* Trans. Lysa Hochroth. Baltimore: Johns Hopkins University Press, 1999.

Forbes, Jack. *Aztecas Del Norte: The Chicanos of Aztlán.* Greenwich, Conn.: Fawcett, 1973.

Foster, Hal. "The 'Primitive' Unconscious of Modern Art." *October* 34 (Autumn 1985): 45–70.

Foster, John Burt Jr. *Heirs to Dionysus: A Nietzschean Current in Literary Modernism.* Princeton, N.J.: Princeton University Press, 1981.

Freeman, Mary. *D. H. Lawrence: A Basic Study of His Ideas.* New York: Grosset & Dunlap, 1955.

Fregoso, Rosa Linda, and Angie Chabram-Dernersesian. "Chicana/o Cultural Representations: Reframing Alternative Critical Discourses." *Cultural Studies* 4 (1990): 203–212.

Friedman, Susan Stanford. "Definitional Excursions: The Meanings of Modern/Modernity/Modernism." *Modernism/Modernity* 8:3 (2001): 493–513.

Gamio, Manuel. *Forjando Patria,* 2nd ed. Mexico: Editorial Porrua, S. A., 1960.

———. "Incorporating the Indian in the Mexican Population." *Aspects of Mexican Civilization. [Lectures on the Harris Foundation 1926].* By José Vasconcelos and Manuel Gamio. Chicago: University of Chicago Press, 1926. 105–127.

———. "The New Conquest." *The Survey Graphic* 50:3 (May 1, 1924): 143–164, 194.

García, Alma M., ed. *Chicana Feminist Thought: The Basic Historical Writings.* New York: Routledge, 1997.

Gaspar de Alba, Alicia. "La Mariscal." *The Mystery of Survival and Other Stories.* Tempe: Bilingual Press, 1993.

Gauguin, Paul. *Letters to His Wife and Friends.* Trans. Henry J. Stenning. Ed. Maurice Malingue. Cleveland: The World Publishing Company, 1949.

George, Rosemary Marangoly. "Homes in the Empire, Empires in the Home." *Cultural Critique* 26 (Winter 1993–1994): 95–127.

Gillespie, Susan. *The Aztec Kings.* Tucson: University of Arizona Press, 1989.

Goldie, Terry. *Fear and Temptation: The Image of the Indigene in Canadian, Australian, and New Zealand Literatures.* Montreal and Kingston: McGill-Queen's University Press, 1989.

Goldwater, Robert. *Primitivism in Modern Art,* rev. ed. New York: Vintage Books, 1967.

Gomez, David F. *Somos Chicanos: Strangers in Our Own Land.* Boston: Beacon Press, 1973.

Gómez-Quiñones, Juan. *Chicano Politics: Reality and Promise, 1940–1990.* Albuquerque: University of New Mexico Press, 1990.

———. *Mexican Students por La Raza: The Chicano Student Movement in Southern California, 1967–1977.* Santa Barbara, Calif.: Editorial La Causa, 1978.

Gonzales, Patrisia, and Roberto Rodriguez. "Zapatistas Inspire Grassroots Leadership Worldwide." June 9, 2004. Indigenous Peoples Literature. www .indigenouspeople.net/ipl_final.html. Accessed June 15, 2005.

González, Corky. "Yo Soy Joaquín." *The Latino Reader: From 1542 to the Present.* Ed. Harold Augenbraum and Margarite Fernández Olmos. Boston: Houghton Mifflin, 1997. 266–279.

González, Jovita, and Eve Raleigh. *Caballero: A Historical Novel.* College Station: Texas A&M University Press, 1996.

González, Rafael Jesús. "Chicano Poetry/Smoking Mirror." *New Directions in Chicano Scholarship.* Ed. Ricardo Romo and Raymund Paredes. Chicano Studies Monograph Series. La Jolla, Calif.: Chicano Studies Program, University of California, San Diego, 1978. 127–138.

Greene, Graham. *The Power and the Glory.* New York: Viking, 1946.

Griffin, Susan. *Woman and Nature: The Roaring Inside Her.* New York: Harper & Row, 1978.

Griswold del Castillo, Richard. *The Treaty of Guadalupe Hidalgo: A Legacy of Conflict.* Norman and London: University of Oklahoma Press, 1990.

Guha, Ranajit. "On Some Aspects of the Historiography of Colonial India." *Selected Subaltern Studies.* Ed. Ranajit Guha and Gayatri Chakravorty Spivak. New York: Oxford University Press, 1988. 37–44.

Gunn, Drewey Wayne. *American and British Writers in Mexico, 1556–1973.* Austin: University of Texas Press, 1974.

Gutiérrez, Donald. "Lapsing Out: Ideas of Mortality and Immortality in Lawrence." *Twentieth Century Literature: A Scholarly and Critical Journal* 24 (1978): 169–187.

Hall, Stuart. "Cultural Identity and Diaspora." *Identity: Community, Culture, Difference.* Ed. Jonathan Rutherford. London: Lawrence & Wishart, 1990.

———. *"Lady Chatterley's Lover:* The Novel and Its Contribution to Lawrence's Work." *New Left Review* 6 (November–December 1960): 32–35.

Harasym, Sarah, ed. *The Post-Colonial Critic: Interviews, Strategies, Dialogues.* New York: Routledge, 1990.

Herrera-Sobek, María. "Introduction." *Beyond Stereotypes. The Critical Analysis of Chicana Literature.* Ed. María Herrera-Sobek. Binghamton, N.Y.: Bilingual Press, 1985. 9–28.

Hill-Boone, Elizabeth. "Collecting the Pre-Columbian Past: Historical Trends and the Process of Reception and Use." *Collecting the Pre-Columbian Past.* Ed. Elizabeth Hill-Boone. Washington, D.C.: Dumbarton Oaks, 1993. 315–350.

Hillman, James. *Re-visioning Psychology.* New York: Harper & Row, 1975.

Hinsley, Curtis. "In Search of the New World Classical." *Collecting the Pre-Columbian Past.* Ed. Elizabeth Hill-Boone. Washington, D.C.: Dumbarton Oaks, 1993. 105–122.

Hu DeHart, Evelyn. "Coolies, Shopkeepers, Pioneers: The Chinese of Mexico and Peru (1849–1930)," *Amerasia Journal* 15:2 (1989): 91–116.

———. "Immigrants to a Developing Society: The Chinese in Northern Mexico, 1875–1932." *Journal of Arizona History,* 21 (Autumn 1980): 49–85.

———. "Racism and Anti-Chinese Persecution in Mexico." *Amerasia Journal* 9:2 (1982): 1–28.

Huerta, Jorge. *Chicano Drama.* Cambridge: Cambridge University Press, 2000.

Humma, John B. *Metaphor and Meaning in D. H. Lawrence's Later Novels.* Columbia and London: University of Missouri Press, 1990.

Johnson, Robert A. *Owning Your Own Shadow: Understanding the Dark Side of the Psyche.* San Francisco: HarperSanFrancisco, 1991.

Joost, Nicholas, and Alvin Sullivan. *D. H. Lawrence and the Dial.* Carbondale: Southern Illinois University Press, 1970.

Josephy, Alvin Jr. *The Indian Heritage of America.* New York: Knopf, 1968.

Jung, C. G. *Mysterium Coniunctionis. An Inquiry into the Separation and Synthesis of Psychic Opposites in Alchemy.* Trans. R. F. C. Hull. *The Collected Works of C. G. Jung,* Vol. 14, 2nd ed. Ed. Sir Herbert Read, et al. Princeton, N.J.: Princeton University Press, 1963.

———. "The Shadow." *Aion. Researches into the Phenomenology of the Self.* Trans. R. F. C. Hull. *The Collected Works of C. G. Jung,* Vol. 9, Part 2. Ed. Sir Herbert Read, et al. New York: Pantheon Books, 1959: 8–10.

Keating, AnaLouise. *Women Reading Women Writing: Self-Invention in Paula Gunn Allen, Gloria Anzaldúa and Audre Lorde.* Philadelphia: Temple University Press, 1996.

Keen, Benjamin. *The Aztec Image in Western Thought.* New Brunswick, N.J.: Rutgers University Press, 1990.

Keller, Gary D. "Introduction: Alurista, Poeta-Antropologo, and the Recuperation of the Chicano Identity." *Return: Poems Collected and New.* By Alurista. Ypsilanti, Mich.: Bilingual Press/Editorial Bilingue, 1982. xi-xlix.

Kinkead-Weekes, Mark. *D. H. Lawrence: Triumph to Exile, 1912–1922.* New York: Cambridge University Press, 1996.

Klor de Alva, Jorge. "Aztlán, Borinquen and Hispanic Nationalism in the United States." *Aztlán: Essays on the Chicano Homeland.* Ed. Rudolfo A. Anaya and Francisco A. Lomelí. Albuquerque: University of New Mexico Press, 1991. 135–171.

———. "California Chicano Literature and Pre-Columbian Motifs: Foil and Fetish." *Confluencia* 1 (Spring 1986): 18–26.

———. "The Invention of Ethnic Origins and the Negotiation of Latino Identity, 1969–1981." *Challenging Fronteras: Structuring Latina and Latino Lives in the U.S.* Ed. Mary Romero, Pierrette Hondagneu-Sotelo, and Vilma Ortiz. New York: Routledge, 1997. 55–74.

Knight, Alan. "Racism, Revolution and Indigenismo: Mexico, 1910–1940." *The Idea of Race in Latin America.* Ed. Richard Graham. Austin: University of Texas Press, 1990. 71–113.

Latorre, Guisela. "Gender, Muralism and the Politics of Identity: Chicana Muralism and Indigenist Aesthetics." *Disciplines on the Line: Feminist Research on Spanish, Latin American, and U.S. Latina Women*. Ed. Anne J. Cruz, Rosilie Hernández-Pecoraro, and Joyce Tolliver. Newark, Del.: Juan de la Cuesta, 2003. 321–356.

Lawrence, D. H. "America, Listen to Your Own." *Phoenix: The Posthumous Papers of D. H. Lawrence*. Ed. Edward D. McDonald. New York: Viking Press, 1936.

———. "Au Revoir, U.S.A." *Phoenix: The Posthumous Papers of D. H. Lawrence*. Ed. Edward D. McDonald. New York: Viking Press, 1936.

———. "Certain Americans and an Englishman." *Phoenix II*. Ed. Warren Roberts and Harry T. Moore. London: Heinemann, 1968. 238–243.

———. *The Escaped Cock*. Ed. Gerald Lacy. Los Angeles: Black Sparrow, 1973.

———. *The Letters of D. H. Lawrence*, Vol. 4. Ed. James T. Boulton, et al. Cambridge: Cambridge University Press, 1979.

———. *Mornings in Mexico*. New York: Alfred A. Knopf, 1927.

———. *The Plumed Serpent*. Ed. L. D. Clark. Cambridge: Cambridge University Press, 1987.

———. "The Woman Who Rode Away." *The Woman Who Rode Away and Other Stories*. London: Martin Secker, 1928.

Leal, Luis. "In Search of Aztlán." Trans. Gladys Leal. *Aztlán: Essays on the Chicano Homeland*. Ed. Rudolfo A. Anaya and Francisco Lomelí. Albuquerque: University of New Mexico Press, 1989. 6–13.

Leavis, F. R. *D. H. Lawrence: Novelist. 1955*. New York: Simon & Schuster, 1969.

León-Portilla, Miguel. *Los antiguos mexicanos a través de sus crónicas y cantares*. México: Fondo de Cultura Económica, 1961.

———. *Aztec Thought and Culture: A Study of the Ancient Nahuatl Mind*. Trans. Jack Emory Davis. Norman: University of Oklahoma Press, 1963.

———. *The Broken Spears: The Aztec Account of the Conquest of Mexico*. Boston: Beacon Press, 1962.

———. *Endangered Cultures*. Trans. Julie Goodson-Lawes. Dallas: Southern Methodist University Press, 1990.

León-Portilla, Miguel, and Earl Shorris, eds. *In the Language of Kings: An Anthology of Mesoamerican Literature—Pre-Columbian to the Present*. New York: Norton, 2001.

Levi-Strauss, Claude. *Myth and Meaning*. Toronto: University of Toronto Press, 1978.

———. *Structural Anthropology*. Trans. Monique Layton. New York: Basic Books, 1963.

Limón, José E. *American Encounters: Greater Mexico, the United States, and the Erotics of Culture*. Boston: Beacon Press, 1998.

———. *Dancing with the Devil. Society and Cultural Poetics in Mexican-American South Texas*. Madison: University of Wisconsin Press, 1994.

———. "La Llorona, the Third Legend of Greater Mexico: Cultural Symbols, Women, and the Political Unconscious." *Renato Rosaldo Lecture Series Monograph 2*. Ed. Ignacio M. Garcia. Tucson: University of Arizona Mexican American Studies and Research Center, 1986. 59–93.

————. *Mexican Ballads, Chicano Poems: History and Influence in Mexican-American Social Poetry*. Berkeley: University of California Press, 1992.

————. "Tex-Sex-Mex: American Identities, Lone Stars, and the Politics of Racialized Sexuality." *American Literary History* 9:3 (Fall 1997): 598–616.

López Austin, Alfredo, and Leonardo López Luján. *El Pasado Indígena*. México: El Colegio de México, 1996: 191.

López, Alma. *Our Lady*. Making Face, Making Soul. A Chicana Feminist Homepage. http://chicanas.com/alma.html. Accessed February 11, 2007.

López, Yolanda M. *Portrait of the Artist as the Virgin of Guadalupe. Chicano Art: Resistance and Affirmation, 1965–1985*. Los Angeles: Wight Art Gallery, 1991. 323.

Lowry, Malcolm. *Under the Volcano*. New York: Vintage, 1958.

Luckert, Karl W. *Olmec Religion: A Key to Middle America and Beyond*. Norman: University of Oklahoma Press, 1976.

Luhan, Mabel Dodge. *Lorenzo in Taos*, 1st ed. New York: Alfred A. Knopf, Inc., 1932.

Mariategui, José Carlos. *Seven Interpretive Essays on Peruvian Reality*. Trans. Marjory Urquidi. Austin: University of Texas Press, 1971.

McKenna, Teresa. *Migrant Song: Politics and Process in Contemporary Chicano Literature*. Austin: University of Texas Press, 1997.

Menchaca, Martha. "Chicano Indianism: A Historical Account of Racial Repression in the United States." *American Ethnologist* 20:3 (1993): 583–603.

————. *Recovering History, Constructing Race: The Indian, Black, and White Roots of Mexican Americans*. Austin: University of Texas Press, 2001.

Mercer, Kobena. *Welcome to the Jungle: New Positions in Black Cultural Studies*. New York: Routledge, 1994.

Meyers, Jeffrey. "*The Plumed Serpent* and the Mexican Revolution." *Journal of Modern Literature* 4 (1974): 55–72.

Michaelsen, Scott. *The Limits of Multiculturalism: Interrogating the Origins of American Anthropology*. Minneapolis: University of Minnesota Press, 1999.

Mirandé, Alfredo, and Evangelina Enríquez. *La Chicana: The Mexican-American Woman*. Chicago: University of Chicago Press, 1979.

Montejano, David. *Anglos and Mexicans in the Making of Texas, 1836–1986*. Austin: University of Texas, 1987.

Montgomery, Robert E. *The Visionary D. H. Lawrence: Beyond Philosophy and Art*. Cambridge: Cambridge University Press, 1994.

Moore, Harry T. *The Priest of Love: A Life of D. H. Lawrence*, rev. ed. New York: Farrar, Straus and Giroux, 1974.

Moore, Henry. "Primitive Art." *Primitivism and Twentieth-Century Art*. Ed. Jack Flam and Miriam Deutch. Berkeley: University of California Press, 2003. 267–271.

Moore, John. "*A Primitivist Primer*." www.primitivism.com/primer.htm. Accessed June 15, 2005.

Mora, Pat. *House of Houses*. Boston: Beacon Press, 1997.

Moraga, Cherríe. *Loving in the War Years: Lo Que Nunca Pasó por sus Labios*. Boston: South End Press, 1983.

————. "Refugees of a World on Fire: Foreword to the Second Edition." *This*

Bridge Called My Back: Writings by Radical Women of Color. Ed. Cherríe Moraga and Gloria Anzaldúa. New York: Kitchen Table, 1981. i-iii.

Muñoz, Carlos Jr. *Youth, Identity, Power. The Chicano Movement.* London: Verso, 1989.

Museum of Modern Art. *Les Demoiselles de Avignon: Conserving a Modern Masterpiece.* 2003. www.moma.org/collection/conservation/demoiselles/index.html. Accessed February 4, 2007.

Nieto-Gómez, Anna. "Chicanas Identify." *Regeneration* 1:10 (1971): 9.

Nixon, Cornelia. *Lawrence's Leadership Politics and the Turn against Women.* Berkeley: University of California Press, 1986.

Novak, Maximillian E. "Primitivism." *The Cambridge History of Literary Criticism, Vol. 4: The Eighteenth Century.* Ed. H. B. Nisbet and Claude Rawson. Cambridge: Cambridge University Press, 1997. 456–469.

Oropeza, Lorena. *¡Raza Si! ¡Guerra No! Chicano Protest and Patriotism During the Viet Nam War Era.* Berkeley: University of California Press, 2005.

Orozco, José Clemente. *José Clemente Orozco: An Autobiography.* Trans. Robert C. Stephenson. Austin: University of Texas Press, 1962.

Ortego, Philip D. "The Chicano Renaissance." *Social Casework* 52:5 (May 1971): 294–307.

Padilla, Genaro. "Discontinuous Continuities. Remapping the Terrain of Spanish Colonial Narrative." *Reconstructing a Chicana/o Literary Heritage: Hispanic Colonial Literature of the Southwest.* Ed. María Herrera-Sobek. Tucson: University of Arizona Press, 1993. 24 36.

———. *My History, Not Yours: The Formation of Mexican American Autobiography.* Madison: University of Wisconsin Press, 1993.

———. "Myth and Comparative Cultural Nationalism: The Ideological Uses of Aztlán." *Aztlán: Essays on the Chicano Homeland.* Ed. Rudolfo A. Anaya and Francisco Lomelí. Albuquerque: University of New Mexico Press, 1989. 111–131.

Pagán, Eduardo Obregón. *Murder at the Sleepy Lagoon: Zoot Suits, Race, and Riot in Wartime L.A.* Chapel Hill: University of North Carolina Press, 2003.

Paredes, Américo. *"With His Pistol in His Hand": A Border Ballad and Its Hero.* Austin: University of Texas Press, 1958.

Parmenter, Ross. *Lawrence in Oaxaca: A Quest for the Novelist in Mexico.* Salt Lake City: Gibbs M. Smith, Inc./Peregrine Smith Books, 1984.

Parry, Benita. "Problems in Current Theories of Colonial Discourse." *Oxford Literary Review* 9:1–2 (1987): 27–58.

Paz, Octavio. "Critique of the Pyramid." *The Other Mexico: Critique of the Pyramid.* Trans. Lysander Kemp. New York: Grove Press, 1972.

———. "Sons of La Malinche." *Labyrinth of Solitude.* Trans. Lysander Kemp, Yara Milos, and Rachel Phillips Belash. New York: Grove Press, 1985. 65–117.

Peña, Manuel. *The Texas-Mexican Conjunto: History of a Working-Class Music.* Austin: University of Texas Press, 1985.

Perez, Emma. *The Decolonial Imaginary: Writing Chicanas into History.* Bloomington: Indiana University Press, 1999.

Pérez-Torres, Rafael. *Mestizaje. Critical Uses of Race in Chicano Culture.* Minneapolis: University of Minnesota Press, 2006.

————. *Movements in Chicano Poetry: Against Myths, Against Margins.* Cambridge Studies in American Literature and Culture. Ed. Eric Sundquist. Cambridge: Cambridge University Press, 1995.

————. "Refiguring Aztlán." *The Chicano Studies Reader: An Anthology of Aztlan.* Ed. Chon Noriega. Los Angeles: UCLA Chicano Studies Research Center, 2001. 213–39.

Pettit, Florence H., and Robert M. Pettit. *Mexican Folk Toys: Festival Decorations and Ritual Objects.* New York: Hastings House Publishers, 1978.

Pizarro, Mark. "Brechtian and Aztec Violence in Valdez's 'Zoot Suit'" *Journal of Popular Film and Television* 26:2 (Summer 1998): 52–61.

Popul Vuh: The Definitive Edition of the Mayan Book of the Dawn of Life and the Glories of Gods and Kings. Trans. Dennis Tedlock. New York: Simon and Schuster, 1985.

Poyo, Gerald E., ed. *Tejano Journey. 1770–1850.* Austin: University of Texas Press, 1996.

Poyo, Gerald E., and Gilberto M. Hinojosa, eds. *Tejano Origins in Eighteenth-Century San Antonio.* Austin: University of Texas Press/Institute of Texan Cultures, 1991.

Pratt, Mary Louise. "Presidential Address 2003: Language, Liberties, Waves, and Webs: Engaging the Present." *PMLA: Publications of the Modern Language Association of America* 119:3 (2004): 417–428.

Prescott, William Hickling. *History of the Conquest of Mexico.* Ed. Harry Block. Mexico City: Heritage Press, 1949.

Price, Sally. *Primitive Art in Civilized Places.* Chicago and London: University of Chicago Press, 1989.

"Quest for a Homeland." *Chicano! History of the Mexican American Civil Rights Movement.* National Latino Communications Center and Galán Productions, 1996.

Quintana, Alvina. *Home Girls: Chicana Literary Voices.* Philadelphia: Temple University Press, 1996.

Read, Herbert. *A Concise History of Modern Sculpture.* New York: Frederick A. Praeger, 1964.

Rebolledo, Tey Diana. *Women Singing in the Snow: A Cultural Analysis of Chicana Literature.* Tucson: University of Arizona Press, 1995.

————. "'Y Dónde Estaban las Mujeres?': In Pursuit of an *Hispana* Literary and Historical Heritage in Colonial New Mexico, 1580–1840." *Reconstructing a Chicana/o Literary Heritage: Hispanic Colonial Literature of the Southwest.* Ed. María Herrera-Sobek. Tucson: University of Arizona Press, 1993. 140–157.

Rebolledo, Tey Diana, and Eliana S. Rivero. "Myths and Archetypes." *Infinite Divisions: An Anthology of Chicana Literature.* Ed. Tey Diana Rebolledo and Eliana S. Rivero. Tucson: University of Arizona Press, 1991. 189–195.

Rendon, Armando B. *Chicano Manifesto. 1971.* Berkeley: Ollin and Assoc., 1996.

Robbins, Rebecca L. "Self-Determination and Subordination: The Past, Present, and Future of American Indian Governance." *The State of Native America: Genocide, Colonization and Resistance.* Ed. M. Annette Jaimes. Boston: South End, 1992. 87–122.

Roberts, Warren, James T. Boulton, and Elizabeth Mansfield, eds. *The Letters of*

D. H. Lawrence, Vol. 4 (June 1921–March 1924). Cambridge: Cambridge University Press, 1987.

Rosenblatt, Daniel. "The Antisocial Skin: Structure, Resistance, and 'Modern Primitive' Adornment in the United States." *Cultural Anthropology* 12:3 (1997): 298–334.

Rubin, William. "Modernist Primitivism. An Introduction." *"Primitivism" in 20th Century Art: Affinity of the Tribal and the Modern*. Exhibition catalog, Vol. 1. New York: Museum of Modern Art, 1984. 1–81.

Ruderman, Judith. *D. H. Lawrence and the Devouring Mother*. Durham, N.C.: Duke University Press, 1984.

Rudnick, Lois Palken. *Mabel Dodge Luhan: New Woman, New Worlds*. Albuquerque: University of New Mexico Press, 1984.

Ruíz de Burton, María Amparo. *The Squatter and the Don*. Houston: Arte Público Press, 1992.

Sáenz, Benjamin Alire. "In the Borderlands of Chicano Identity, There Are Only Fragments." *Border Theory: The Limits of Cultural Politics*. Ed. Scott Michaelsen and David E. Johnson. Minneapolis: University of Minnesota Press, 1997.

Saldaña-Portillo, Josefina. "Who's the Indian in Aztlán? Re-Writing Mestizaje, Indianism, and Chicanismo from the Lacandón." *Latin American Subaltern Studies Reader*. Ed. Ileana Rodríguez. Durham: Duke University Press, 2001.

Saldívar, José David. *Border Matters: Remapping American Cultural Studies*. Berkeley: University of California Press, 1997.

Saldívar-Hull, Sonia. "Feminism on the Border: From Gender Politics to Geopolitics." *Criticism in the Borderlands: Studies in Chicano Literature, Culture, and Ideology*. Ed. Hector Calderón and José David Saldívar. Durham and London: Duke University Press, 1991.

———. "Introduction to the Second Edition." *Borderlands/La Frontera: The New Mestiza*. By Gloria Anzaldúa. San Francisco: Aunt Lute Books, 1999. 1–15.

Salinas, Luís Omar, and Lillian Faderman. *From the Barrio: A Chicano Anthology*. San Francisco: Canfield Press, 1973.

Sánchez, George I. "Pachucos in the Making—1943." *Readings on La Raza: The Twentieth Century*. Ed. Matt S. Meier and Feliciano Rivera. New York: Hill and Wang, 1974. 122–126.

Sánchez, Marta Ester. *Contemporary Chicana Poetry: A Critical Approach to an Emerging Literature*. Berkeley: University of California Press, 1985.

Sánchez, Rosaura. "Reconstructing Chicana Gender Identity." *American Literary History* 9:2 (Summer 1997): 350–363.

———. *Telling Identities: The Californio Testimonios*. Minneapolis: University of Minnesota Press, 1995.

Sandoval, Chela. "Mestizaje as Method: Feminists-of-Color Challenge the Canon." *Living Chicana Theory*. Ed. Carla Trujillo. Series in Chicana/Latina Studies. Berkeley: Third Woman Press, 1998. 444.

Schroeder, Susan. "The Annals of Chimalpahin." *Sources and Methods for the Study of Postconquest Mesoamerican Ethnohistory, Provisional Version*. Ed. James Lockhart, Lisa Sousa, and Stephanie Wood. http://whp.uoregon.edu/Lockhart/Schroeder.pdf. Accessed June 9, 2007.

Schwartz, Stuart B. *Victors and Vanquished: Spanish and Nahua Accounts of the Conquest of Mexico.* Boston: Bedford, 2000.

Sedgwick, Eve Kosofsky. *Between Men: English Literature and Male Homosocial Desire.* New York: Columbia University Press, 1992.

Segade, Gustavo. "Identity and Power: An Essay on the Politics of Culture and the Culture of Politics in Chicano Thought." *Aztlán* 9 (1978): 85–99.

———. "An Introduction to Floricanto." *Festival De Flor Y Canto: An Anthology of Chicano Literature.* Ed. Alurista. Los Angeles: University of Southern California Press, 1976. 1–5.

Séjourné, Laurette. *Burning Water: Thought and Religion in Ancient Mexico.* Trans. Irene Nicholson. New York: Vanguard Press, 1957.

———. *El Universo del Quetzalcóatl.* México: Fondo de Cultura Económica, 1962.

Sharpe, Jenny. *Allegories of Empire: The Figure of the Woman in the Colonial Text.* Minneapolis: University of Minnesota Press, 1993.

Slotkin, Richard. "Myth and the Production of History." *Ideology and Classic American Literature.* Ed. Sacvan Bercovitch and Myra Jehlen. Cambridge: Cambridge University Press, 1986. 70–90.

Smith, Sidonie. *Subjectivity, Identity and the Body: Women's Autobiographical Practices in the Twentieth Century.* Bloomington: Indiana University Press, 1993.

Snow, Sinclair. "Introduction." *Barbarous Mexico.* Ed. John Kenneth Turner. Austin: University of Texas, 1969. ix–xxvii.

Sosa-Riddell, Adaljiza. "Chicanas and El Movimiento." *Aztlán* 5:1–2 (Spring/Fall 1974): 155–165.

Soustelle, Jacques. *Daily Life of the Aztecs on the Eve of the Spanish Conquest.* Trans. Patrick O'Brian. Stanford: Stanford University Press, 1962.

Spence, Lewis. *Gods of Mexico.* London: Eyre & Spottiswoode, 1967.

Spivak, Gayatri Chakravorty. "Can the Subaltern Speak?" *Marxism and the Interpretation of Culture.* Ed. Cary Nelson and Lawrence Grossberg. Urbana: University of Illinois Press, 1988. 271–313.

———. "Marginality in the Teaching Machine." *Outside in the Teaching Machine.* New York: Routledge, 1993. 53–76.

———. "Theory in the Margin: Coetzee's *Foe* Reading Defoe's *Crusoe/Roxana.*" *Consequences of Theory.* Ed. Jonathan Arac and Barbara Johnson. Baltimore: Johns Hopkins University Press, 1990.

Stephen, Lynn. *Zapotec Women.* Texas Press Sourcebooks in Anthropology. Austin: University of Texas Press, 1991.

Tafolla, Carmen. "La Malinche." *Infinite Divisions: An Anthology of Chicana Literature.* Ed. Tey Diana Rebolledo and Eliana S. Rivero. Tucson: University of Arizona, 1993. 198–199.

———. "La Malinche." *Tejidos* 4:4 (1977): 1–2.

Templeton, Wayne. "'Indians and an Englishman': Lawrence in the American Southwest." *The D. H. Lawrence Review* 25:1–3 (1993 and 1994).

Tenorio-Trillo, Mauricio. *Mexico at the World's Fairs: Crafting a Modern Nation.* The New Historicism: Studies in Cultural Poetics. Ed. Stephen Greenblatt. Berkeley: University of California Press, 1996.

Thompson, E. P. "Revolution Again! Or Shut Your Ears and Run." *New Left Review* 6 (November–December) (1960): 18–31.

Thompson, Edward H. *People of the Serpent. Life and Adventure Among the Mayas.* Boston: Houghton Mifflin, 1932.

Tindall, William York. *D. H. Lawrence and Susan His Cow.* New York: Columbia University Press, 1939.

Torgovnick, Marianna. *Gone Primitive: Savage Intellects, Modern Lives.* Chicago: University of Chicago, 1990.

———. *Primitive Passions: Men, Women and the Quest for Ecstasy.* New York: Alfred A. Knopf, 1996.

Townsend, Richard F. *The Aztecs.* London: Thames and Hudson, Ltd., 1992.

Travis, Leigh. "D. H. Lawrence: The Blood-Conscious Artist." *American Imago* 25 (1968): 163–190.

Trilling, Lionel. "On the Teaching of Modern Literature." *Beyond Culture.* New York: Viking Press, 1965. 3–30.

Turner, John Kenneth. *Barbarous Mexico.* Austin: University of Texas, 1969.

Valdez, Luis. "The Dark Root of a Scream." *From the Barrio: A Chicano Anthology.* Ed. Luis Omar Salinas and Lillian Faderman. San Francisco: Canfield Press, 1967. 79–98.

———. *Pensamiento Serpentino: A Chicano Approach to the Theatre of Reality.* n.p.: Cucaracha Publications/El Teatro Campesino, 1973.

———. "The Tale of La Raza." *Bronze* 1:1 (1968): 2–4.

Valliant, George. *Aztecs of Mexico: Origin, Rise and Fall of the Aztec Nation,* rev. ed. Garden City, N.Y.: Doubleday & Company, Inc., 1962.

Van Gogh, Vincent. *Complete Letters of Vincent Van Gogh,* Vol. 3. London: Thames and Hudson, 1958.

Van Hoosier-Carey, Kimberley. "Struggling with the Master: The Position of Kate and the Reader in *Quetzalcoatl* and *the Plumed Serpent*." *D. H. Lawrence Review* 25:1–3 (1993 and 1994): 104–118.

Vasconcelos, José. *The Cosmic Race: A Bilingual Edition.* Trans. Didier T. Jaén. Race in the Americas. Ed. Robert Reid-Pharr. Baltimore and London: Johns Hopkins University Press, 1979.

———. "The Race Problem in Latin America." *Aspects of Mexican Civilization [Lectures on the Harris Foundation 1926].* By José Vasconcelos and Manuel Gamio. Chicago: University of Chicago Press, 1926. 75–102.

Vaughan, Mary Kay. *Cultural Politics in Revolution: Teachers, Peasants, and Schools in Mexico, 1930–1940.* Tucson: University of Arizona Press, 1997.

Vidal, Mirta. *Chicanas Speak Out. Women: New Voice of La Raza.* New York: Pathfinder Press, Inc., 1971.

Villanueva, Alma Luz. "Free Women." *Weeping Woman: La Llorona and Other Stories.* Tempe, Ariz.: Bilingual Press, 1994. 69–80.

Villarreal, José Antonio. *Pocho.* New York: Anchor Books, 1989.

Von Hendy, Andrew. *The Modern Construction of Myth.* Bloomington: Indiana University Press, 2002.

Walker, Ronald. *Infernal Paradise: Mexico and the Modern English Novel.* Berkeley: University of California Press, 1978.

Walls, Andrew F., and Lamin Sanneh. *"Missions and Human Rights: A Conference Prospectus.* 2001." Yale-Edinburgh Group on the History of the Missionary Movement and Non-Western Christianity. www.library.yale.edu/div/theme2 .htm. Accessed June 8, 2007.

Waters, Frank. *Book of the Hopi. Drawings and Source Material Recorded by Oswald White Bear Fredericks.* New York: Viking Press, 1963.

Wertheimer, Eric. *Imagined Empires: Incas, Aztecs, and the New World of American Literature, 1771–1876.* Cambridge: Cambridge University Press, 1999.

White, Hayden. "The Forms of Wildness: Archaeology of an Idea." *The Wild Man Within: An Image in Western Thought from the Renaissance to Romanticism.* Ed. Edward Dudley and Maximillian E. Novak. n.p.: University of Pittsburgh Press, 1972. 3–38.

Widmer, Kingsley. "The Primitivistic Aesthetic of D. H. Lawrence." *The Journal of Aesthetics and Art Criticism* 17:3 (1959): 344–353.

Williams, Raymond. *Culture and Society: 1780–1950.* New York: Columbia University Press, 1960.

———. *The English Novel from Dickens to Lawrence.* London: Chatto & Windus, 1970.

———. *Keywords: A Vocabulary of Culture and Society,* rev. ed. New York: Oxford University Press, 1976.

Worthen, John. *D. H. Lawrence: A Literary Life.* New York: St. Martin's Press, 1989.

Yarbro-Bejarano, Yolanda. "From Acto to Mito: A Critical Appraisal of the Teatro Campesino." *Modern Chicano Writers: A Collection of Critical Essays.* Ed. Joseph Sommers and Tomás Ybarra-Frausto. Englewood Cliffs, N.J.: Prentice-Hall, Inc., 1979: 176–185.

Ybarra-Frausto, Tomás. "Alurista's Poetics: The Oral, the Bilingual, the Pre-Columbian." *Modern Chicano Writers: A Collection of Critical Essays.* Ed. Joseph Sommers and Tomás Ybarra-Frausto. Englewood Cliffs, N.J.: Prentice-Hall, Inc., 1979. 117–132.

Zamudio-Taylor, Victor. "Inventing Tradition, Negotiating Modernism. Chicano/a Art and the Pre-Columbian Past." *The Road to Aztlan: Art from A Mythic Homeland.* Ed. Virginia M. Fields and Victor Zamudio-Taylor. Los Angeles: LA County Museum of Art, 2001.

"Zoot Suit Riots." *American Experience.* Boston: WGBH, 2002.

Index

142, 186n14; and Mexican state indigenism, 45; and primitive art, 16,
169n7; sexual fantasy of, 156; and
subversion of Chicana/o indigenist
nationalism, 144–145
communitarian social structures, 18
conjunto music, 140
Conquest of Americas: and Catholic
Church, 90, 92; and Chicana/o
identity, 162; and Chicana/o literary indigenism, 140–141, 145; and
Chicana subjectivity, 120; documentation of, 10, 31; dominant
representations of, 106, 110, 126;
Indigenous accounts of, 79, 111,
178n18, 182n11; myth predating
European accounts of, 11; Prescott
on, 76, 176n35; and rape metaphor,
139, 185n11; and representation of
Indigenous population, 77; and
Spanish domination of Native
people, 63; violence of, 58–59; and
women's roles, 58–59, 175n30
consumerism, 96, 97–98, 102, 160
Cooper Alarcón, Daniel, 50, 73,
177n38
corridos, 149, 150–151
Cortés, Hernán: Cuahtemoc executed
by, 180n32; and La Malinche, 105,
107, 108, 110, 120, 157–158; mistaken for Quetzalcoatl, 79, 110,
178n18; Prescott on, 176n35
cosmovisions, 3
Cotera, Martha, 107
Coyolxauhqui, 106, 176n35, 181nn2, 4
Creole elites, 24–25
Cuahtemoc (Aztec ruler), 113, 120,
180n32, 182n13
Cucaracha Publications, 85
Culler, Jonathan, 12–13
cultural revitalization: and Carrasco,
2; and Chicana/o indigenist nationalism, 107; and Chicano movement
politics, 74, 77, 102; and Valdez,
86, 93, 94

danzas, 179n27
Davies, Nigel, 178n18

death, and representations of Mexican
culture, 19, 55, 56, 57
deep ecology, 16–17
DeHart, Evelyn Hu, 171n26
del Castillo, Adelaida: and academic
background, 164; on La Malinche,
39, 103, 106, 110, 111–112; rejection
of Aztec pantheon, 113, 131, 161;
"Malintzin Tenépal," 106, 110
De León, Arnoldo, 139, 184n2
Deloria, Vine, Jr., 180n40
Denver Youth Conference, 72, 101
Derain, André, 169n9
El Despertador Mexicano, 36
d'Harnoncourt, René, 176n33
Día de los Muertos (Day of the Dead),
56
Díaz, José, 75
Díaz del Castillo, Bernal, 43
Diego, Juan, 181n1
Dobie, J. Frank, 135
Duarte, Ignacio Magaloni, 85
Dunbar-Ortiz, Roxanne, 27–29
Durán, Diego, 4, 73
Duran Ayres, Edward, 75–76

Eagleton, Terry, 45
educational curricula, 35, 76
Egyptian art, 19, 20
Ejército Zapatista de Liberación
Nacional (EZLN), 35–37
Ellis, David, 48, 172n5, 173n17, 175n29
Emplumada (Cervantes): and Chi-
cana/o identity, 134; and Chicana/o
subjectivity, 145–153; and Indige-
nous ancestry, 147–149, 152; and
migration, 146–147, 149–150, 151,
153, 186n16; and Quetzalcoatl,
178n16; and Spanish language, 145–
146, 147, 149; tensions in, 151
English language, and Cervantes, 146,
151
Enlightenment, 18
Enloe, Cynthia, 142, 186n14
Enríquez, Evangelina, 107
Errington, Shelly, 4, 5
Esquibel, Catrióna Rueda, 155–156,
157, 186n21